Christmas 2018

Sawyer,
PaPa and I wanted
you to enjoy your
Farm-to-table recipes.
With all our love,
Granny and PaPa

The White House Kids' "State Dinner" Cookbook

The White House Kids' "State Dinner" Cookbook

WINNING RECIPES FROM
THE HEALTHY LUNCHTIME
CHALLENGE

THE WHITE HOUSE HISTORICAL ASSOCIATION
WASHINGTON, D.C.

THE WHITE HOUSE HISTORICAL ASSOCIATION is a nonprofit educational Association founded in 1961 for the purpose of enhancing the understanding, appreciation, and enjoyment of the Executive Mansion. All proceeds from the sale of the Association's books and products are used to fund the acquisition of historic furnishings and art work for the permanent White House collection, assist in the preservation of public rooms, and further its educational mission.

First Edition

10 9 8 7 6 5 4 3 2 1

Library of Congress Control Number: 2016951585

ISBN 9781931917742

Printed in the U.S.A.

ABOUT THE PHOTOGRAPHS

FRONT COVER: A 2016 Kids' "State Dinner" place setting; BACK COVER: First Lady Michelle Obama greets guests at the Kids' "State Dinner" in the East Room, 2015 (Official White House Photo by Lawrence Jackson); PAGE 3: First Lady Michelle Obama and guests watch a performance during the Kids' "State Dinner" in the White House, 2012 (Official White House Photo by Sonya N. Hebert); PAGE 5: Bell peppers growing in the Kitchen Garden, 2016 (White House Historical Association); PAGE 6: First Lady Michelle Obama addresses audience during the dedication of the White House Kitchen Garden, October 5, 2016 (Photo by Cheriss May/NurPhoto via Getty Images); PAGE 13: Place setting at the 2016 Kids' "State Dinner" (White House Historical Association); PAGE 14: The Cross Hall decorated for the Kids' "State Dinner," 2016 (White House Historical Association); Pages 16–561: Photographs of plated food: 2015–16: Jeff Elkins for WGBH; 2014: Jeff Elkins of Jeff Elkins Photography for Epicurious; 2013: Sara Bonisteel; PAGES 562–67: AP Photos; PAGES 568–69: Official White House Photo by Amanda Lucidon; PAGES 570–73: White House Historical Association; PAGES 572–75: Bruce White for the White House Historical Association; PAGE 576: Official White House Photo by Amanda Lucidon

THE WHITE HOUSE
WASHINGTON

THE WHITE HOUSE

My passion for helping our kids grow up healthy began long before I became First Lady. In fact, the idea for *Let's Move!* – our nationwide effort to raise a healthier generation – was actually born back when Barack was first running for President.

I was sitting at our kitchen table in Chicago one night, trying to wrap my head around what I would do if he actually managed to win, and I started thinking about the challenges that my family and so many others were facing as we tried to raise healthy kids. We often just didn't understand the impact that the food we ate was having on our bodies, and we didn't have the time or information we needed to buy and prepare healthy food. That's when I had this crazy idea—what if we planted a garden on the White House lawn to start a conversation about where our food comes from and how it impacts our health?

That conversation evolved into *Let's Move!*, and since we launched this initiative in 2010, we have seen a transformational culture change across this country. Major companies now race to market healthier versions of their products. Many convenience stores now sell fresh fruit. You can even get apples and skim milk in kids' meals at fast food places. Today, tens of millions of kids are eating healthier meals and snacks in schools and daycares and getting more physical activity every day. And childhood obesity rates in this country have stopped rising, and they've even started falling for our youngest kids.

And it is not just the adults that are making a difference. Kids themselves are becoming role models for their peers, inspiring and motivating their friends and families to eat well and get active. Kids understand that they need to take care of their bodies and minds to be healthy and strong today and for years to come.

Since 2012, the Healthy Lunchtime Challenge has been central to these efforts, prompting thousands of our country's youngest chefs to come up with their own healthy and creative recipes. Over the years, we received 6,000 recipe submissions and were blown away by the energy, imagination, diversity, and culinary skills reflected in each and every one. After the recipes were prepared, tasted, and rated by a panel of judges, more than 270 young people and their families representing every state and territory in America were selected to attend our White House Kids' "State Dinners" and show off their dishes. This cookbook contains their healthy – and delicious! – winning submissions.

The idea behind the Healthy Lunchtime Challenge, the Kids' "State Dinners," and everything we do through *Let's Move!* is very simple—to empower kids and families to live healthier lives. We wanted to show kids where their food comes from and teach them the importance of putting good fuel in their bodies. And we hope that this recipe collection will inspire more young people to get into the kitchen and start cooking.

So grab your friends and family, head into the kitchen, find a new recipe, and get cooking!

Michelle Obama

Contents

Guam

Hawaii

Idaho

Illinois

Indiana

Iowa

Kansas

Kentucky

Louisiana

Maine

Maryland

Massachusetts

Michigan

Minnesota

Mississippi

Missouri

Montana

Nebraska

Nevada

New Hampshire

New Jersey

New Mexico

New York

North Carolina

North Dakota

Northern Mariana Islands

Ohio

Oklahoma

Oregon

Pennsylvania

Puerto Rico

Rhode Island

South Carolina

South Dakota

Tennessee

Texas

U.S. Virgin Islands

Utah

Vermont

Virginia

Washington

West Virginia

Wisconsin

Wyoming

Preface

THE WHITE HOUSE HISTORICAL ASSOCIATION has grown and evolved over half a century since its founding in 1961, enjoying the enthusiasm and collaboration of each successive administration.

Flower gardening has been of interest at the White House off and on from earliest times, most famously when President Kennedy created the Rose Garden so familiar to us today, just outside the Oval Office. But vegetable gardening on the grounds is more unique. Until First Lady Michelle Obama created the White House Kitchen Garden, there had been no substantial working vegetable garden at the White House since the 1870s. President Woodrow Wilson planted a small one during World War I, to encourage home gardening, and likewise a small "victory garden" was planted during World War II.

Mrs. Obama, however, wanted to start a national conversation around healthy living and returned to an older White House tradition—one dating to President John Adams, first occupant of the White House—in planting fruits and vegetables for the first family's meals. She inspired Americans everywhere to do the same. Unlike that of President Adams, whose single administration ended before his garden grew, the White House Kitchen Garden abounds in seasonal fruits and vegetables throughout the year, such as tomatoes, cucumbers, lettuce, turnips, corn, beans, okra, strawberries, and sweet potatoes.

This cookbook is the result of *Let's Move!*, a comprehensive initiative that Mrs. Obama launched, which has succeeded in encouraging healthy eating and physical activity across America. It proved to be a Saturn with many rings, one of which was the Healthy Lunchtime Challenge. For this, schoolchildren were invited to submit their own recipes in a competition for the tastiest, most affordable, and healthiest lunch dishes. Over five years, one winner was selected from each state and territory to attend the Kids' "State Dinner" and to be included in an online cookbook. Those appealing and creative recipes from young chefs across the country are included here for your enjoyment.

Our historical Association is proud to present the 273 kid-crafted recipes in this cookbook in honor of Mrs. Obama's vision and in celebration of the national impact and legacy of her healthy eating mission.

Stewart D. McLaurin
President
White House Historical Association

Mr. McLaurin

SEAL OF THE PRESIDENT OF THE UNITED STATES

Introduction

Between 2012 and 2016, First Lady Michelle Obama, the U.S. Department of Education, and the U.S. Department of Agriculture teamed up with a media partner to host the Healthy Lunchtime Challenge, a nationwide recipe challenge for kids, which promoted cooking and healthy eating as part of Mrs. Obama's *Let's Move!* initiative. For the first three years, Epicurious was the media partner, and for the two years following, PBS flagship station WGBH Boston served as the media partner.

Over the five years, the Healthy Lunchtime Challenge invited 8 to 12-year-olds across the nation to create a healthy, affordable, original, and delicious lunch recipes. Entrants were encouraged to reference ChooseMyPlate.gov to ensure recipes met the USDA's recommended nutrition guidance by representing each of the food groups—including fruits, vegetables, whole grains, lean protein, and low-fat dairy—either in one dish or as parts of a lunch meal.

Once the recipes were submitted, finalists were chosen based on the challenge requirements. DC Central Kitchen then prepared the finalists' recipes for judging. Winners representing all 50 states, the U.S. territories, and the District of Columbia were selected to attend a Kids' "State Dinner" at the White House hosted by Mrs. Obama. The aspiring young chefs and a parent or guardian joined Mrs. Obama for a healthy lunch, featuring a selection of the winning recipes, followed by a visit to the White House Kitchen Garden.

Alabama

Yummy Summer Soup

Falcon Wiles, age 9 in 2012

"I came up with my recipe because tomatoes and yellow bell peppers are in season and they are really good for you. And Alabama's tomatoes are both delicious and nutritious," says Falcon. "I like a toasted turkey and cheese sandwich with my soup to include all the Choosemyplate food groups."

Makes 8 to 10 servings

INGREDIENTS

3 pounds tomatoes, halved

2 yellow bell peppers, seeded, stemmed, and quartered

2 garlic cloves

2 tablespoons olive oil

Salt

Pepper

8 fresh basil leaves

6 cups chicken stock or low-sodium chicken broth

1/2 cup light whipping cream or 1 percent milk

Parmesan cheese, shaved or grated

PREPARATION

1. Preheat the oven to 450°F.
2. Place the tomatoes, peppers, and garlic on 2 large baking sheets or roasting pans, drizzle with olive oil, and sprinkle with a pinch of salt and pepper. Roast until the peppers are slightly dark and the tomatoes are bubbling and slightly brown, about 40 minutes. Let the vegetables cool.
3. Once the veggies are cool, put them in a blender, along with the basil, and blend until coarsely chopped.
4. Put the chopped veggies in a large pot and add the chicken stock. Bring to a boil, then lower the heat to a simmer and slowly add the cream or milk. Continue simmering until the soup is hot, about 15 minutes. Carefully spoon the soup into bowls and top with shaved or grated Parmesan cheese.

Kale, Broccoli, Chicken, and Apple Salad

KINDALL SEWELL-MURPHY, age 10 in 2013

"I love salad!! And me and my aunt were playing around in the kitchen and combined two of our favorite recipes," says Kindall. "I would include on the side a whole wheat tortilla because all the other food groups are in it."

Makes 6 to 8 servings

INGREDIENTS

3 cups rotisserie chicken, cut into bite-size pieces

3 cups kale, torn into bite-size pieces

2 cups broccoli florets, cut into bite-size pieces

2 cups broccoli slaw

1 cup thinly sliced Brussels sprouts

1 medium plum tomato, chopped

1 cup shredded low-fat Mexican-blend cheese (or your favorite low-fat cheese)

1/2 cup chopped red onion

1/2 cup dried fruit and nut mix or pumpkin or sunflower seeds

1/4 cup dried cranberries

1 1/2 cups cored, peeled, and chopped Honeycrisp apples or your favorite apple variety

Juice from 1/2 lemon

1 cup creamy poppy seed dressing or your favorite low-fat dressing

6 to 8 whole wheat tortillas

PREPARATION

1. In a large bowl, toss together the chicken, kale, broccoli florets, broccoli slaw, Brussels sprouts, tomato, cheese, red onion, fruit and nut mix, and dried cranberries.

2. In a small bowl, toss together the apples and lemon juice. Add the apples to the salad, drizzle with salad dressing, and toss well. Serve as a salad or use the whole wheat tortillas to make wraps.

536 calories; 31g protein; 51g carbohydrates; 23g fat (5g saturated fat); 653mg sodium

VEGGIE SPAGHETTI WITH ALABAMA GULF SHRIMP

INGREDIENTS

1 large (or 2 small) spaghetti squash
1 tablespoon olive oil
1 yellow onion, peeled and chopped
6 cloves garlic, peeled and finely chopped
4 tomatoes, coarsely chopped
1 teaspoon sugar
1 teaspoon coarse sea or kosher salt
12 fresh basil leaves, cut into thin strips
8 dried whole chiles de árbol
24 large raw Alabama Gulf shrimp, peeled and deveined
2 ½ cups kale, chopped

PREPARATION

Pierce the squash with a large-pronged fork in several spots. Microwave the squash on high for 15 minutes, or until it feels soft to the touch. Let cool for 5 minutes. Cut the squash in half lengthwise; remove and discard seeds. With a fork, scrape spaghetti squash into a bowl and set aside.

In a large sauté pan, warm the oil on medium heat. Add the onion and garlic and sauté until the onions are clear and the garlic is slightly browned, about 6 minutes. Add tomatoes, sugar, and salt. Cover with a lid and cook for 10 minutes. Turn the heat to low, add the basil and chiles, and continue cooking for 8 to 10 minutes. Add shrimp, increase the heat to medium, and cook for 5 minutes. Add kale on top of the sauce mixture, cover the pan, and cook for 5 more minutes. The shrimp should be pink and the kale wilted.

Place 1 ½ cups of the cooked spaghetti squash on the plate and top with the tomato/shrimp sauce.

Jane Battle, age 10 in 2014

"I watch cooking shows on the Food Network. The show *Chopped* is all about how to create a dish out of different ingredients," says 10-year-old Jane. "For this recipe, I tried to think that way about ingredients that I love--tomatoes, kale, and pasta. I basically tried to replace a traditional meat spaghetti dish with vegetables. For the pasta, I used spaghetti squash. It's fun to scrape it into the bowl, and it looks like a science experiment! From there, I knew that fresh flavor plus healthy Alabama Gulf shrimp as a healthy protein would be perfect. My secret ingredient is the dried red pepper."

Makes 4 servings • 167 calories • 5g fat • 24g carbohydrates • 10g protein

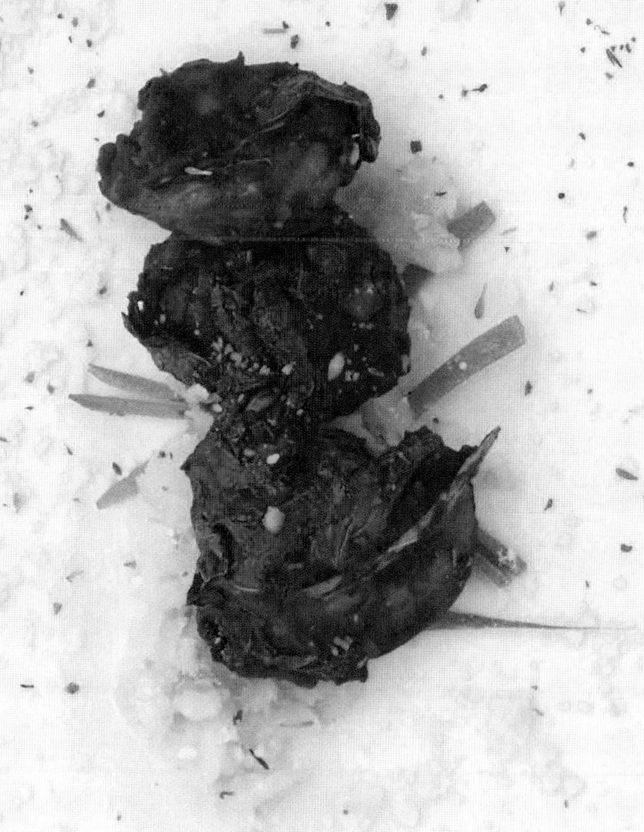

CHEF JANE

Alabama Fancy Fish Tacos

Makes 4 Servings • 393 calories • 5g fat • 56g carbohydrates • 33g protein

INGREDIENTS

4 fresh or frozen tilapia fillets
Salt to taste
1 cup quinoa, rinsed
1 large carrot, peeled and thinly sliced
1 large cucumber, thinly sliced
½ cup red cabbage
1 cup broccoli, chopped
¼ cup fresh cilantro
Juice of 1 lime
4 whole-wheat tortillas or wraps

PREPARATION

1. **Preheat the oven to 350°F.** On a large baking sheet, place the tilapia, and add salt to taste (if frozen, defrost the fish first). Bake for 25 minutes, or until the fish flakes easily with a fork.
2. **Meanwhile, in a medium pot,** bring 2 cups of water and the quinoa to a boil over medium heat; reduce heat to low and cook for about 20 minutes, or until tender.
3. **In a large bowl,** combine the vegetables and cilantro. When the fish is done, squeeze lime juice over each fillet. Fill each whole-wheat tortilla with fish and about ¼ cup vegetables. Roll up and serve.

Chef Jay Wolanzyk,

age 10 in 2015

"I wanted to make something healthy that gave me energy to play sports," says Jay. "I play outside a lot after school or I have a ballgame and I wanted something good to fill me up. I'm kind of a picky eater, but I love fish and I knew I wanted it to be the main ingredient. My mom adds vegetables in food that I may not see, so I like these better because they are different colors and I can tell which ones I'm eating!"

Green Chicken Wrap and Fruit-tacular Salad

Makes 6 servings • 452 calories • 15g fat • 59g carbohydrates • 22g protein

INGREDIENTS

For the Green Chicken Wraps:

2 cups shredded chicken
1 large avocado, peeled, pitted, and thinly sliced
¼ cup fresh spinach, chopped
⅛ cup cilantro, chopped
⅛ cup chopped onion
¼ cup low-fat mayonnaise
½ teaspoon garlic powder
Salt and pepper (optional)
6 10-inch whole-grain tortillas

For the Fruit-tacular Salad *(not pictured)***:**

2 apples, peeled, cored, and diced
1 banana, peeled and diced
1 kiwi, peeled and diced
2 tangerines, peeled and separated
½ cup diced strawberries
2 tablespoons honey
2 tablespoons fresh lemon juice

PREPARATION

1. **To make the Green Chicken Wrap:** In a large salad bowl, combine all of the ingredients together except the wraps. Place in the refrigerator for 15 minutes to chill. Once the mixture is chilled, serve with the whole-grain tortillas.
2. **To make the Fruit-tacular Salad:** In a large salad bowl, combine all of the fruit, stir in the honey and lemon juice, and combine thoroughly.

CHEF

Lael Jefferson

age 11 in 2016

"I love cooking and I love my vegetables. Avocado and spinach are two of my favorites and they are also good for your body," says Lael. "I have been making this recipe for a while but made it a bit more green. Some of the veggies and fruits were purchased at my local farmers market, along with the honey. I am the daughter of an Air Force member and Air Force veteran. Cooking is one of my many passions."

Alaska

Teriyaki Salmon Wrap

Aaron Blust, age 9 in 2012

Aaron tells us that they eat a lot of salmon in Alaska. He and mom Jeanne say these wraps taste great with smoked salmon but you can also use cooked or canned salmon, or other types of fish, such as halibut, rockfish, or even canned tuna. "This is a great way to use up leftover salmon, rice, and whatever vegetables are in the refrigerator," says Jeanne.

Aaron would serve this wrap with a glass of nonfat milk and a bowl of blueberries with 1/4 cup nonfat Greek yogurt and 1 teaspoon of honey.

Makes 4 servings

INGREDIENTS

8 ounces cooked, canned, or smoked salmon

3 tablespoons cream cheese

3 tablespoons teriyaki sauce

1/2 teaspoon freshly ground black pepper

4 (10-inch) corn or whole-wheat tortillas

1 cup cooked brown or white rice, at room temperature

4 leaves Romaine lettuce, cut into thin strips

For garnish:

Thinly sliced raw vegetables such as red bell pepper, cucumber, zucchini, tomato, and red onion

PREPARATION

1. In a large bowl, combine the salmon (if using canned, drain first), cream cheese, teriyaki sauce, and pepper, and stir thoroughly to combine.
2. In a microwave on a paper towel, warm the tortillas for about 10 seconds each.
3. Place the warm tortillas on individual plates and evenly spread 1/4 cup of rice in the middle of each. Spread 1/4 cup the salmon mixture on top of the rice, then top each wrap with lettuce and any sliced vegetables.
4. Tightly roll each tortilla around the filling from bottom to top, overlapping one end, burrito style. Slice the wraps in half if desired.

Alaskan Ceviche with Mango

ROWAN BEAN, age 9 in 2013

"I came up with this because it's a dish that has mostly fresh fruits and vegetables. It also has Alaskan fish and Alaskan spot prawns, which is the best seafood in the world. These are all things that I like," says Rowan. "I would put whole-grain tortilla chips and low-fat milk to balance it out for a healthy meal."

Makes 6 to 8 servings

INGREDIENTS

1/2 cup fresh grapefruit juice

1 to 2 Alaskan rockfish fillets, or any white, firm fish, skin removed and chopped into bite-size pieces

10 Alaskan spot prawns or large shrimp, peeled, cleaned, and tails removed, then cut into bite-size pieces

6 plum tomatoes, chopped

1 mango, peeled and chopped

3/4 cup chopped fresh cilantro leaves

1/2 cup chopped white onion

1/2 cup freshly squeezed lime juice

1/4 cup freshly squeezed lemon juice

1/4 cup freshly squeezed orange juice

1 teaspoon minced jalapeño or serrano chile (optional)

1 teaspoon kosher salt

PREPARATION

1. In a medium saucepan over moderate heat, bring the grapefruit juice to a boil. Add the rockfish and prawns, reduce the heat to a simmer, and poach the fish and prawns until just tender, about 3 minutes. Transfer the fish and prawns to a non-aluminum bowl, cover, and chill in the refrigerator up to 3 hours.

2. In a large bowl, toss together the tomatoes, mango, cilantro, and onion. Add the lime, lemon, and orange juices, the jalapeño or serrano chile, if using, and salt. Add the chilled seafood, stir to combine, and taste to see if you want to add more salt, citrus, or spiciness. Serve immediately or chill up to 2 hours for later use.

101 calories; 11.6g protein; 11g carbohydrates; 1g fat (0g saturated fat); 232mg sodium

Michael Halpern, age 10 in 2014

"Being an Alaskan-born kid, I love salmon! I like the salmon my dad prepares, but decided to break out and take it to the next level," explains Michael. "So, I decided to combine some of the ingredients from foods I enjoy to create an original recipe. I also have a friend who is gluten-intolerant, so I made this recipe gluten-free. I would include a mandarin orange, steamed asparagus, and a glass of skim milk to complete the meal."

Makes 6 servings • 357 calories • 15g fat • 34g carbohydrates • 22g protein

MAPLE-PECAN SALMON DELIGHT

INGREDIENTS

♥ For the Salmon:
1 pound wild Alaskan salmon
½ lemon
1 clove garlic, peeled and minced
1 inch fresh ginger, peeled and grated
¼ cup maple syrup
1 tablespoon low-sodium soy sauce
¼ cup chopped pecans
♥ For the Quinoa:
1 cup quinoa
1 cup carrots, peeled and chopped
1 cup peas

PREPARATION

Preheat oven to 400°F. Place the salmon in a baking dish skin-side down. Squeeze the lemon juice onto the salmon. In a small bowl, mix together garlic, ginger, maple syrup, and soy sauce. Pour the mixture over the salmon. Marinate in the refrigerator for 20 minutes.

While salmon is marinating, prepare the quinoa: In a small saucepan, boil 2 cups of water over high heat. Add the quinoa, carrots, and peas and reduce the heat to low, and cover. Cook for 15 minutes or until quinoa and carrots are tender.

Sprinkle pecans over the salmon and bake uncovered for 15 to 20 minutes or until its golden and flaky towards the edges.

Chef Sable Scotton,

age 10 in 2015

"I really like vegetables. In the summer, I wander through the garden eating peas, carrots, broccoli, and even flowers like nasturtiums," says Sable. "I also love to fish for wild salmon and other types of whitefish with my family, so this recipe brings together my two favorite worlds. This recipe is for one of my favorite foods because it is so delicious and healthy. It uses wild salmon that we harvest from the Yukon River and then jar ourselves. However, any species of canned salmon can be used."

Deliciousness over Rice

Makes 6 Servings • 341 calories • 13g fat • 35g carbohydrates • 22g protein

INGREDIENTS

2 cups chopped cauliflower
2 cups chopped broccoli
2 carrots, peeled and thinly sliced
1 cup snap peas
2 cups rainbow chard leaves, cut into 1-inch strips
1 garlic clove, peeled and minced
1 tablespoon avocado or olive oil
1 teaspoon black pepper
½ teaspoon salt
2 tablespoons unsalted butter
¼ cup peeled and diced onion
¼ cup diced celery
2 tablespoons all-purpose flour
2 cups 1% milk
1 (15-ounce) can salmon
3 cups cooked brown rice

PREPARATION

1. **Preheat the oven to 350°F.** In large bowl, combine cauliflower, broccoli, carrots, snap peas, rainbow chard, garlic, avocado or olive oil, pepper, and salt. Place in a 13- by 9-inch baking pan and bake for about 20 minutes, or until the veggies are just soft.
2. **In a large saucepan**, melt the butter over medium heat. Add the onion and celery and sauté for 5 minutes, stirring frequently. Add the flour and stir until bubbly. Add the milk, whisking to mix, until the sauce begins to bubble and thicken, about 10 minutes. Add the salmon and roasted vegetables and stir to combine. Divide the rice and salmon-veggie mix among 6 bowls and serve.

CHEF

Denali Schijvens

age 9 in 2016

"I thought of this dish because it has a lot of Alaska elements in it, like the blueberries I eat off the bush in summer while hiking, and the halibut we catch while boating," says Denali. "The rest of the components seemed to blend in perfectly with the dish. The tartness of the blueberries goes amazing with the halibut and crunch of the lettuce. I decided to pair this dish with a smoothie, because I've seen school lunches served with chocolate milk with so much sugar, and I thought a nice refreshing healthy smoothie made with fruits and a vegetable would be the perfect thing to wash down this meal."

Wrapped Alaska Denali Style and Spinach Smoothie

Makes 6 servings • 404 calories • 12g fat • 46g carbohydrates • 31g protein

INGREDIENTS

For the Whole-Wheat Crepes:
1 ¼ cups low-fat milk
2 tablespoons unsalted melted butter
½ cup whole-wheat flour
½ cup all-purpose flour
Butter, oil, or nonstick cooking spray
3 eggs
Dash of sea salt

For the Blueberry Sauce:
1 pound blueberries
Dash of sea salt
Juice of ¼ fresh lemon

For the Halibut:
1 tablespoon butter
12 (2-ounce) halibut fillets
(you can substitute with cod)
1 tablespoon low-sodium soy sauce
Juice of ½ lemon
Sea salt

Garnish:
3 tablespoons low-fat sour cream
6 lettuce leaves

For the Spinach Smoothie ***(not pictured)*****:**
¾ peeled banana
15 pieces diced fresh or frozen mango
6 pineapple chunks
5 peach slices
½ cup orange juice
¾ cup low-fat plain yogurt
1 ½ cups fresh spinach

PREPARATION

1. **For the Whole-Wheat Crepes:** In a medium bowl, beat together milk, eggs, and butter. Add the flours and salt and whisk until smooth. In a nonstick pan over medium heat, melt a small amount of butter, oil, or nonstick cooking spray. Pour approximately ¼-cup batter into pan. Cook for 1 to 2 minutes, gently flip over with a spatula and cook for 1 more minute. Transfer to plate and continue making the rest of the crepes.
2. **For the Blueberry Sauce:** In a small saucepan, warm the blueberries, covered, over medium heat until the berries are boiling. Remove the cover, reduce the heat to low, add sea salt to taste and lemon juice, and stir. Let blueberries slowly reduce until the rest of the meal is ready, stirring occasionally.
3. **For the Halibut:** In a large nonstick pan, melt the butter over medium heat. Cook the halibut for 2 minutes, sprinkle with sea salt, soy sauce, and lemon juice, and cook for 4 more minutes, or until golden brown.
4. **For the Smoothie:** Combine all ingredients in a blender. Blend together until smooth.
5. **To Assemble the Crepes:** Put a crepe on each plate, smear ½ tablespoon of low-fat sour cream on top, add lettuce, 2 halibut pieces, and top with a generous spoonful of blueberry sauce. Eat unwrapped, with a fork, or wrap up and eat with your hands.

American Samoa

Breadfruit, Taro, and Garlic Chicken Trio

CHEF
Amelie Chen
age 9 in 2016

"In American Samoa, we eat taro and breadfruit as our starch," says Amelie. "We eat it with coconut cream and other food. My recipe has taro and breadfruit, two local foods found in the Pacific. We also have lots of coconut trees and coconut cream. It tastes great together."

Makes 2 servings • 363 calories • 6g fat • 44g carbohydrates • 35g protein

INGREDIENTS

For the Garlic Chicken:
1 skinless boneless chicken breast, halved
1 tablespoon minced garlic
¼ teaspoon sugar
Salt

For the Breadfruit and Taro:
6 ounces taro
(you can substitute with parsnip or sweet potato)
5 ounces breadfruit
(you can use canned or substitute with plantains)
6 ounces broccoli
¼ cup lite coconut cream
2 tablespoons water
1 tomato, quartered
Salt and freshly ground black pepper

PREPARATION

1. **To make the Garlic Chicken:** In a small bowl, combine the chicken, garlic, sugar, and salt to taste, and marinate for ½ hour in the refrigerator. In a medium nonstick pan, cook the chicken breast on medium heat for 3 minutes on each side or until golden brown.
2. **To make the Breadfruit and Taro:** In a large stockpot, fill with water, taro, and breadfruit and bring to a boil over high heat. Boil for 6 minutes, add the broccoli, and boil another 4 minutes. Drain the water from the pot, moving the broccoli to a plate, but leaving the taro and breadfruit in the pot. Add in the coconut cream, water, tomato, salt, and pepper to taste, and stir. Cook 2 minutes more.
3. **To Assemble:** Divide all of the food onto two plates. Pour any leftover coconut cream sauce onto taro and breadfruit and serve.

Arizona

Quinoa, Black Bean, and Corn Salad

Haile Thomas, age 11 in 2012

Haile's family gave up eating white rice after learning her dad is diabetic, so they began experimenting with quinoa. Haile's recipe adds the protein-packed grain to the family's favorite black bean and corn salsa, and they serve the salad hot or cold with tacos or just about anything else, like shrimp, chicken, pork, fish, or lean red meats. Haile's mom, Charmaine, reports the secret to its success is that "all the kids love it, the ingredients are affordable, it's easy to make, and it's just plain good."

Makes 6 servings

INGREDIENTS

2 (15-ounce) cans organic black beans, drained and rinsed

4 cups fresh corn

1 pint cherry tomatoes, quartered

2 cups cooked quinoa

1 medium red onion, chopped

1/2 bunch fresh cilantro or flat-leaf parsley

1 medium red onion, chopped

2 avocados, pitted, peeled, and cut into cubes

1 tablespoon extra-virgin olive oil

1 lemon, halved

Sea salt

PREPARATION

In a large bowl, combine the black beans, corn, tomatoes, quinoa, cilantro or parsley, red onion, avocados, and olive oil. Squeeze the lemon halves and add their juice to the bowl. Toss to combine then season to taste with salt and serve.

Cook's Note: To make this dish hot, warm it on the stovetop or in a microwave, or sauté all the vegetables together and add the avocado and cilantro or parsley after it's plated.

Banana's Black Bean Burritos

ALEXANDRA NICKLE, age 10 in 2013

"My nickname is Banana. My mom has called me Banana ever since I was a baby because I always ate bananas. Shhh... Don't tell any other kids in Arizona that this is my nickname," says Alexandra. "Kids in Arizona love bean burritos. My version is healthier than you can find in most restaurants. I love mangoes. A good mango is a great food for any day of the year. As a side dish, I would suggest a mango soy smoothie made with frozen bananas."

Makes 6 servings

INGREDIENTS

For the mango salsa:

2 ripe mangoes, peeled and chopped

1/2 red onion, chopped

1 tablespoon finely chopped fresh cilantro leaves

1 tablespoon freshly squeezed lime juice

1 teaspoon olive oil

1/4 teaspoon salt

1/4 teaspoon freshly ground black pepper

For the black beans:

2 teaspoons olive oil

1/2 red onion, chopped

3 medium tomatoes, diced

1 1/2 teaspoons ground cumin

1 1/2 teaspoons dried oregano

1 teaspoon salt

2 (15-ounce) cans black beans, drained and rinsed

6 large romaine lettuce leaves

6 whole-grain tortillas (warm)

1/4 cup shredded low-fat Monterey Jack cheese

PREPARATION

Make the mango salsa:

1. In a large bowl, toss together the mango, red onion, cilantro, lime juice, olive oil, salt, and pepper. Set aside.

Make the black beans:

1. In a medium sauté pan over moderate heat, warm 1 teaspoon olive oil. Add the red onion and sauté until translucent, about 5 minutes. Add the tomatoes, cumin, oregano, and salt. Remove the mixture from the heat and let cool for a few minutes. Transfer the tomato mixture to a blender and pulse until smooth with some lumps.

2. In a medium sauté pan over moderate heat, warm the remaining teaspoon olive oil. Add the beans and the tomato purée and cook until thickened, about 10 minutes.

3. To assemble burritos, arrange 1 large romaine lettuce leaf on top of each tortilla and top with a scoop of the black bean and tomato mixture. Sprinkle with cheese and wrap the burritos with the salsa inside, on top, or on the side of the burrito.

325 calories; 12g protein; 52g carbohydrates; 7g fat (1g saturated fat); 597mg sodium

SHRIMP TACOS WITH WATERMELON JICAMA SALAD

INGREDIENTS

♥ For the Watermelon Jicama Salad:

1 small seedless watermelon, chopped

½ cup jicama, peeled and julienned

¼ cup chopped cilantro

½ fresh jalapeño, de-seeded and finely diced

Juice from 1 lime

♥ For the Shrimp Tacos:

2 tablespoons finely diced pickled jalapeños

1 cup plain Greek yogurt

½ pound shrimp, peeled and deveined

Salt and pepper, to taste

Red chili powder, to taste

Ground cumin, to taste

¼ cup extra virgin olive oil

1 dozen 5-inch white corn tortillas

2 cups shredded cabbage

1 avocado, sliced

1 lime, quartered

Salsa, optional

PREPARATION

In a small bowl, combine the pickled jalapeños with the plain Greek yogurt. Place in the refrigerator.

To make the Watermelon Jicama Salad: In a large bowl, mix all the ingredients.

In a large bowl, lightly season the shrimp with salt, pepper, red chili powder, and cumin. In a medium sauté pan, warm the olive oil. Add the shrimp and cook until pink and lightly browned, 6 to 8 minutes. Warm the tortillas on a grill, in a pan, or in the microwave.

Place three shrimp in the tortilla and top with a drizzle of your jalapeño yogurt sauce; top with cabbage and avocado and serve with a lime wedge. Feel free to top with your favorite salsa.

Cody Vasquez, age 11 in 2014

"My mom and dad own a small Mexican food restaurant, so I always go in the kitchen and try to make something new with the ingredients we have," says Cody. "This is a great dish since I live in Arizona, because it is not only delicious and healthy but also very refreshing on warm summer days."

Makes 4-6 servings • 382 calories • 22g fat • 35g carbohydrates • 15g protein

Oodles of Zoodles with Avocado Pistachio Pesto

Makes 5 Servings • 310 calories • 31g fat • 8g carbohydrates • 3g protein

---

INGREDIENTS

For the Pesto:

1 ripe avocado
1 packed cup fresh basil
1 packed cup fresh cilantro
1 jalapeño, ribs and seeds removed
2 garlic cloves, peeled
Juice of 1 lime
½ cup olive oil
1 teaspoon salt, or to taste
½ cup pistachios

For the Zoodles:

4 zucchinis, peeled
2 cups cherry tomatoes, halved
2 cups peeled, shredded carrots
½ medium red onion, peeled and thinly sliced

PREPARATION

1. **To make the Pesto:** In a blender or food processor, blend 1 cup water with all the pesto ingredients, except the pistachios, until incorporated. Add the pistachios and blend until mostly smooth. Taste and adjust seasoning if needed. Set aside.
2. **To make the Zoodles:** Use a grater, peeler, mandoline slicer, or spiralizer to turn the zucchini into zoodles. (I used a spiralizer to get the noodle A.K.A. zoodle shape.) In a large bowl, mix the zoodles with the tomatoes, carrots, and red onion. Arrange the salad in bowls. Top with the pesto and serve.

Chef Nia Thomas,

age 10 in 2015

"I am not a big fan of cooked zucchini, but when my sister made zucchini noodles one day with a tomato sauce, I loved it," says Nia. "So, I started experimenting and came up with a very delicious pesto sauce by using lots of flavors that I love, like avocado, spinach, and pistachios. It turned out so delicious and when I made it for dinner for my family, they loved it. It is crunchy fresh, and the sauce is just awesome."

Scarlet's Southwest Barack-A-Bowl

Makes 4 servings • 365 calories • 16g fat • 33g carbohydrates • 26g protein

INGREDIENTS

½ pound chicken tenders
¾ of 7-ounce can chipotles in adobo sauce
4 teaspoons extra-virgin olive oil
2 ears of corn or 1 cup frozen corn
½ cup quinoa
¼ head of cauliflower
¼ red onion, peeled and finely chopped
2 garlic cloves, peeled and minced
½ cup canned black beans, rinsed and drained
¼ cup finely chopped cilantro
1 avocado, peeled, pitted, and thinly sliced
¼ cup Cotija cheese, grated
(Parmesan can be substituted)
¼ cup roasted, salted pumpkin seeds
Juice of ½ fresh lime

PREPARATION

1. **Place chicken and chipotles** in 1-gallon freezer bag, refrigerate, and marinate for at least 1 hour, but preferably overnight.
2. **Preheat the grill.** When it's hot, sprinkle ½ teaspoon olive oil on each ear of corn, wrap in foil, place on the side of the grill, and cover. (You can also boil the corn; place in cold water and bring to a boil over medium heat. Drain and remove the kernels.) Cook for 10 minutes, turn the corn over; remove the chicken from the plastic bag and place onto the grill. Cook for 6 minutes on each side. Turn the grill off. Remove the chicken and corn, then unwrap the corn and place back on the grill for a few minutes to get grill marks. After corn has cooled, cut the kernels off the ears by holding cobs vertically and slicing downwards. Cut chicken into bite-size pieces.
3. **Meanwhile, cook quinoa** according to package instructions in a large saucepan. In a food processor, add cauliflower and process until it's a rice-like consistency.
4. **In a large nonstick pan,** warm 1 tablespoon olive oil over medium heat, then add the onions and garlic and cook for 3 minutes, or until softened.
5. **Into the quinoa pan,** add cauliflower, chicken, corn, onion, garlic, black beans, and cilantro. Warm over medium heat for about 4 minutes. Remove from heat and add Cotija cheese. Garnish with avocado slices, pumpkin seeds, and lime juice and serve!

CHEF

Scarlet Summers

age 10 in 2016

"Much of the food we eat is inspired by southwest flavors, which is why I chose to create a healthy southwest dish loaded with power foods for energy," says Scarlet. "Due to the beautiful weather in Arizona, we grill outdoors year round, so I wanted to include grilled chicken and corn. Our family is trying to be healthier in our food choices, so I suggested to my mom that we substitute white rice with cauliflower 'rice,' and when we mixed it with the quinoa, I couldn't even tell it wasn't white rice!" Scarlet likes to serve this with a prickly pear smoothie.

Arkansas

Kickin' Chicken Salad

Trey Sims, age 12 in 2012

"This is one of Trey's favorite salads," says mom Carrie. "We serve it with a whole-grain baguette to get all of the food groups in. This is a great-tasting, healthy lunch that my kids enjoy because there are so many flavors and textures." Trey likes this with raspberry vinaigrette, but a simple olive oil and balsamic vinegar dressing would be delicious, too.

Makes 8 servings

INGREDIENTS

6 ounces fresh baby spinach

1 head lettuce, torn into bite-size pieces

2 cups chopped grilled chicken

1 pint grape tomatoes, halved

1/2 cup sliced strawberries

1/2 cup blueberries

1/2 cup grapes, halved

1/2 cup grated carrots

1/2 cup sliced avocado

1/2 cup sliced cucumber

1 cup mozzarella cubes

1 cup honey-roasted pecans

Low-fat salad dressing

PREPARATION

In a large bowl, combine the spinach, lettuce, chicken, tomatoes, strawberries, blueberries, grapes, carrots, avocado, cucumber, mozzarella, and pecans. Toss to combine, or stack in layers, and serve with your favorite low-fat salad dressing.

Confetti Spring Rolls with Orange-Cilantro Sauce

EMMA-KATE SCHAEFER, age 8 in 2013

"I created this recipe because I love to eat healthy. Quinoa is a grain and was grown about 5,000 years ago in the Andes Mountains. This grain is tasty and it's combined with my favorite vegetables, shrimp, and pineapple," says Emma-Kate. "This is a fun healthy lunch for school. I would serve it with a glass of 2% milk."

Makes 5 servings

INGREDIENTS

For the spring rolls:

2 1/4 cups low-sodium chicken broth

3/4 cup black quinoa, rinsed

1 1/2 tablespoons coconut oil

1/2 cup diced red bell pepper

1/2 cup diced yellow bell pepper

1 cup asparagus tips

2 cups medium shrimp, peeled, cleaned, and tails removed

3/4 cup diced fresh pineapple

10 rice paper wrappers

For the orange-cilantro dipping sauce:

1/4 cup sesame oil

1/4 cup freshly squeezed orange juice

1 1/2 teaspoons freshly grated orange zest

2 tablespoons soy sauce

2 tablespoons chopped fresh cilantro leaves

2 tablespoons agave nectar

1 teaspoon chopped garlic

PREPARATION

Make the spring rolls:

1. In a large pot over moderate heat, combine the chicken broth and quinoa and bring to a boil. Reduce the heat and simmer until the quinoa is tender, about 15 minutes. Transfer the cooked quinoa to a large bowl.

2. In a large saucepan over moderate heat, warm the coconut oil. Add the red and yellow bell pepper and the asparagus tips and cook until tender, about 3 minutes. Add the cooked vegetables to the quinoa. Do not clean the saucepan.

3. Using the same saucepan, sauté the shrimp over moderate heat unttil fully cooked through, about 2 minutes. Add the shrimp to the quinoa-vegetable mixture then add the pineapple and toss to combine.

Make the orange-cilantro dipping sauce:

1. In a blender, combine the sesame oil, orange juice, orange zest, soy sauce, cilantro, agave nectar, and garlic. Pulse until smooth.

Assemble the spring rolls:

1. Add 2 tablespoons of the dipping sauce to the quinoa, vegetable, and shrimp mixture and mix well.

2. Fill a pie dish with warm water. Immerse 1 rice paper wrapper in the water until pliable, about 15 seconds, then transfer it to a cutting board. Place a generous teaspoon of filling into the middle of a rice paper wrapper. Fold the bottom over the filling then fold both sides into the center, and roll the wrapper up tightly to form a spring roll. Transfer the spring roll to a plate and keep covered with a damp paper towel. Repeat with the remaining filling and rice paper wrappers. Serve with dipping sauce.

393 calories; 17g protein; 40g carbohydrates; 17g fat (5g saturated fat); 500mg sodium

ARKANSAS MEETS ASIA CATFISH SLIDERS

INGREDIENTS

♥ For the Catfish:
¼ cup low-sodium soy sauce
2 tablespoons fresh lemon juice
2 tablespoons minced ginger
2 teaspoon toasted sesame oil
½ pound catfish fillets, quartered
Pepper, to taste

♥ For the Asian Slaw:
2 cups of packaged undressed cabbage slaw
½ Granny Smith apple, peeled and thinly sliced
1 tablespoon fresh lemon juice
1 tablespoon minced ginger
1 tablespoon honey
1 tablespoon rice vinegar
3 tablespoons low-sodium soy sauce
3 tablespoons light olive oil
Zest of 1 lemon
1 tablespoon sesame seeds

PREPARATION

Preheat oven to 450°F. Prepare fish: In a small bowl, mix the soy sauce, lemon juice, ginger, and sesame oil until well combined. Cut four 12-inch aluminum foil squares and place a fillet in each. Spoon the marinade over each and season with pepper. Fold foil to make a sealed packet and bake for 15 minutes, or until fish is tender and flakey.

In a large bowl, toss the slaw with the apple. In a separate bowl, combine the lemon juice, ginger, honey, vinegar, soy sauce, and olive oil. Add lemon zest and sesame seeds and whisk until well combined. Toss the slaw ingredients with the mixture. Place the catfish fillet in a whole-wheat bun, top with slaw, and enjoy.

Hart Irby, age 10 in 2014

"I live right outside of Little Rock, and I love going into the city and seeing the Asian Gate and Garden along the Arkansas River," notes Hart. "I learned that it represents the cultural exchanges between two countries (America and South Korea) and two cities (Little Rock and Hanam City). I was inspired by this, and thought it would be neat to blend two cultures together with food. Arkansas is known for its catfish, and I love Asian food! I like to eat this with fruits and milk for a healthy lunch."

Makes 4 servings • 254 calories • 17g fat • 16g carbohydrates • 12g protein

Arkansas Baked Almond Catfish

Makes 6 Servings • 273 calories • 11g fat • 16g carbohydrates • 28g protein

INGREDIENTS

2 pounds catfish fillets
½ cup low-fat milk
1 large egg
1 teaspoon salt
¼ teaspoon black pepper
1 cup breadcrumbs or panko (Japanese breadcrumbs)
½ cup sliced almonds
¼ onion, peeled and minced
1 tablespoon unsalted butter, melted

PREPARATION

1. **Preheat the oven to 500°F.** Cut the catfish fillets roughly in half, so you have enough to feed 6 people evenly. Lightly grease a large baking sheet.
2. **In a medium bowl,** whisk together the milk, egg, salt, and pepper. In a separate bowl, combine the breadcrumbs, almonds, and onion.
3. **Dip the fish pieces in the milk and egg mixture,** then dredge them in the breadcrumb mixture, making sure they are evenly coated on both sides. Place the fish pieces on the baking sheet, drizzle with the melted butter and bake for 15 minutes, or until the fish flakes easily with a fork.

Chef Aspen Smith,

age 11 in 2015

"My family loves catfish, especially fried, but my dad and other family members have heart problems," says Aspen. "I wanted something that was healthier for all of us to enjoy. I love to cook and bake and this is really healthy, good, and easy to prepare. I watch cooking shows all the time and put a few ideas together in this recipe. I love it and hope you do, too!"

Asian in Arkansas

Makes 4 servings • 523 calories • 16g fat • 70g carbohydrates • 28g protein

INGREDIENTS

For the Spring Rolls:

4 ounces vermicelli rice noodles
1 tablespoon olive oil
½ pound shrimp, peeled, tails removed, and de-veined
8 brown-rice wrappers
8 basil leaves, whole
1 cup shredded carrots
1 cucumber, peeled and cut into thin strips
8 sprigs of mint, leaves chopped
Ponzu sauce, for dipping (optional)

For the Edamame Salad:

1 pound frozen shelled edamame, thawed
½ red onion, peeled and diced
1 tomato, diced
2 garlic cloves, peeled and minced
1 tablespoon olive oil
2 teaspoons low-sodium soy sauce
2 tablespoons rice wine vinegar
1 teaspoon grated fresh ginger

For the Watermelon Skewers *(not pictured)*:

1 cup watermelon cubes
16 sprig mint leaves, halved
8 bamboo skewers

PREPARATION

1. **To make the Spring Rolls:** In a medium saucepan, cook vermicelli noodles according to package instructions; rinse, drain, and cool. Meanwhile, in a large nonstick pan, warm the olive oil over medium heat. Add the shrimp and sauté until pink and cooked through, about 6 minutes. Let cool and then coarsely chop.
2. **To Assemble:** Place a rice wrapper in a bowl of warm water until softened, then lay on a flat surface. Place one basil leaf first. Then add vermicelli noodles, ⅛ of shrimp, carrots, cucumber, and mint. Fold in the sides of the wrapper and then roll. Continue with remaining 7 wrappers. Serve with Ponzu sauce for dipping.
3. **To make the Edamame Salad:** In a large stockpot of boiling water, cook the edamame over medium-high heat, until just softened; drain. Into a large bowl, add the onion, tomato, edamame, and garlic. In a separate small bowl, whisk thoroughly the olive oil, soy sauce, rice wine vinegar, and ginger. Pour the dressing over the salad and let sit in the refrigerator for 15 minutes, or until the dressing is absorbed.
4. **To make the Watermelon Skewers:** Alternate watermelon and 2 whole mint leaves on skewers. Serve 2 skewers with 2 Spring Rolls and Edamame Salad.

CHEF

Lily Radtke

age 11 in 2016

"Lily is small in stature, but big in heart, and cooking is a place where she feels especially skilled," says Lily's mom, Catherine. "She loves southern cuisine, but enjoys experimenting with recipes from around the world. Lily and I are able to bike to a farmers market every Saturday. Rice and soybeans are huge crops in Arkansas, so Lily decided to showcase these two things in her recipe. She also wanted to feature watermelon in her dish. Lily makes this recipe on the weekends so she can take it to school for lunch."

California

3-Pepper Soup

Sean Reichbach, age 9 in 2012

"I went to the store with my mom and saw a red, an orange, and a yellow bell pepper and had an idea to make a three-pepper soup! The secret is the three peppers and that we use three different kinds of peppers: fresh bell peppers, ground black pepper, and a little chili pepper powder," says Sean. "When I get a cold, we make this soup and I feel better." Mom Andrea notes you can use any whole-wheat pasta or soup pasta if you prefer.

Makes 4 servings

INGREDIENTS

8 ounces vermicelli noodles, broken in half

2 tablespoons olive oil

3 Roma or plum tomatoes, diced

1 small red onion, diced

1 red bell pepper, diced

1 yellow bell pepper, diced

1 orange bell pepper, diced

1 Idaho or baking potato, peeled and diced

1 1/2 cups baby carrots, diced

8 ounces boneless, skinless chicken breast, cut into 1/2-inch pieces

1 teaspoon chili powder

1 teaspoon sea salt

1 teaspoon freshly ground black pepper

2 cups organic chicken stock or low-sodium chicken broth

Whole-wheat rolls, for serving

PREPARATION

1. In a large soup or pasta pot, bring salted water to a boil. Add the vermicelli noodles and cook until al dente. Drain and reserve.
2. In the same pot, heat the olive oil over moderate heat. Add the tomatoes, red onion, bell peppers, potato, and carrots and sauté until softened and lightly browned, 5 to 7 minutes.
3. Add the chicken, chili powder, salt, and pepper and sauté until the chicken is cooked through, about 5 minutes.
4. Add the chicken stock and bring to a boil, then lower the heat and simmer for 10 minutes.
5. While the soup is simmering, warm the whole-wheat rolls in the oven or toaster oven. Ladle the hot soup into bowls, adding the vermicelli noodles according to people's taste.

Pork and Tofu Lettuce Cups

ROSE SCOTT, age 12 in 2013

"When my little brother Galen was a baby, he was allergic to a lot of foods. He couldn't eat wheat, dairy, or eggs. That meant no pizza or macaroni and cheese. My mom spent a lot of time trying to find nutritious foods that he could eat," says Rose. "She used to serve a pork and tofu dish over rice. I was inspired by that dish when I made this recipe. It can be served with brown rice, but I like to eat it with lots of veggies and sliced oranges on the side. You can also make this with ground beef or turkey."

Makes 6 servings

INGREDIENTS

3 tablespoons reduced-sodium soy sauce

1 tablespoon sesame oil

1 tablespoon cornstarch

2 teaspoons white or rice vinegar

2 teaspoons grated ginger

2 teaspoons sugar

2 cloves garlic, minced

2 teaspoons olive oil

1 pound lean ground pork

1 block firm tofu, drained well and cut into 1/2-inch cubes

2 heads romaine lettuce, cleaned and separated into leaves

Toppings: 1 bag broccoli slaw (undressed), plus bean sprouts, fresh cilantro, fresh mint, and lime slices

PREPARATION

1. Make the sauce: In a small bowl, whisk together the soy sauce, sesame oil, cornstarch, vinegar, ginger, sugar, and garlic.

2. In a medium sauté pan over moderately high heat, warm the olive oil. Add the ground pork and cook, stirring to break up the meat, until brown, 5 to 7 minutes. Drain any excess oil from the pan then add the sauce to the pan and cook, stirring frequently, until thickened, about 3 minutes. Add the tofu and cook until heated through, about 2 minutes.

3. To serve, scoop several heaping tablespoons of the pork and tofu mixture into each romaine lettuce "cup" then top with broccoli slaw, bean sprouts, cilantro, mint, and lime slices.

180 calories; 22g protein; 5g carbohydrates; 7g fat (1.5g saturated fat); 283mg sodium

Genene Savall Wedd, age 10 in 2014

"I love cooking with my mom. It is fun spending time with her and talking about my day," says Genene. "This is one of my favorite recipes because it reminds me of Ethiopia, my birthplace, and is a very healthy meal for my body. We added our favorite traditional ingredients together to create this comfort food to suit our tastes. When we make this recipe, we love to serve it with *injera*, a type of breadlike sourdough that you can use to pick up the Ethiopian Kik Alitcha with your fingers." *(Please note: Photo was styled differently than the recipe.)*

Makes 4 servings • 253 calories 4g fat 38g carbohydrates 14g protein

ETHIOPIAN KIK ALITCHA

INGREDIENTS

I tablespoon olive oil
3 cups onions, peeled and chopped
1 cup diced carrots
6 cloves of garlic, peeled and
finely chopped
1 teaspoon minced fresh ginger
½ teaspoon turmeric
½ teaspoon salt
¼ teaspoon ground pepper
1 cup dried yellow split peas, washed
and soaked overnight
Lettuce leaves

PREPARATION

In a large pot over medium-low heat, warm the oil. Add the onions and cook until soft and translucent, about 8 minutes. Add the carrots, garlic, and ginger and cook 2 minutes. Add the turmeric, salt, ground pepper, and 3 ½ cups of water and turn heat to high.

Bring water to a boil, add the split peas, and reduce heat to medium-low. Place a lid partially on the pot, but leave a gap for steam to escape. Simmer for 40 to 60 minutes, stirring occasionally, until the yellow split peas are tender. Add more water if the water boils off too quickly.

When the peas are softened, remove from heat and mash them gently with a fork. Serve on a bed of lettuce.

Chef Aria Pelaez,

age 9 in 2015

"I was inspired to make this recipe because my family makes bland tacos," says Aria. "I took leftover BBQ pineapple, tomatoes, orange peppers, and red onions and made a taco with them. I added grilled fish and I made a guacamole yogurt sauce to give it a strong taste. This dish makes my mouth water. You rock, Mrs. Michelle Obama!

P.S. This is gluten free! My granddad has Celiac so I try to eat gluten free, too, in his honor."

California Rainbow Taco with Mic-kale Obama Slaw and Barack-amole

Makes 4 Servings • 482 calories • 22g fat • 55g carbohydrates • 25g protein

INGREDIENTS

For the Tacos:

1 tablespoon vegetable oil
1 cup fresh pineapple, cut into 1-inch chunks
1 red onion, peeled and cut into 1-inch chunks
1 orange, red, or green bell pepper, seeded and cut into 1-inch chunks
24 cherry tomatoes
2 fresh tilapia fillets
8 corn tortillas
½ cup low-fat Mexican cheese blend

For the Slaw:

½ cup shredded cabbage
½ cup finely chopped kale
¼ cup peeled shredded carrots
¼ cup fresh cilantro
¼ cup red onion, peeled and diced
1 tablespoon vegetable oil
Juice from 3 limes
Salt and pepper to taste

For the Dip:

2 avocadoes, pitted
1 cup yogurt
1 garlic clove, peeled and minced
¼ cup chopped fresh cilantro
Juice from 3 limes
Salt and pepper to taste

Equipment:

4 skewers

PREPARATION

1. **Grill the veggies and fish:** Grease the grill lightly with vegetable oil to prevent sticking and preheat to medium-high. Place the fruit and veggies on 4 skewers, alternating the pineapple, onion, bell pepper, and cherry tomatoes. Cook the veggies and fish, turning once, about 5 minutes per side, or until cooked through and browned on the outside.
2. **Meanwhile, make the slaw:** In a large bowl, combine all the slaw ingredients and mix thoroughly.
3. **Make the dip:** In a blender or food processor, combine all the dip ingredients. Blend until just mixed, then season to taste with salt and pepper.
4. **Warm each tortilla in a frying pan over low heat.** Flip then sprinkle with 1 tablespoon of cheese and heat until the cheese melts. Place each tortilla on a plate and top with ¼ piece of fish and a few grilled vegetables. Top each with 1 big spoonful of cabbage slaw, drizzle with Guacamole-Yogurt dip, roll up, and serve.

CHEF

Cannon Meiers

age 8 in 2016

"Cannon created this recipe because he loves eating fruits, vegetables, lean protein, and whole grains," says Cannon's mom, Amanda. "He couldn't always eat whole grains because of a rare food allergy that he's since outgrown. Cannon also has a very rare genetic disorder called Mosaic Trisomy 14 and Uniparental Disomy 14, so eating healthy and exercising is a top priority for us! Cannon has been making this recipe for a little over a year, changing things along the way. Living in California, we are so lucky to have a variety of fruits and veggies that are easily accessible."

Cannon's California Rolls

Makes 6 to 8 servings • 389 calories • 16g fat • 31g carbohydrates • 31g protein

INGREDIENTS

1 teaspoon salt
Juice of 2 fresh lemons
1 ½ pounds chicken tenders
1 avocado, peeled, pitted, and thinly sliced
½ cup low-fat Greek yogurt
½ cup toasted sliced almonds
¼ cup raisins
1 apple, peeled, cored, and chopped
2 teaspoons chia seeds
1 celery stalk, finely chopped
2 green onions, peeled and thinly sliced
8 whole-wheat tortillas or thin, wide slices of cucumber

PREPARATION

1. **In a large stockpot,** combine 4 cups of water with ½ teaspoon salt and the juice from 1½ lemons. Bring to a boil over medium-high heat and add the chicken. Cover with a lid, reduce heat, and simmer for 10 minutes or until the chicken is cooked through. Drain the water and shred the chicken.
2. **Meanwhile, in a large bowl,** combine the avocado with the Greek yogurt. Add the almonds, raisins, apple, chia seeds, celery, green onions, and remaining lemon juice and salt. Add the chicken and mix well.
3. **Dividing evenly,** spread the chicken mixture on a tortilla or in the cucumber slices and roll up. Slice the tortilla into bite-sized pieces or secure the cucumbers with a toothpick. Serve with grapes or your favorite fruit or veggie!

Colorado

Rainbow Salad with Black Beans, Mint, and Lemon

Aidan Gould, age 12 in 2012

"It all started when I broke my arm and was feeling forlorn," says Aidan. "I wasn't allowed to play soccer, ride my unicycle, run, or do anything fun. My mom got me four mint plants to cheer me up. I planted them as best I could with one arm. The mint soon filled the pot, and, by the time I got my cast off, even started to flow over the rim. I started to make mint tea, but still had too much mint. So I made up Rainbow Salad for my family. It's a bright and tasty salad that is easy and fun to make because you get to use the food processor to cut the vegetables. I love salad!" Aidan enjoys this with whole-wheat crackers.

Makes 6 servings

INGREDIENTS

2 (15-ounce) cans black beans, rinsed and drained

6 carrots, grated

3 tomatoes, diced

1 yellow bell pepper, sliced

1/4 small purple cabbage, thinly sliced (about 3 1/2 cups total)

1 cup fresh mint, finely chopped

Zest and juice of 3 lemons

1/4 cup olive oil

Salt

PREPARATION

1. In a large bowl, combine the beans, carrots, tomatoes, pepper, cabbage, and mint. Toss to combine.
2. In a small bowl, whisk together the lemon zest, lemon juice, and olive oil. Season to taste with salt.
3. Drizzle the dressing over the salad and toss to coat the vegetables in dressing.

Sushi Salad

NICHOLAS HORNBOSTEL DE MOURA E SILVA
age 8 in 2013

"I have loved sushi since I was little! I wanted to make sushi something even healthier, and I did!" writes Nicholas. "I got the idea from thinking about eating sushi and then the next day I thought about eating salad. Then I put the two together and it equaled a sushi salad! That night we tested the recipe and it was amazing! My parents rated it a 9 and I was proud of myself. You can serve it with brown rice and oranges for dessert."

Makes 4 servings

INGREDIENTS

1/4 cup plus 1 tablespoon canola oil

1 pound skinless salmon fillets

2 teaspoons seasoned rice vinegar

1/2 teaspoon sesame oil

1/2 teaspoon salt

1 cup warm cooked brown rice

2 tablespoons black sesame seeds

1 tablespoon reduced-sodium soy sauce

8 cups prewashed mixed greens, including baby spinach

1 small pitted avocado, cut into 1/2-inch cubes (optional)

1 orange

4 seaweed sheets cut with scissors into 1/2-inch squares

PREPARATION

1. In a sauté pan over moderate heat, warm 1 tablespoon of the canola oil. Add the salmon and cook for 4 minutes. Flip the salmon over and cook for an additional 4 minutes. Transfer the salmon to a bowl and gently shred into 1-inch pieces.

2. In a small jar or bowl, combine the remaining 1/4 cup canola oil with the vinegar, sesame oil, and salt. Cover and shake the jar to mix the salad dressing or whisk it together.

3. In a large bowl, stir together the cooked rice, sesame seeds, and soy sauce. Add the mixed greens, avocado, and salmon. Drizzle with salad dressing and a squeeze of the orange, and sprinkle with seaweed pieces. Yum!

545 calories; 32g protein; 25g carbohydrates; 36g fat (3.7g saturated fat); 403mg sodium

GRILLED SALMON WITH FARRO & WARM SWISS CHARD SALAD

INGREDIENTS

♥ For the Salmon:
1 cup farro
2 tablespoons olive oil
4 salmon fillets (about 1 pound)
2 tablespoons herbes de Provence
Salt and pepper, to taste
Pinch garlic powder
Pinch onion powder
1 lemon, thinly sliced

♥ For the Salad:
½ tablespoon olive oil
Bunch Swiss chard, roughly chopped
1 large carrot, julienned
1 large red bell pepper, julienned
1 tablespoon balsamic vinegar
Salt and pepper to taste
Crumbled feta cheese, to taste

♥ For the Smoothie:
1 cup orange juice
1 cup lite coconut milk
2 cups low-fat vanilla yogurt
1 teaspoon vanilla extract
2 frozen bananas
1 cup frozen cut mango
½ teaspoon fresh ground nutmeg

PREPARATION

In a large pot, boil 2 cups of water over high heat. Add the farro and bring back to a boil. Reduce the heat to low, cover, and simmer for 30 minutes, until grains are tender and all water is absorbed.

Preheat the grill. Drizzle the olive oil on salmon. Mix the spices in a small bowl and sprinkle evenly to coat salmon. Grill salmon fillet for up to 5 minutes per side, depending on how thick the salmon is. After flipping the salmon on the grill, lay lemon slices on the fish.

To make the Salad: In a large pan, warm the olive oil over medium heat. Add the Swiss chard and cook for 2 minutes. Add the carrot and red pepper and cook for 2 minutes. When Swiss chard wilts, add balsamic vinegar, salt, and pepper, and feta cheese, if you want.

To make the Smoothie: Add liquid ingredients to the blender first. Add rest of ingredients. Blend and enjoy!

Kiana Farkash, age 8 in 2014

"I made grilled salmon because it is one of my very favorite dishes," says Kiana. "I made the salad because it is very colorful and it reminds me of spring. I like warm, tropical places, so I decided to serve this with a tropical breeze smoothie because it reminds me of our family trip to Florida. I used farro because it's a healthy whole grain and I like the nuttier flavor it has!"

Makes 4 servings • 453 calories • 21g fat • 33g carbohydrates • 30g protein

CHEF KIANA

Rain's Turkey Chili

Makes 10 Servings • 288 calories • 6g fat · 40g carbohydrates • 23g protein

---

INGREDIENTS

2 tablespoons olive oil
1 pound lean ground turkey
1 medium red bell pepper, deseeded and diced
1 small zucchini, diced
1 white onion, peeled and diced
1 cup carrots, peeled and diced
3 kale leaves with stems removed, chopped finely
2 (14.5-ounce) cans fire-roasted diced tomatoes in juice
1 (15-ounce) can dark red kidney beans, drained and rinsed
1 (15-ounce) can pinto beans, drained and rinsed
4 cups low-sodium chicken broth
1 cup old-fashioned rolled oats
2 tablespoons of chili powder (or to taste)
1 tablespoon honey
1 garlic clove, peeled and minced
1 teaspoon onion powder
1 teaspoon ground cumin
2 teaspoons dried oregano
1 teaspoon salt
½ teaspoon pepper

PREPARATION

1. **In a large stockpot,** heat the olive oil over medium heat. Add the turkey and cook, breaking up the meat with a wooden spoon for about 12 minutes, or until light brown and cooked through.
2. **Add the vegetables to the stockpot,** cover, and cook for 10 minutes. Add the remaining ingredients, reduce the heat to low, and simmer for 40 minutes. Enjoy your delicious chili!

Chef Rain Adams,

age 11 in 2015

"This chili is a vegetable-packed super food that follows MyPlate guidelines," says Rain. "Vegetables make up 50% of each serving, the turkey 25%. My secret ingredient, oats, makes up the grain, and completes this great tasting, healthy meal." Rain recommends that this turkey chili be served with baked tortilla chips and apple slices.

Hannah's Sweet and Savory Chicken and Peaches

Makes 4 servings • 594 calories • 10g fat • 55g carbohydrates • 71g protein

INGREDIENTS

4 boneless, skinless chicken breasts
1 tablespoon curry powder
Salt and freshly ground black pepper
2 peaches, pitted and halved
2 tablespoons honey
1 tablespoon olive oil
½ onion, peeled and finely chopped
1 8-ounce package sliced mushrooms
1 garlic clove, peeled and minced
1 cup reduced-sodium chicken broth
½ teaspoon cinnamon
1 Gala apple, peeled, cored, and chopped
1 cup low-fat milk
2 ½ tablespoons all-purpose flour
½ teaspoon oregano
2 cups cooked basmati, white, or brown rice
½ cucumber, sliced
Optional toppings:
Raisins, cashews, peanuts, sliced bell pepper

PREPARATION

1. **Preheat the grill to medium-high heat.** Season chicken breasts each with ½ teaspoon curry powder, salt, and pepper, and add to the grill. Cook for 6 minutes on each side, or until golden brown. Remove chicken then add peach halves, cut side down, and cover. Grill until peaches are soft and tender, about 4 minutes. Remove from the grill, plate, and drizzle with honey.
2. **In a large nonstick pan,** warm oil over medium heat. Add onion, mushrooms, and garlic and cook for about 5 minutes, stirring occasionally, until vegetables are tender. Add ¾ cup broth, cinnamon, and apple to pan and warm through.
3. **In a blender,** combine milk, flour, remaining 1 teaspoon curry powder, ¼ cup broth, oregano, salt, and pepper to taste. Blend until smooth and creamy. Transfer to a small saucepan, heat over medium heat, continuously stirring with a whisk, until slightly thickened.
4. **Divide** the cooked rice and chicken amongst 4 plates. Top chicken with vegetables and sauce. Arrange cucumbers along rim. Serve with grilled peaches.

CHEF
Hannah Skalicky
age 10 in 2016

"Every year since I was 4 years old, I have helped my dad at the Rotary Peach Festival," says Hannah. "We help sell Palisade peaches, which grow in the foothills of the Rockies. I learned how to make grilled peaches from my Dad, who grills a lot. The curried chicken recipe was created because I wanted to make an Indian dish. My friend's mom is Indian and teaches cooking classes that include lots of curry and cumin, which are native to India. She has inspired me to experiment while cooking. These two foods complement each other and make for a delicious summer lunch."

Connecticut

Heavenly Lunch Wrap

Betsy DaSilva, age 10 in 2012

"Every day (and trust me, every day it annoys me) I eat this because it's good for my health," says Betsy. "This recipe has one very important and new ingredient, which is quinoa. My mom grew up eating this amazing Incan food. Whenever I eat this food, I know that I've been blessed with the energy to focus more at school." Betsy has this with a slice of watermelon, a hard-boiled egg, some cucumber slices, and low-fat milk.

Makes 1 serving

INGREDIENTS

1 (10-inch) whole-grain wrap

1 teaspoon mayonnaise

1 tablespoon cooked quinoa

6 fresh baby spinach leaves

4 slices tomato

3 slices turkey breast

PREPARATION

1. Place the wrap on a plate and evenly spread the mayonnaise over the entire surface. Spoon the quinoa in the middle of the wrap, then top with spinach, tomato, and turkey.
2. Tightly roll the wrap around the filling, from bottom to top, overlapping one end, burrito style.

Quinoa "Risotto" with Shrimp and Kale

JOHN BREITFELDER, age 9 in 2013

"My mom's side of the family is Italian and we all love cooking together," says John. "For years, my mom has been hiding vegetables in our risottos. Now that I've caught on to her sneaky ways, I've kicked it up a notch and added quinoa in place of rice. This is now one of my favorites—and it's gluten-free, too! For dessert, a bowl of raspberries and blueberries swirled around vanilla Greek yogurt is a fun red, white, and blue treat!"

Makes 6 servings

INGREDIENTS

3 tablespoons olive oil

3 cloves garlic, minced

1 pound large shrimp, peeled and deveined

Salt and freshly ground black pepper

1/2 yellow onion, diced

1 cup well-rinsed quinoa

2 1/4 cups chicken stock or low-sodium chicken broth

1 cup chopped kale

1/2 cup frozen peas

1/2 cup frozen corn

1 medium plum tomato, chopped

1/4 cup grated Parmesan

PREPARATION

1. In a large sauté pan over moderate heat, warm 2 tablespoons olive oil. Add the garlic and shrimp, along with a pinch of salt and pepper, and sauté, stirring occasionally, until the shrimp turn pink, about 5 minutes. Transfer to a bowl. Do not clean pan.

2. In the same sauté pan over moderate heat, warm the remaining 1 tablespoon olive oil. Add the onion and sauté until translucent, about 3 minutes. Add the quinoa and cook, stirring occasionally, for about 1 minute. Add the chicken stock and bring to a boil, stirring occasionally. Reduce the heat and simmer for 5 minutes. Add the kale, peas, corn, and tomato and cook until the quinoa is tender, about 5 minutes. Add the cooked shrimp and gently stir to combine. Add the Parmesan, and season with salt and pepper. Serve hot!

317 calories; 21g protein; 30g carbohydrates; 12g fat (2.6g saturated fat); 383mg sodium

QUINOA CHICKEN BURGER WITH KALE & POTATO CHIPS

INGREDIENTS

4 teaspoons olive oil
10 ounces lacinato kale, stemmed and chopped
1 yellow potato, sliced thinly
½ pound skinless boneless chicken, chopped
¾ cup cooked quinoa
2 teaspoons teriyaki
1 tablespoon vegetable oil
4 whole-wheat slider buns
Salt

PREPARATION

Make the Kale and Potato Chips: Preheat oven to 325°F. In a large bowl, mix 2 teaspoons olive oil with the kale and sprinkle with salt to taste. Spread the leaves out on a baking pan. In another large bowl, toss potato with remaining 2 teaspoons of olive oil and sprinkle with salt to taste. Spread the potato slices on a baking pan. Bake both kale and potatoes for 20 minutes, switching tray positions halfway through, until kale is crispy and potatoes are light golden brown.

Make the Chicken Quinoa Burgers: In a food processor or blender, grind the chicken, pulsing until the chicken is finely ground. In a large bowl, combine the chicken with the cooked quinoa, and teriyaki. Combine thoroughly and shape into 4 patties. In a large sauté pan, warm the oil over moderate heat. Add the patties and cook for 5 minutes per side, until the chicken is cooked through and light brown. Place cooked on a bun and serve with kale and potato chips.

Cecilia Vinas, age 10 in 2014

"I came up with my dish by thinking about a food that a lot of Americans enjoy--I came up with a hamburger," says Cecilia. "Next I thought of how I can make this dish healthier but still taste really good. I thought of a quinoa base for grain with chicken for a lean protein, then kale and potato for veggies."

Makes 4 servings • 427 calories • 19g fat • 36g carbohydrates • 20g protein

CHEF CECILIA

Hannah's Eggy Potato Scramble

Makes 2 Servings • 437 calories • 19g fat • 43g carbohydrates • 25g protein

---

INGREDIENTS

2 sweet potatoes
1 cup Brussels sprouts
1 garlic clove, peeled and crushed
1 tablespoon olive oil
1 teaspoon apple cider vinegar
Pinch of salt
Pinch of pepper
½ cup mushrooms, chopped
4 large eggs
2 tablespoons milk
¼ cup low-fat cheese
¼ cup whole-wheat breadcrumbs
¼ cup ham, shredded

PREPARATION

1. **Preheat the oven to 400°F.** Wash and dry the sweet potatoes, place on a large baking sheet, and bake for 40 minutes.
2. **Meanwhile, in a baking dish,** toss the Brussels sprouts with the garlic, olive oil, apple cider vinegar, salt, and pepper. Add to the oven where the sweet potatoes are baking. After 10 minutes, add the mushrooms, and cook for another 10 minutes, or until the veggies are slightly browned.
3. **In a small bowl,** whisk together the eggs and milk. Cook in a nonstick pan over medium heat for about 2 minutes, or until the eggs are scrambled.
4. **When the potatoes and veggies are cooked,** remove from the oven (leave the oven on) and carefully cut the sweet potatoes in half lengthwise, being careful not to rip the skin. Scoop out the sweet potato flesh and place in a medium bowl. Add the Brussels sprouts-mushroom mixture and the scrambled eggs, mix together well, and place into the potato skins. Sprinkle the cheese, breadcrumbs, and shredded ham on top of each potato half. Bake for 5 minutes, or until the cheese has melted.

Chef Hannah Betts,

age 10 in 2015

"I came up with my recipe, because I wanted a meal that was filling and healthy, and also included sweet potatoes as I really love them," says Hannah. "I do gymnastics and swimming, so I need food that is going to fill me up and give me lots of energy. I love to cook and I help my mom out in the kitchen all the time. Even my little brother Daniel (who wants to be president one day) says it is delicious. I hope you enjoy it, too."

Springtime Lunchtime

Makes 4 servings • 200 calories • 8g fat • 16g carbohydrates • 16g protein

INGREDIENTS

For the Egg Bird's Nests:

4 eggs
½ cup cooked chicken
½ cup shredded carrots
⅔ cup alfalfa sprouts
8 sprigs cilantro
8 yellow cherry tomatoes, halved

For the French Toast Flowers:

1 egg
1 tablespoon milk
¼ teaspoon cinnamon
¼ tablespoon butter
2 slices whole-wheat bread
1 cherry tomato, halved
2 blueberries

For the Apple Bird's Nest:

1 medium apple, peeled and cored
Handful of blueberries

PREPARATION

1. **To make the Egg Bird's Nest:** Preheat the oven to 350°F. Oil 4 muffin cups and place in a muffin tin pan. In a small bowl, mix one egg with a fork. Pour the egg into a muffin cup. Repeat with the next three muffin cups. Place muffin pan in the oven for 4 minutes. Remove from the oven and add ¼ of chicken, carrots, sprouts, cilantro, and tomatoes into each egg. Then place muffin pan back into oven and cook for another 15 minutes. Take out and let cool for 3 minutes; cover to keep warm.
2. **To make French Toast Flowers:** Meanwhile, mix the egg in a bowl with milk and cinnamon. In a large nonstick skillet, melt the butter on low heat. Use a flower-shaped cookie cutter to cut 2 flower shapes out of each slice of bread. Dip and cover the bread flowers in the egg mixture. Add to the pan and cook for 2 minutes on each side or until golden brown. Transfer to plates. Add a halved cherry red tomato in the center of 2 of the French toast flowers and a blueberry in the center of the other 2 French toast flowers.
3. **To make the Apple Bird's Nest:** Cut the apple into spirals or cut around as if peeling to make the bird's nests out of the apple. It will make four small bird's nests. Top each bird's nest with blueberries. Serve 1 Egg Bird's Nest, 1 French Toast, and 1 Apple Bird's Nest on each plate.

CHEF

Kalaya Moody

age 10 in 2016

"Thinking of the word spring made Kalaya think of Connecticut's state bird, the Robin, which tries to make a nest on top of our front door wreath every spring," says Kalaya's mom, Beverly. "One year we allowed the Robin to nest there and we enjoyed the upbringing of three baby Robins. It also brought to mind her grandmother's backyard vegetable garden. Kalaya helps her grandmother to pick the many different types of tomatoes during the summer. While most of Kalaya's free time for the past three-and-a-half years has been devoted to gymnastics, entering the Healthy Lunchtime Challenge is Kalaya's way of making her dream of becoming a chef a reality." Kalaya serves this meal with a fruit smoothie.

Delaware

Stuffed Tomatoes

Jourdann Latney, age 12 in 2012

"My aunt introduced me to chickpeas, and I grow tomatoes and mint in the yard," reports Jourdann. "This is a high-protein vegetarian lunch. I serve sliced cucumbers with this, and grapes or orange slices for dessert. Beverage choice is plain or flavored water or seltzer water."

Makes 4 servings

INGREDIENTS

1 (15-ounce) can chickpeas, drained and rinsed

1 garlic clove

2 tablespoons lemon juice

1 tablespoon extra-virgin olive oil

Pinch of dried red pepper

Salt

4 medium tomatoes, halved

8 fresh mint leaves

PREPARATION

1. In a blender, combine the chickpeas, garlic, lemon juice, olive oil, red pepper, and 1 tablespoon water. Blend until thoroughly incorporated. If the hummus is too thick, gradually add more water to make it slightly thinner. Season to taste with salt.

2. Scoop as much pulp as possible out of each tomato half. Divide the hummus among the tomato halves and garnish with mint leaves.

Tortilla Bowl Deluxe

BRAEDEN MANNERING, age 9 in 2013

"I like tacos, but they are messy and don't hold a lot, so I chose a corn tortilla bowl," notes Braeden. "That way you can eat the bowl, too. Grilled chicken is good and it's healthy. To add color and vegetables I picked avocado because I don't like lettuce and I wanted it to have some green. I also picked orange sweet peppers and tomatoes. To top the bowl you could add shredded lactose-free cheese. (I am lactose-intolerant.) On the side would be fruit. Pineapples, mangoes, cantaloupe, grapes, and watermelon would be colorful and delicious."

Makes 1 serving

INGREDIENTS

1 medium (4-ounce) boneless, skinless chicken breast, grilled or cooked as desired, and cut into bite-size pieces

1/4 cup diced avocado

1/4 cup diced orange bell pepper

1/4 cup diced tomato

1/4 cup shredded Monterey Jack cheese

Salt and freshly ground black pepper

1 corn tortilla bowl

PREPARATION

1. In a medium bowl, toss together the chicken, avocado, bell pepper, tomato, and cheese. Season with salt and pepper, scoop into the tortilla bowl, and serve immediately.

563 calories; 48g protein; 45g carbohydrates; 20g fat (7g saturated fat); 921mg sodium

Roisin Liew, age 9 in 2014

"Well, I am both Chinese, from my father's side, and Irish, from my mother's side. My mom loves shepherd's pie, and I love the taste of Chinese food," says Roisin. "So, one day while eating shepherd's pie I thought, "What if I used ground turkey instead of beef. I bet it would be delicious! And it was!" Roisin likes this Get Your Goat for dessert."

Makes 6 servings • 417 calories • 17g fat • 39g carbohydrates • 22g protein

CHI-IRISH SHEPHERD'S PIE & GET YOUR GOAT DESSERT

INGREDIENTS

♥ For the Salmon:
2 tablespoons extra-virgin olive oil
1 small white onion, peeled and chopped
1 tablespoon peeled and finely chopped ginger
4 garlic cloves, peeled and finely chopped
1 pound ground turkey
3 tablespoons tamari or low-sodium soy sauce
3 tablespoons hoisin sauce
3 tablespoons Chinese five-spice powder
½ cup frozen green peas
½ cup frozen corn
6 medium potatoes, coarsely chopped
¼ cup 1% milk
3 tablespoons butter
1 tablespoon fresh thyme, finely chopped
Pepper and salt to taste

♥ For Get Your Goat Dessert:
4 cups vanilla Greek yogurt
1 cup blueberries
¼ cup honey
¼ cup granola

PREPARATION

For Chi-Irish Shepherd's Pie: In a large pan, warm the olive oil. Add the onion, ginger, and garlic and cook on medium heat for 6 minutes, or until the onions are soft.

Add the turkey, tamari, hoisin sauce, and Chinese five-spice powder and stir well, breaking up the turkey with a wooden spoon. Cook until the turkey is cooked through, about 10 minutes. Add in the peas and corn and cook, covered, for 10 minutes.

Bring a pot of water to a boil over high heat. Add the potatoes, cover, and cook for about 10 minutes, or until they are tender. Drain. Mash potatoes with milk, butter, thyme, and salt and pepper to taste.

Preheat oven to 400°F. Put the turkey into a baking pan and top with mashed potatoes. Smooth over the top with a fork. Bake for 15 minutes, until brown on top.

For Get Your Goat dessert: Divide the yogurt among the bowls and top with fruit, honey, and granola.

Spinach Power Salad with Mandarin Vinaigrette

Makes 4 Servings • 362 calories • 22g fat • 27g carbohydrates • 16g protein

---

INGREDIENTS

For the Dressing:

Juice from 1 snack-size cup of mandarin oranges in natural juice (reserve the oranges)
2 tablespoons apple cider vinegar
¼ cup olive oil
¼ cup pure cane sugar
½ small onion, peeled and chopped
1 tablespoon spicy brown mustard
1 tablespoon yellow mustard
½ teaspoon salt
½ teaspoon pepper

For the Salad:

8 ounces skinless, boneless chicken breast
5 ounces baby spinach
1 large carrot, peeled and shredded
24 red seedless grapes
Reserved mandarin oranges (from above)
1 ½ ounces shelled walnuts, chopped coarsely
Salt and pepper to taste

PREPARATION

1. **To make the Dressing:** In a blender, combine all of the dressing ingredients. Pour into a decorative bottle with a lid.
2. **Preheat the grill to medium-high.** Grill the chicken, flipping once, for about 10 minutes total, or until cooked through. Chop into bite-sized pieces.
3. **To make the Salad:** Divide the spinach among 4 bowls. Top each bowl with shredded carrots, grapes, chicken, mandarin oranges, and walnuts. Season with salt and pepper. Shake the dressing to ensure it's mixed well and drizzle desired amount on top of salad.

Chef Emilie Monnig,

age 12 in 2015

"I was inspired to make this salad because a couple weeks ago my dad made a spinach salad that was really good," says Emilie. "I decided that I wanted to make my own spinach salad with homemade dressing. I chose spinach because it is a high source of iron, fiber, and vitamin C. I also think kids would like to eat this salad because of its fun colors."

Caribbean Fiesta!

Makes 1 serving • 371 calories • 21g fat • 22g carbohydrates • 24g protein

INGREDIENTS

1 tablespoon olive oil
1 chicken tender, cut into bite-sized pieces
Dash of seasonings like curry, allspice, and scotch bonnet pepper sauce (optional)
8 blue or yellow corn tortilla chips
¼ cup pinto and/or black beans, rinsed and drained
4 grape tomatoes, chopped
½ orange bell pepper, seeded and diced
⅓ green onion, peeled and chopped
1 ounce low-fat shredded cheddar jack cheese

PREPARATION

1. **In a nonstick skillet,** warm the olive oil over medium heat. Add the chicken, season with optional spices, and cook for about 5 minutes, or until cooked through.
2. **Evenly spread** the tortilla chips on a plate and evenly distribute chicken, beans, tomatoes, bell peppers, and green onions. Top with cheese and microwave for 1 minute or until cheese is melted.

CHEF

Jamal Bin-Yusif

age 11 in 2016

"Jamal's maternal grandparents are Jamaican and the Caribbean flavors are a normal part of our food," says Jamal's mom, Kathy. "He also loves tacos, but the shells can be high in sodium. Jamal found a way to significantly lower the sodium of his favorite dish by using the blue corn tortilla chips and because the dish is open, he adds even more vegetables and beans. Jamal already had a high blood pressure reading and we have a very strong family history of high blood pressure and diabetes on both sides. Jamal is very aware of the health concerns of his family and ethnicity. If he can make his food healthier, then he believes he'll live a more active life where he can keep doing all the fun things he loves to do." Jamal likes to serve this dish with a fruit salad.

District of Columbia

Mexican Delight

Iliana Gonzales-Evans, age 11 in 2012

"I came up with my recipe by watching my grandma make tortillas," says Iliana. "One day I came up with the Mexican Delight. To go along with my main course, I would serve a healthy serving of brown rice and a delicious fruit smoothie."

Makes 4 servings

INGREDIENTS

For the filling:

1 pound turkey bacon

1/2 head green leaf lettuce, chopped

1 green bell pepper, diced

1 tomato, diced

1/2 onion, diced

For the whole-wheat tortillas:

2 cups of whole-wheat flour

1 tablespoon baking powder

1 teaspoon salt

1/2 cup vegetable oil, plus more for cooking

For serving:

3 cups cooked brown rice

PREPARATION

Make the filling:

1. Working in batches, cook the turkey bacon in a large, heavy skillet over moderate heat, flipping occasionally, until brown and crisp, 6 to 8 minutes. Transfer to a paper-towel-lined plate to drain, then transfer to a clean plate.
2. Arrange the pepper, tomato, and onion in separate bowls.

Make the tortillas:

3. In a large bowl, stir together the flour, baking powder, and salt. Add ½ cup oil and 2/3 cup water, and stir to combine. On a lightly floured work surface, knead the dough until smooth and elastic, about 4 minutes. Dust your hands with flour if the dough is sticky. Divide the dough into 8 equal portions, roll each portion into a ball, and cover with plastic wrap.
4. On a lightly floured work surface, use a rolling pin to roll each ball of dough into an 8- to 10-inch round.
5. Lightly oil a large, heavy skillet and place over moderate heat. Carefully place one tortilla in the skillet and cook until it bubbles and puffs, about 45 seconds. Flip the tortilla and cook the other side until it bubbles and puffs. Carefully transfer the tortilla to a plate and cover with foil to keep warm. Continue cooking the remaining tortillas.
6. Set up a buffet with the vegetables, bacon, and tortillas, and let everyone make their own tacos. Serve brown rice on the side.

Inga Binga's Salmon Salad

INGRID GRUBER, age 9 in 2013

"The way I came up with my recipe was that I read the rules with my mom. We thought a little, jotted down some ideas, and came up with one we liked," says Ingrid. "And now I know for real that my mom and I make a really great cooking pair. The salmon recipe was my great-grandfather's recipe. But the salad recipe is mine. It's gluten-free, which is important, because I have celiac disease. But I think anyone would like it."

Makes 4 servings

INGREDIENTS

For the salmon:

1 pound salmon fillets

Juice of 1 lemon

Beau Monde Seasoning, or any seasoning you like, to taste

For the quinoa:

1 cup quinoa, rinsed

2 cups water

2 cups cherry tomatoes, cut into quarters

2 cups minced arugula

3 tablespoons plain Greek-style yogurt

2 tablespoons freshly squeezed lemon juice

2 tablespoons olive oil

1 clove garlic, crushed

Sea salt

PREPARATION

Make the salmon:

1. Preheat the oven to 375°F or preheat the grill to medium. Brush both sides of the salmon with lemon juice and sprinkle with the Beau Monde Seasoning. Arrange the salmon in a large baking dish or place it directly on the grill. Bake or grill the salmon until cooked through, about 25 minutes in the oven or 10 minutes on the grill.

Make the quinoa:

1. In a medium saucepan, bring the quinoa and water to a boil. Reduce the heat to low and simmer until the quinoa is tender, about 15 minutes. Let the quinoa cool then add the tomatoes and arugula and stir to combine.

2. In a small bowl, whisk together the yogurt, lemon juice, olive oil, garlic, and salt. Add the yogurt mixture to the quinoa salad, and stir to combine. To serve, place a small (4-ounce) piece of salmon on top of some salad. (Salmon can be served hot or cold over the salad.)

442 calories; 33g protein; 38g carbohydrates; 18g fat (2g saturated fat); 169mg sodium

Maxwell Wix, age 10 in 2014

"My dad makes something like this for dinner a lot, and I love to take the leftovers to school the next day for lunch," says Maxwell. "I modified his recipe to make it healthier, adding different grains and more and different vegetables. I would serve some plain 2% Greek yogurt drizzled with honey with this dish, because it completes the meal with some dairy. I have also always loved Greek yogurt with honey."

Makes 6 servings • 335 calories • 14g fat • 36g carbohydrates • 9g protein

HEALTHY GRAINS, SQUASH, APPLES, SAUSAGE, & KALE

INGREDIENTS

1 large butternut squash, peeled and cut into small cubes
1 bunch of lacinato kale, chopped finely
3 tablespoons olive oil
Salt and pepper
2 Granny Smith apples, peeled and diced
4 ounces spicy Italian sausage, casings removed
½ cup Israeli couscous
½ cup quinoa, rinsed
2 cups vegetable broth or chicken broth
1 tablespoon white wine vinegar

PREPARATION

Preheat oven to 450°F. On a large baking pan, spread the squash and kale. Drizzle with 2 tablespoons of olive oil, and season to taste with salt and pepper. Bake for 15 minutes, then add apples and bake another 15 minutes.

In a large pan, warm the remaining 1 tablespoon oil over moderate heat. Add the sausage and cook for 6 minutes, or until cooked through. Transfer to a plate, reserving the pan drippings. Add the couscous and quinoa and cook for 2 minutes. Add broth, bring to a boil, then lower the heat and cover. Cook for about 20 minutes, until broth is absorbed and couscous-quinoa is tender.

Remove pan from heat and let sit covered for 5 minutes. Add back in the sausage, squash, apples, and kale. Season with vinegar, salt, pepper and serve.

Chef Timothy Burke,

age 8 in 2015

"I like to make my wraps myself. Everyone can put what they like inside, and you can eat a whole meal in just a roll," says Timothy. "I also like spicy food, but I am picky about vegetables. When we chop the veggie mix up into confetti, it looks fancy, but I can't really tell what is there, and then when it is wrapped inside rice paper, I can't even see it! The best part is that I am getting many different veggies in every bite, but when I eat it, I mostly taste the mint and the hoisin sauce!"

Vegetable Confetti Spring Rolls

Makes 12 Servings • 133 calories • 7g fat • 14g carbohydrates • 6g protein

---

INGREDIENTS

1 cup brown rice
¼ cup olive oil plus 2 tablespoons
½ teaspoon lime zest
¼ cup lime juice
½ teaspoon sea salt
2 skinless, boneless chicken breasts
2 cups chopped rainbow chard with stems
½ cup chopped red bell pepper
½ cup chopped orange bell pepper
½ cup chopped yellow bell pepper
½ cup peeled and chopped carrot (purple if possible)
½ cup chopped fresh mint leaves
1 package rice paper
Hoisin sauce
⅓ cup chopped peanuts

PREPARATION

1. **In a large stockpot,** combine 1 ½ cups water with the brown rice and bring to a boil over medium-high heat. Reduce the heat to a simmer and cook for 20 to 30 minutes, or until the rice is tender.
2. **In a medium bowl,** mix ¼ cup of the olive oil with the lime zest, lime juice, and sea salt. Add the chicken, cover, and marinate in the refrigerator for 30 minutes.
3. **In a large sauté pan,** heat the remaining 2 tablespoons olive oil over medium-high heat. Add the chicken and cook for 8 minutes, or until cooked through and golden down. Let cool, then dice into small pieces and place in a small serving bowl. In a large bowl, combine all of the vegetables.
4. **Soak rice paper in hot water** as directed on package. Lay out on the plate. In the center of each paper, put 1 teaspoon hoisin sauce, 1 tablespoon rice, 1 teaspoon chicken, 3 tablespoons vegetable confetti, and 1 teaspoon peanuts (optional).
5. **Fold 2 sides into the center,** then roll tightly from one end to the other, being careful not to rip the rice paper.

CHEF

Elena Sotobashi

age 8 in 2016

"My grandfather is Japanese and my family likes to eat sushi," says Elena. "D.I.Y. Sushi has pretty much the same ingredients but everyone gets to make their own rolls. It is good for school lunches because the seaweed is separate and doesn't get soggy. I like it because it is easy to make and you can choose what you want. In summer we can get the carrots and cucumbers from our garden. It is fun to make."

D.I.Y. Sushi

Makes 4 servings • 427 calories • 11g fat • 66g carbohydrates • 17g protein

INGREDIENTS

For the Rice Balls:

1 ½ cups short grain sushi rice (use brown rice if available)

2 cups water

⅓ cup seasoned rice vinegar

Rice press or rice mold (optional)

For the Crab Salad:

8 ounces imitation crabmeat, chopped

3 tablespoons mayonnaise

Wasabi (optional)

For the Vegetable Fillings:

½ cucumber, peeled and thinly sliced

1 avocado, peeled, pitted, and thinly sliced

½ cup shredded carrots

1 bell pepper, seeded and thinly sliced

Pickled ginger

For Wrapping and Dipping:

6 sheets of nori or seaweed paper, cut into 2-inch strips

Low-sodium soy sauce (optional)

Wasabi (optional)

PREPARATION

1. **To make the Rice:** In a large saucepan, combine the rice and water and bring to a boil over medium-high heat. Cover, reduce the heat to low and cook for 20 minutes. Turn off the heat and leave the rice covered for 10 minutes. Fluff the rice and gently stir in the seasoned rice vinegar. Scoop rice into the rice mold, press down with the lid to pack it in, then gently push the rice out of the mold. (It helps to dunk the rice mold in a bowl of cold water in between pressings.) Repeat until you have pressed all the rice. If you do not have a rice press, you can mold the rice with your hands into little balls, dipping your fingers into cold water to keep rice from sticking. You should have about 20 balls or rice cakes.

2. **To make the Crab Salad:** Meanwhile, in a medium bowl, combine the crab meat with mayonnaise and a dash of wasabi and combine thoroughly.

3. **To Assemble:** Arrange the rice balls, crab salad, vegetable fillings, and seaweed on a serving platter. Now it's the fun part! Place one rice ball on a seaweed sheet, choose your fillings, wrap it up, and EAT! You can try different combinations on each roll. Serve with dipping sauces.

Florida

"Triple F" Fake Fast Food

Deborah Goncalves, age 12 in 2012

"I came up with this lunch because my grandmother always made this for my mother and taught the recipe to her," says Deborah. She likes to serve this with a baby arugula and greens salad with a blue-cheese vinaigrette and watermelon cut up to look like fries.

Makes 6 servings

INGREDIENTS

2 cups bulgur wheat

1 tablespoon olive oil, plus more for greasing

1 medium onion, finely chopped

1/4 cup finely diced red bell pepper

2 garlic cloves, minced

1/2 teaspoon ground cumin

2 pounds lean ground beef

1/4 cup finely chopped fresh flat-leaf parsley

Salt and pepper

4 slices melting cheese, such as mozzarella

2 carrots, peeled and grated

2 cups fresh baby spinach, chopped

PREPARATION

1. Preheat the oven to 400°F and grease an 8-inch-square baking pan with olive oil.
2. In a medium saucepan, bring 4 cups of water to a boil. Add the bulgur, cover, remove from the heat, and let stand for 15 minutes, then drain in a sieve.
3. In a small skillet over moderate heat, warm the olive oil. Add the onion, bell pepper, and garlic, and sauté, stirring occasionally, until soft, about 4 minutes. Stir in the cumin and cook 2 more minutes. Let cool.
4. In a large bowl, combine the ground beef, cooked onion mixture, parsley, and the bulgur. Season with salt and pepper, and mix until you don't see the difference between the beef and bulgur. Add half of the beef-bulgur mixture to the greased baking pan and press into an even layer. Add the cheese in an even layer on top. Sprinkle the carrot and spinach over the cheese, and season lightly with salt. Crumble the remaining beef-bulgur mixture on top.
5. Bake the casserole until bubbling and lightly browned on top, about 35 minutes. Let rest for 5 to 10 minutes before you cut.

Summer Salmon

NICOLE MEDINA, age 10 in 2013

"I came up with this recipe after I found out my cholesterol levels were high. I started to eat healthier and salmon is one of the foods that help lower my cholesterol," says Nicole. "Since I live in Florida and orange is our state fruit, my aunt helped me create this dish using orange in the salmon sauce. I love to cook with my aunt and uncle. For dessert I like a dish created by my aunt called Cielo, with layers of fresh strawberries and egg white whipped cream."

Makes 2 servings

INGREDIENTS

Juice from 1 orange

1 tablespoon extra-virgin olive oil

1 teaspoon honey

1 teaspoon mustard

Kosher salt and freshly ground black pepper

1 (6-ounce) skinless salmon fillet

1/4 cup whole wheat linguine

6 asparagus spears, chopped

1/4 medium onion, chopped

1 clove garlic, minced

4 sprigs fresh parsley, leaves removed and chopped

2 fresh basil leaves, thinly sliced

1 teaspoon freshly grated Pecorino

PREPARATION

1. In a small bowl, whisk together the orange juice, 1 teaspoon olive oil, honey, and mustard. Season with salt and pepper.

2. In a medium sauté pan over moderate heat, warm 1 teaspoon olive oil. Add the salmon and cook for 4 minutes. Flip the salmon over, add the orange sauce, and continue to cook until the salmon is golden and cooked through, about 4 more minutes. Season with salt and pepper and transfer to a plate.

3. In a medium pot of boiling salted water, cook the pasta until al dente, about 5 minutes. Add the asparagus and continue cooking for 2 more minutes. Drain the pasta and asparagus and transfer to a bowl.

4. In a medium sauté pan over moderate heat, warm the remaining 1 teaspoon of olive oil. Add the onion, garlic, parsley, and basil and sauté, stirring occasionally, about 3 minutes. Add the onion and garlic mixture to the pasta, sprinkle with cheese, season with salt and pepper, and toss to combine. Serve the salmon alongside the pasta with asparagus.

273 calories; 22g protein; 14g carbohydrates; 14g fat (2g saturated fat); 157mg sodium

Gabriel Medina, age 10 in 2014

"I came up with this fish recipe because I love fish," notes Gabriel. "In this recipe that I invented, I also included other foods that I love, which are tomatoes and mushrooms. When I eat fish, I like it simple with not a lot of stuff, so that is why I decided to make it in a paper bag so it could cook in its juices. While it was cooking in the parchment paper, I also included the side—potatoes. This fish also goes well with brown rice, which is healthier than white rice."

Makes 1 serving • 372 calories • 14g fat • 29g carbohydrates • 31g protein

FISH CARTUCHO AL GABUSHO

INGREDIENTS

15-inch sheet of parchment paper
½ lemon, sliced
5 ounces mahimahi fillet
½ tablespoon butter
½ tablespoon olive oil
Pinch salt and pepper
1 small Yukon Gold potato, chopped
¼ cup cherry tomatoes, chopped
¼ cup mushrooms, chopped
1 twig parsley
1 twig oregano
Steamed brown rice (optional)

PREPARATION

Preheat oven to 400°F. Fold the paper in half and trim with scissors to make a heart shape when unfolded.

On one half of the parchment heart place half the lemon slices, the fish, butter, and olive oil, and season with salt and pepper. Pile on the remaining lemon, potatoes, tomatoes, mushrooms, parsley, and oregano.

Fold the parchment paper over and fold in the ends all around, creating a pouch that lies on its side. Place on a baking sheet and bake for 20 minutes or until the fish is flaky and potatoes are tender. Serve with brown rice, if desired.

Chef Bobby Sena,

age 12 in 2015

"Last year I wanted to surprise my mom with a gift on Mother's Day, but I didn't have money to buy her anything and my sister didn't want to sing a song with me, so I decided that making something that she would like to eat and that was healthy for her, would be the ideal gift," says Bobby. "She is from the Dominican Republic and we live in Florida, so I thought why not prepare a dish that is Caribbean and Floridian! She also has high cholesterol, so I had to research the best foods to help reduce cholesterol levels. I thought what better way to honor her culture, our agriculture in Florida, and her good health!"

Caribbean Delight

Makes 4 Servings • 484 calories • 13g fat • 68g carbohydrates • 30g protein

INGREDIENTS

1 sweet plantain, peeled and sliced
¾ pound fresh tilapia fillets
½ lemon
1 garlic clove, peeled and minced
1 teaspoon balsamic vinegar
¼ teaspoon adobe
1 medium kiwi, peeled and diced
2 cups fresh pineapple, diced
1 avocado, pitted and diced
1 mango, pitted and diced
1 tomatillo, peeled and diced
1 red tomato, diced
½ red onion, peeled and diced
4 whole-wheat flour tortillas
1 cup shredded low-fat mozzarella, or smoked provolone, Asiago, or Romano cheese
1 bunch fresh cilantro
8 strawberries, sliced

PREPARATION

1. **Preheat the oven to 350°F.** Place the sweet plantain on a foil-lined baking sheet and bake for 30 minutes. Let cool, then slice and set aside.
2. **Meanwhile, place the tilapia in a large bowl** and squeeze ½ lemon over the fillets. Add the garlic, balsamic vinegar, and adobo and stir to combine. Let sit for 10 minutes while you prepare the salsa.
3. **In a large bowl,** combine ½ the kiwi with the pineapple, avocado, mango, tomatillo, tomato, and red onion. Cover and chill in the refrigerator.
4. **Place the tilapia fillets** on a parchment-lined baking sheet, and bake for 20 minutes, or until a fork can easily flake the fish. Ten minutes into baking, wrap the tortillas in foil and bake on the same baking sheet for 10 minutes.
5. **Let the fish cool for 2 minutes** then flake the tilapia into pieces. Place some tilapia in the middle of each tortilla and top with cheese, salsa, and cilantro. Place on a dish with the plantains, sliced strawberries, and the remaining kiwi. Serve with milk and enjoy!

CHEF
Olivia LaRochelle
age 12 in 2016

"My mom and I created this healthy seafood recipe, giving it a Latin twist since my grandparents are from Cuba," says Olivia. "We decided to use tropical fruits and vegetables to make the salsa. The avocado and mango grow right in my grandparents' backyard. We also added orange and lime because fish goes great with citrus. Living in Florida, it is very easy to find the most delicious, sweet oranges. I love oranges and it really helps to brighten the flavors in this dish! My grandparents said the fish cakes were so delicious."

Bountiful Florida Fish "BFF" Cakes

Makes 4 servings • 341 calories • 8g fat • 45g carbohydrates • 24g protein

INGREDIENTS

For the Fish Cake:

¾ pound skinless large-mouth bass, or any white meat fish such as cod, cut into small pieces
1 egg white
1 cup cooked brown rice
½ cup black beans, rinsed and drained
1 teaspoon smoked paprika
¼ teaspoon garlic powder
¼ teaspoon kosher salt or to taste
½ cup whole-wheat panko breadcrumbs

For the Salsa:

1 ¼ cups diced mango
1 ¼ cups diced strawberries
1 cup diced avocado
¾ cup diced cucumber
¼ cup chopped cilantro
2 tablespoons fresh lime juice

For the Orange-You-Glad Yogurt Sauce *(not pictured)*:

½ cup low-fat plain yogurt
3 tablespoons orange juice
½ teaspoon orange zest
Orange wedges, for garnishing

PREPARATION

1. **To make the Fish Cakes:** Preheat oven to 375°F. In a large bowl, combine all ingredients except breadcrumbs. Form mixture into 4 patties, pressing each patty together so it holds its shape. Line a medium baking sheet with parchment paper. Put breadcrumbs on a plate and roll the patties in the breadcrumbs. Place each patty on baking sheet and bake for 20 minutes or until light golden brown and fish is cooked through.
2. **To make the Salsa:** In medium bowl, toss salsa ingredients until well combined.
3. **To make Orange-You-Glad Yogurt Sauce:** In a small bowl, stir together all ingredients.
4. **To Assemble:** Top each fish cake with Salsa and drizzle with Orange-You-Glad Yogurt sauce. Sprinkle with additional cilantro if you wish. Serve with orange wedges and a glass of low-fat milk.

Georgia

Stuffed Zucchini Boats

Haley Matthews, age 12 in 2012

Haley was inspired by her garden to create this menu. The family has been growing a summer and winter crop for three years now. "This recipe is fun to make and is fun to serve to my family. It is pretty on a plate and is full of color and flavors." The family likes to serve this with a Caprese Salad, which has fresh mozzarella, tomatoes, and basil, drizzled with olive oil and balsamic vinegar.

Makes 4 servings

INGREDIENTS

4 large zucchini, trimmed and halved lengthwise

2 tablespoons olive oil

1/2 cup diced red bell pepper

1/2 cup diced yellow onion

2 garlic cloves, chopped

1/2 pound ground chicken sausage or ground chicken

1 cup cooked brown rice

1 large egg

1/2 cup ricotta cheese

1 teaspoon chopped fresh thyme

1 teaspoon chopped fresh flat-leaf parsley

1 teaspoon salt

1 teaspoon freshly ground black pepper

1/4 cup freshly grated Parmesan cheese

1/4 cup panko breadcrumbs

PREPARATION

1. Preheat the oven to 375°F. Lightly grease a large baking sheet with olive oil.
2. Scoop out the pulp of the zucchini and discard. Place the zucchini boats on the prepared baking sheet with the scooped-out sides facing up.
3. In a large sauté pan over moderate heat, warm 1 tablespoon of the olive oil, then add the red bell pepper and onion and sauté, stirring occasionally, for 5 minutes. Add the garlic and sauté, stirring occasionally, 2 more minutes.
4. In a second sauté pan over moderate heat, warm the remaining 1 tablespoon olive oil. Add the ground chicken sausage or ground chicken and sauté, stirring occasionally, until cooked through, about 5 minutes. Remove from the heat and add the cooked vegetables, rice, egg, ricotta, thyme, parsley, salt, and pepper. Stir until well combined.
5. Divide the mixture into equal portions and stuff into the zucchini boats.
6. In a small bowl, stir together the Parmesan cheese and panko breadcrumbs. Sprinkle this mixture over the stuffed zucchini boats, then bake until the zucchini are soft and the cheese and crumbs are browned, about 30 minutes.

Sweet Potato Turkey Sliders

REGAN MATTHEWS, age 12 in 2013

"I am a member of my gardening club at middle school. We are growing sweet potatoes and many other fruits and vegetables. Once the plants are ready to be harvested we will dig them out and our school will use them for our lunches," says Regan. "My mom challenged me to create a yummy, healthy recipe. I choose sweet potato sliders because they are a fun and healthy lunch. My sweet potato sliders are very yummy and taste great. I enjoy my sliders with a fruit smoothie and sweet potato chips."

Makes 6 servings

INGREDIENTS

For the sweet potato turkey sliders:

1 sweet potato, peeled and thickly sliced crosswise

1 pound lean ground turkey

1/2 cup oats

1 medium onion, finely chopped

3 cloves garlic, minced

1 large egg

1/2 cup ricotta cheese

1/2 cup chopped fresh parsley leaves

2 teaspoons maple syrup

1 teaspoon cayenne pepper

1 teaspoon salt

1/2 teaspoon freshly ground black pepper

12 mini whole wheat buns

6 slices provolone cheese, cut in half

For garnish: Spinach, pickles, tomato, mustard, and ketchup

For the sweet potato chips:

1 sweet potato, peeled and thinly sliced crosswise

Cooking spray

Salt and freshly ground black pepper

PREPARATION

Make the sweet potato turkey sliders:

1. Preheat the oven to 375°F and line a large baking sheet with parchment paper or aluminum foil.

2. Bring a medium pot of water to a boil. Add the sweet potato slices and cook until tender, about 7 minutes. Transfer the sweet potato slices to a bowl and use a fork to mash them. Add the ground turkey, oats, onion, garlic, egg, ricotta cheese, parsley, maple syrup, cayenne pepper, salt, and pepper and stir to combine. Shape the mixture into 12 meatball-size sliders and place them on the prepared baking sheet. Bake the sliders, turning them once, for 35 minutes.

3. Top each slider with half a piece of cheese and serve them on the mini whole wheat buns. Garnish with spinach, pickles, tomato, mustard, and ketchup.

Make the sweet potato chips:

1. Preheat the oven to 425°F and line a large baking sheet with parchment paper or aluminum foil.

2. Arrange the sweet potato slices on the prepared baking sheet and spray with cooking spray. Bake until tender, about 15 minutes. Season with salt and pepper and serve hot.

315 calories; 30g protein; 32g carbohydrates; 9g fat (4g saturated fat); 690mg sodium (not including chips)

Mira Solomon, age 10 in 2014

"At my school, I have always enjoyed when we have outdoor grilled lunches. But as a vegetarian, there is not really much for me to eat, as the menu is always hot dogs and hamburgers," says Mira. "I decided to create a healthy, delicious, and vegetarian grilled lunch. Vegetarians and meat-eaters alike will devour this scrumptious meal!" Mira likes to have this with a spinach and dried-cranberry salad and frozen mango-banana smoothie.

Makes 5 servings • 393 calories • 15g fat • 43g carbohydrates • 15g protein

CHEF MIRA

GRILLIN' OUT, VEGGIE STYLE

INGREDIENTS

♥ For the Black Bean Burgers:
2 tablespoons olive oil
½ onion, peeled and chopped
2 garlic cloves, peeled and minced
1 (15-ounce) can black beans, rinsed and drained
1 teaspoon chili powder
Pinch salt and pepper
1/3 cup cilantro
½ cup whole-wheat breadcrumbs
2 eggs whites
5 whole-wheat buns

♥ For the Carrot Salad:
2 pounds carrots, peeled and shredded
2 cups peeled fresh pineapple chunks, chopped
¾ cup raisins
1 tablespoon honey
¼ cup low-fat plain Greek yogurt

♥ For the Avocado Spread:
1 avocado
1 lime (zest and juice)
Pinch of salt

PREPARATION

Make the Black Bean Burgers: In a small sauté pan, warm the olive oil. Add the onions and garlic and cook for 3 minutes, or until the onion is soft. Add the beans, chili powder, salt and pepper, and cilantro. Let cool for 5 minutes, then place in a food processor. Pulse about 5 times, or until coarsely chopped. Pour into a bowl and add the breadcrumbs and egg whites and combine thoroughly. Let sit in the refrigerator for 30 minutes.

Make the Carrot Salad: In a large bowl, combine carrots, pineapple, and raisins. In a separate small bowl, stir honey and yogurt until blended. Toss with salad. Let sit for 30 minutes.

Preheat the grill. Shape the burger mix into 5 patties and grill on grill topper/ basket until cooked through and crispy on each side, about 5 minutes per side.

Make the Avocado Spread: Blend avocado and zest and juice of one lime with salt to taste in a food processor until smooth, about 30 seconds. Spread over Black Bean Burgers and serve with Carrot Salad.

Chef Corey Jackson Jr.,

age 10 in 2015

"Corey and I began creating great gluten-free recipes about five years ago," says Corey's mom, Dora. "After Corey was diagnosed with Autism, he was placed on a gluten-free diet. In the early years, we tried every gluten-free recipe we could find. But most were not kid-friendly. So, Corey ate his favorite two foods, chicken and rice, often. As with many autistic people, he was skeptical about any changes, including when it came to his meals. We slowly introduced variations to his two favorite foods, by adding coconut milk and mangoes."

Mango-Cango Chicken

Makes 4 Servings • 744 calories • 36g fat • 83g carbohydrates • 38g protein

---

INGREDIENTS

1 (14-ounce) package classic slaw
1 (13.5-ounce) can lite coconut milk
¼ cup mayonnaise
2 tablespoons brown sugar
1 teaspoon lime juice
1 teaspoon vanilla extract
1 cup jasmine rice
2 large skinless, boneless chicken breasts
½ teaspoon salt
1 (15-ounce) can pear halves
1 (15-ounce) can diced mangoes
4 red leaf lettuce leaves

PREPARATION

1. **In a medium bowl,** thoroughly mix the slaw with 1 cup coconut milk, the mayonnaise, 1 tablespoon brown sugar, and the lime juice. Chill for 20 minutes.
2. **In a medium saucepan,** combine 1 ⅓ cups water with the remaining ⅔ cup coconut milk and bring to a gentle boil over low heat. Add the vanilla and jasmine rice. Cover, turn off the heat, and let stand for 25 minutes.
3. **Preheat the grill to medium-high.** Grill the chicken, flipping once, for about 10 minutes total, or until it's cooked through. Sprinkle with salt.
4. **Meanwhile, in a medium saucepan,** combine the pears and mangoes with their juices and the remaining 1 tablespoon brown sugar and cook over medium heat for about 8 minutes.
5. **Arrange a lettuce leaf on each plate,** and top with slaw. Add some coconut rice and chicken. Top with the fruit sauce and serve.

CHEF

Jackson Kelly

age 8 in 2016

"Jackson heard that a classmate cooks once a week for her family and wanted to try cooking for us," says Jackson's mom, Nour. "He loves his dad's traditional spaghetti with sausage but wanted to try to make his own with more of a meat sauce. Since we try not to eat pasta often, we decided to make this with spaghetti squash instead. He added his favorite veggies, which include mushrooms, carrots, and our local staple, Vidalia onions, to a basic Bolognese sauce and substituted ground turkey for beef." Jackson serves this with whole-wheat toast drizzled with olive oil, and mango for dessert.

Spaghetti Squash and Turkey Bolognese

Makes 6 servings • 306 calories • 17g fat • 26g carbohydrates • 18g protein

INGREDIENTS

2 medium spaghetti squash, halved and seeded
Dash of sea salt
1 teaspoon Herbes de Provence (optional)
3 tablespoons olive oil
1 Vidalia onion, peeled and chopped
2 carrots, peeled and finely chopped
8 ounces sliced mushrooms
1 garlic clove, peeled and minced
1 pound ground turkey
1 28-ounce can crushed tomatoes
1 8-ounce can tomato paste
8 ounces water
1 tablespoon dried basil
1 teaspoon dried oregano
1 teaspoon salt
1 teaspoon freshly ground black pepper
1 teaspoon garlic powder
Freshly grated Parmesan cheese

PREPARATION

1. **Preheat the oven to 425°F.** Sprinkle spaghetti squash with sea salt and Herbes de Provence, if using, and drizzle with 1 tablespoon olive oil. Place on a baking sheet or pan, cut side up, and cover tightly with foil. Bake for 25 minutes, uncover and continue baking for 45 minutes or until the flesh can be scooped out with a fork.
2. **Meanwhile, in a large nonstick pan,** warm the remaining 2 tablespoons olive oil over medium heat and add the onions and carrots. Sauté over medium heat until softened, about 6 minutes. Add the mushrooms and garlic and sauté for 3 minutes or until lightly brown. Add the turkey and cook about 8 minutes, or until no longer pink. Add the tomatoes, tomato paste, water, basil, oregano, salt, pepper, and garlic powder. Bring to a boil, reduce heat to low, then simmer for about 30 minutes.
3. **To Assemble:** Scoop out the flesh of the spaghetti squash, divide amongst the plates, and top with the sauce and Parmesan (if desired). Serve with a slice of garlic whole-wheat toast.

Guam

Lily Vinch, age 8 in 2014

"This recipe has evolved with my family learning about trying new foods and tastes," says Lily. "We started with only a few of the spices and then added the cinnamon and cloves for a tastier dish. We have also experimented with different dried fruits and veggies to add in. We have even wrapped the mixture into lumpia wrappers along the way."

Makes 4-6 servings • 393 calories • 15g fat • 43g carbohydrates • 15g protein

MO-ROCKIN' MONDAY SPECIAL

INGREDIENTS

1 (10-ounce) box quick couscous
1 tablespoon olive oil
½ onion, peeled and minced
½ teaspoon minced garlic
1 (12-ounce) package ground veggie soy crumbles
½ teaspoon chili powder
½ teaspoon salt
¼ teaspoon cinnamon
¼ teaspoon cumin
¼ teaspoon ground ginger
¼ teaspoon ground cloves (optional)
2 cups shredded carrots
1 can chickpeas, drained
1 cup chopped dried apricots, or dates or golden raisins
1 (5-ounce) bag baby spinach
About 8 romaine lettuce leaves, for serving

PREPARATION

Prepare couscous according to directions on box. Fluff with fork, cover, and set aside.

In a large skillet warm the olive oil over moderate heat. Add the onions and garlic and sauté until soft, about 3 minutes. Add veggie crumbles and heat until warmed, about 3 minutes. Add chili powder, salt, cinnamon, cumin, ground ginger, and ground cloves and thoroughly combine. Add carrots, chickpeas, and dried fruit to skillet and stir until warmed through, about 5 minutes.

Put into large bowl and add couscous and spinach. Serve with romaine leaves for scooping and eating the Mo-Rockin' meal!

Y'obama Yakisoba

Makes 4 Servings • 243 calories • 3g fat • 46g carbohydrates • 13g protein

INGREDIENTS

7 ounces whole-wheat or multi-grain thin spaghetti
1 garlic clove, peeled and minced
2 ½ teaspoons low-sodium soy sauce
½ teaspoon sugar-free grape jelly
½ cup vegetable broth
1 cup shredded or chopped cabbage
1 cup shelled edamame
1 cup peeled shredded carrots
Optional: ½ cup chopped cashews

PREPARATION

1. **Fill a large pasta pot with water** and bring to a boil. Add the spaghetti and boil for about 7 minutes, or until al dente. Drain and set aside.
2. **Meanwhile, in a small bowl,** whisk together the garlic, soy sauce, and grape jelly. Set aside.
3. **In a large stockpot,** bring the broth to a boil. Add the cabbage, edamame, and carrots and boil for 3 minutes, or until tender. Add the drained noodles and sauce, and stir until evenly distributed; top with cashews (optional). Eat and enjoy!

Chef Gracie Giles,

age 9 in 2015

"The dish I created is about two things I love very much. I love noodles and I love my dad," says Gracie. "My dad is Japanese. I wanted to create a dish that represented my Japanese heritage and love for all noodles. I remember how much fun I had as a little child, slurping up noodles and popping edamame out of their shells. This dish is about having fun eating the food I love and spending time with my dad. Both of these things are very special to me!"

Quinoa-Crusted Katsu Curry with Cauliflower Rice

Makes 4 servings • 456 calories • 8g fat • 54g carbohydrates • 43g protein

INGREDIENTS

1 sweet potato
2 skinless, boneless chicken breasts, halved
2 egg whites
½ cup almond or quinoa flour, for dredging
2 cups cooked quinoa
2 tablespoons olive oil or nonstick cooking spray
1 teaspoon minced, fresh garlic
3 carrots, peeled and cut into bite-sized pieces
½ cup grated apple
2 cups low-sodium vegetable broth
2 tablespoons curry powder
1 tablespoon reduced-sodium Worcestershire sauce
1 head cauliflower, stem removed and chopped
1 teaspoon garam masala (or coriander seed)
1 teaspoon cumin
1 teaspoon freshly ground black pepper

PREPARATION

1. **Preheat the oven to 425°F.** Place sweet potato on a baking sheet, poke holes into the sweet potato with a fork, and bake for 45 minutes or until soft when pierced with a fork.
2. **Meanwhile, pound chicken flat to tenderize.** Place egg whites in a wide shallow bowl, and flour and cooked quinoa on plates. Dredge chicken in flour, dip in the egg whites, then in the cooked quinoa, coating well. Place on a large baking sheet and bake in the oven, while the sweet potato is cooking, for 25 minutes or until cooked through.
3. **While chicken and sweet potato are cooking,** in a large nonstick skillet, warm 1 tablespoon olive oil over medium heat, add the garlic and cook for 1 minute. Then add the carrots and apple and cook for another 5 minutes. Add the broth, curry powder, and Worcestershire sauce. Let simmer for 10 minutes. When the sweet potato is cooked, scoop out the sweet potato and add to the vegetable-curry broth.
4. **Into a food processor,** add the cauliflower and pulse to process into a rice-like consistency. (A hand grater will also work.) In a nonstick skillet, warm the remaining tablespoon oil over medium heat, add the cauliflower rice, and cook for about 5 minutes. Season to taste with garam masala, cumin and pepper.
5. **To Assemble:** Divide the cauliflower rice, quinoa-crusted chicken, and curry broth among the four plates, placing the broth next to the rice. Enjoy!

CHEF

Grayson Giles

age 8 in 2016

"I love to eat good food and I love to play soccer," says Grayson. "It's important for me to be able to run fast so I can help my team and make lots of goals—my favorite part! When I played with the Guam National Academy, I needed lots of energy to feel good at practice. I am part Japanese and one of my favorite meals is Katsu Curry Rice. I decided to make a healthy version of it so I could eat what I love but still have lots of energy to run! I love eating this meal with my family."

Hawaii

Scrumptious Salmon Salad

Stefani Shimomura-Sakamoto, age 11 in 2012

"I created this recipe because I love to eat salmon. I decided to combine some of my other favorite foods to make a healthy lunch," says Stefani. "My recipe is served with half a cup of brown rice topped with furikake (seasoned seaweed). I enjoy drinking fruit smoothies, so I blended strawberries, bananas, milk, and some low-fat yogurt!" We're providing both of Stefani's recipes, because her smoothie is a classic recipe that you can improvise on with different fruits as well as by adding wheat germ, flaxseed, or peanut butter.

Makes 1 serving

INGREDIENTS

1 tablespoon vegetable or olive oil

1 (4-ounce) salmon fillet

1 garlic clove, minced

Salt

Pepper

1 cup organic spring greens

1/2 cup cooked brown rice

1 teaspoon furikake (seasoned seaweed)

For garnish:

Sliced pineapple, strawberries, seedless grapes, bananas, lychees, oranges, and apples

Strawberryana Smoothie:

1 cup low-fat milk

1 cup low-fat plain or vanilla yogurt

1 cup frozen strawberries

1 frozen banana, peeled

PREPARATION

1. In a large sauté pan over moderate heat, warm the vegetable or olive oil. Add the salmon and garlic, and cook until the salmon is golden brown, about 2 minutes. Flip the salmon and continue cooking until golden brown and just cooked through, about 4 more minutes. Season to taste with salt and pepper.

2. Arrange the spring greens on a plate and top with the salmon. Surround the salad with your favorite fruit or serve separately. Serve with a scoop of brown rice seasoned with furikake.

Strawberryana Smoothie:

3. In a blender, combine the milk, yogurt, strawberries, and banana. Blend until thoroughly combined.

Curried Chicken Salad and Taste of the Tropics Fruit Bowl

ELEANOR COWELL, age 8 in 2013

"I had lunch with my mom at California Pizza Kitchen, and we ordered a Moroccan Chicken Salad. I loved the curry-spiced chicken and the fresh, crisp greens. Later that night I was inspired to create this recipe," says Eleanor. "I wanted to include lots of fruits and veggies, too, because they're good for you, and sometimes sweeter than candy. Accompany your meal with raita, organic salad greens, or crudités, and Taste of the Tropics Fruit Bowl."

Makes 6 servings

INGREDIENTS

For the curried chicken salad:

2 tablespoons ground coriander

2 teaspoons ground cumin

2 teaspoons ground turmeric

1 teaspoon paprika

1/2 teaspoon ground cinnamon

1/2 teaspoon ground ginger

2 tablespoons canola oil

1/2 cup plain Greek-style yogurt

1/4 cup light mayonnaise

1 tablespoon water

2 cups diced cooked chicken

1 1/2 cup cooked quinoa

1 red bell pepper, seeded and diced

1/2 cup raisins

1/2 cup toasted slivered almonds

2 scallions, chopped

1/4 teaspoon salt

6 butter lettuce leaves

Garnish: 42 baby carrots; 30 grape tomatoes, cut in half

For the Taste of the Tropics fruit bowl:

3 apricots, pitted and diced

3 bananas, peeled and sliced

6 large strawberries, trimmed and cut into quarters

6 tablespoons vanilla or plain Greek-style yogurt

4 1/2 tablespoons shredded unsweetened coconut

PREPARATION

Make the curried chicken salad:

1. In a small sauté pan over low heat, toast the coriander, cumin, turmeric, paprika, cinnamon, and ginger, stirring frequently, until fragrant. Add the canola oil and stir to create a paste. Remove the pan from the heat and let the spice paste cool.

2. In a large bowl, stir together the spice paste, yogurt, mayonnaise, and water. Add the cooked chicken, cooked quinoa, red bell pepper, raisins, almonds, and scallions and stir to combine. Season with salt.

3. To serve, scoop the chicken salad into lettuce leaves. Each person should have one curried chicken lettuce cup. Garnish each plate with baby carrots and grape tomato halves, shaped into flowers.

Make the Taste of the Tropics fruit bowl:

1. In a medium bowl, stir together the apricots, bananas, and strawberries. Scoop the fruit salad into small bowls and top each with 1 tablespoon yogurt. Garnish with shredded coconut and serve with the curried chicken salad.

522 calories; 27g protein; 68g carbohydrates; 19g fat (3.8g saturated fat); 297mg sodium (includes both salad and fruit bowl)

‘AINA HOLOKA’I (FEAST FOR A SEAFARING VOYAGE)

INGREDIENTS

♥ For the Mahi-Mahi:
6 4-ounce mahi-mahi fillets
Juice of 2 lemons
Sea salt and ground pepper, to taste

♥ For the Canoe:
6 whole-wheat pita pockets
1 carrot, peeled and cut into 8 matchsticks

♥ For the Tabbouleh:
½ cup bulgur
Juice of 1 lemon
1 teaspoon olive oil
Sea salt and ground pepper, to taste
2 large tomatoes, diced
1 cucumber, peeled and diced
1 large bunch parsley, chopped

♥ For the Hummus:
1 (15-ounce) can low-sodium garbanzo beans, drained and rinsed
1 tablespoon sesame tahini
1 lemon
½ cup plain nonfat yogurt
1 teaspoon olive oil
1 tablespoon minced garlic

♥ For the Papaya Boat:
3 papayas, sliced in half and seeds removed
½ cup blueberries
6 slices pineapple

♥ Tropical Strawberry Banana Secret Smoothie:
2 frozen bananas
5 fresh strawberries
1 cup nonfat vanilla yogurt
1 cup nonfat milk
1 handful baby spinach

PREPARATION

To make the Mahi-Mahi: In a medium bowl, combine fish with lemon juice, salt, and ground pepper and let sit for 1 hour. Preheat the grill, cook the fish on each side for 3 minutes, or until flaky at the edges and cooked through.

Cut whole-wheat pita into two pieces, one larger than the other for the canoe and the outrigger. Toast pita, and slice off the very bottom so canoe will stand.

To make the Tabbouleh: In a microwave-proof bowl, combine the bulgur with 1 cup of water and cover. Microwave for 3 minutes. Let cool. In a large bowl, combine the bulgur, lemon juice, olive oil, and salt and pepper to taste, tomatoes, cucumber and parsley.

To make the Hummus: Mix all ingredients in a food processor until smooth.

To make the Papaya Boat: Place blueberries inside the papaya. Cut a sail shape from the pineapple slices, and position above the papaya boat.

To make the Canoe: 1 whole-wheat pita sliced in two, 2 carrot sticks to connect, 1 mahi-mahi fillet and tabbouleh in one half, hummus in the other. Serve all pieces of the scene on 1 plate.

To make the Smoothie: Add all ingredients and blend until smooth.

Grady Garzo, age 9 in 2014

"In my third-grade class we study about Hawaiian culture. I thought it would be a great idea to create a recipe that combined local Hawaiian foods with the foods of my family's ethnic background," says Grady. "We have been studying about the Hokule'a (a voyaging canoe) as it takes its journey around Polynesia, which is what inspired this delicious meal. So my recipe theme is seafaring navigation, a mahi-mahi, tabbouleh, and hummus outrigger canoe, accompanied by a papaya fruit boat like a Phoenician galloi, driven by a pineapple sail, and a tropical smoothie." *(Please note: For purposes of judging, recipe pictured was made as a sandwich rather than sailboat.)*

Makes 6 servings • 472 calories • 6g fat • 37g carbohydrates • 40g protein

East Meets West! Chinese Pot Stickers and Tuscan Salad with Aloha Sorbet

Makes 8 servings • 292 calories • 10g fat • 35g carbohydrates • 18g protein

---

INGREDIENTS

For the Pot Stickers:

1 tablespoon sesame oil
1 large onion, peeled and chopped
1 pound ground chicken breast
1 pound chopped frozen spinach
3 tablespoons ground flaxseed
1 large egg
48 pot sticker wrappers
1 tablespoon olive oil
2 tablespoons low-sodium soy sauce

For the Kale Salad:

1 bunch Tuscan kale, stems removed, leaves torn into bite-sized pieces
3 garlic cloves, peeled and minced
Juice of 1 large lemon
¼ cup olive oil
¼ cup grated Parmesan cheese
Salt and pepper to taste

For the Sorbet:

½ pineapple, peeled and cut, plus 1 slice cut into quarters for garnish
1 papaya, chopped, plus ½ papaya for serving
Juice of ½ large lemon
¼ cup honey

PREPARATION

1. **To make the pot stickers:** In a large sauté pan heat the sesame oil over medium-high heat. Add the onion and sauté for 3-4 minutes, or until softened. Add the chicken and cook, breaking the meat up with a wooden spoon, for about 10 minutes, or until cooked through. Squeeze out the excess water in the spinach then add to the pan. Add the flaxseed and egg and cook for another 5 minutes.
2. **Place a tablespoon of the mixture** on each pot sticker wrapper, fold in half, and seal the edges with water. Gently pleat the sides of the dough round to create a crescent shape.
3. **In a nonstick frying pan,** heat the olive oil over medium heat. Place a layer of pot stickers in the pan and cook, allowing the bottoms to crisp, for 3 minutes. Add ½ cup of water and steam for another 7 minutes. Repeat with the remaining pot stickers. Serve with a small dish of soy sauce for dipping.
4. **To make the Kale Salad:** Place the kale in a large bowl. In a small bowl, combine the garlic and lemon juice. Gradually add the olive oil, whisking until combined. Drizzle the dressing on the kale, add the Parmesan cheese, season to taste with salt and pepper, and toss to combine. Serve with the pot stickers.
5. **To make the Sorbet:** In a juicer or blender, process the ½ pineapple and the papaya (you will net about 2 cups of juice). Add the lemon juice and honey and blend. Add the mixture to an ice cream machine and process according to the manufacturer's instructions (or scoop into muffin tins, cover with plastic wrap, and freeze for 1 hour). Scoop out the soft mixture and freeze until firm, at least 1 hour. Serve a large scoop of sorbet in a papaya half. Garnish with quartered slices of pineapple.

Chef Luca Casano,

age 11 in 2015

"The recipe I made is a family recipe. It represents my ethnic heritage, both the Italian and Chinese sides," says Luca. "It also represents my home state of Hawai'i. I have made this recipe with my mom ever since I was in preschool. My mom says this is my favorite way of eating lots of spinach! The Tuscan Kale Salad is really yummy because of the garlic and the Parmesan cheese."

Poke Me Ke Aloha

Makes 4 servings • 521 calories • 31g fat • 47g carbohydrates • 20g protein

INGREDIENTS

For the Tomato Poke:
9 grape tomatoes, halved
¼ cup diced sweet onion
¼ cup sliced green onions
Dash shoyu or low-sodium soy sauce
Dash sesame oil
1 teaspoon sesame seeds
Sea salt

For the Tofu Poke:
14 ounces firm tofu, drained and cut into ½-inch cubes
½ teaspoon kosher salt
½ teaspoon garlic powder
1 tablespoon cornstarch
2 tablespoons coconut oil

For the Edamame Poke:
1 cup cooked, shelled edamame
Dash shoyu or low-sodium soy sauce
Dash sesame oil
2 tablespoons toasted sesame seeds
Salt, pepper and hot sauce

For the Ulu Poke:
½ ulu, steamed and cut into ½-inch cubes (you can substitute 2 steamed sweet potatoes)
2 tablespoons coconut oil or olive oil
Sea salt
1 thinly sliced green onion
1 tablespoon shoyu or low-sodium soy sauce
2 teaspoons sesame oil
2 tablespoons furikake
Juice and zest from ½ fresh lime
3 tablespoons ground macadamia nuts

Quinoa:
2 cups cooked quinoa

PREPARATION

1. **To make the Tomato Poke:** In a small bowl, season the tomatoes lightly with salt. Let tomatoes sit at room temperature for 10 minutes, then drain. Add remaining ingredients and gently toss.
2. **To make the Tofu Poke:** Season each tofu cube with salt and garlic powder, then dust with cornstarch. Heat a nonstick saucepan over medium heat and add the coconut oil. Add the tofu and sear for 2 to 3 minutes on each side, or until golden brown. Drain on paper towels and keep warm.
3. **To make the Edamame Poke:** In a large bowl, gently mix ingredients together. Season to taste.
4. **To make the Ulu Poke:** In a large bowl, season the ulu or sweet potato with oil and sea salt. Add the remaining ingredients and stir.
5. **To Assemble:** Serve quinoa and all the pokes.

CHEF

Kaira Grace Pan

age 9 in 2016

"Poke means to slice, to cut into pieces, in Hawaiian," explains Kaira. "Traditional poke is made with raw fish, Hawaiian salt, limu (seaweed), inamona (roasted, ground kukui nut), chiles, and onions. It is a favorite Hawaiian dish and my family loves making and sharing poke at family gatherings. I named my dish Poke Me Ke Aloha (poke with love) because I put all the things I love in it. I serve the poke with quinoa because it is healthier than white rice." Kaira also serves guacamole and a banana-kale sorbet for dessert with this meal.

Idaho

Fiesta Casserole

Elena Guylay, age 11 in 2012

Elena's mom, Kathryn, tells us this recipe was served for the 5th-grade class at Community School of Sun Valley, Idaho, and the kids all gave it the thumbs-up! Elena uses all different types of beans to keep it colorful (such as kidney, pinto, and black) and serves it with crunchy raw carrots, celery, jicama, and avocado slices, with apple slices for dessert. The recipe can easily be halved to serve a small crowd.

Makes 16 servings

INGREDIENTS

1 cup brown rice

1 1/2 cups quinoa, rinsed

2 (16-ounce) jars your favorite salsa

4 (15-ounce) cans assorted beans, rinsed and drained

2 (16-ounce) containers cottage cheese

Juice of 2 limes

2 teaspoons chili powder

2 teaspoons ground cumin

1 bunch fresh cilantro, coarsely chopped

8 ounces shredded cheese of your choice (Elena likes the Mexican blend)

Salt

For serving:

Sliced carrots, celery, jicama, and avocado

SPECIAL EQUIPMENT

2 (9- by 12-inch) baking dishes

PREPARATION

1. Preheat the oven to 350°F.
2. In two saucepans, cook the rice and quinoa according to the package directions.
3. In a large bowl, combine the rice, quinoa, salsa, beans, cottage cheese, lime juice, chili powder, cumin, and cilantro. Spread the mixture in 2 (9- by 12-inch) baking dishes, cover with foil, and bake until the rice and quinoa are light brown, about 40 minutes.
4. Carefully remove the foil from both pans and sprinkle the cheese on top of each casserole.
5. Return to oven and bake until the cheese is melted and bubbling, about 5 minutes. Season to taste with salt, and serve with sliced veggies.

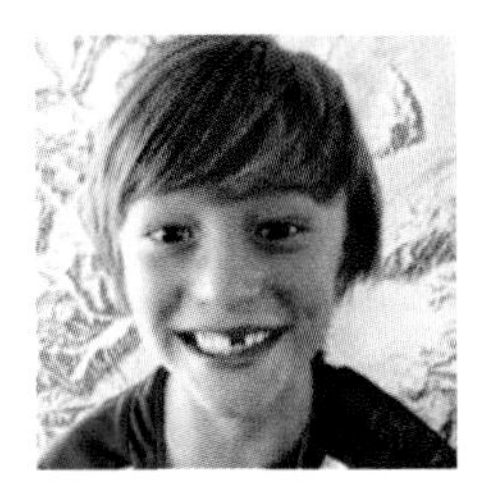

Veggie Barley Salad with Orange-Honey Vinaigrette

MAC WIRTH, age 8 in 2013

"My mom and I make this to have something ready fast when we have busy mornings," says Mac. "We change it up all the time depending on what vegetables we have. We use rice or pasta, too, if it's left over. Sometimes we add basil, pesto, and cheese. We could also add some beans or cut-up chicken. We make a bigger recipe and have some for dinner and pack the rest in our lunches. To fill up my lunch box, I like to add an apple, grapes, or a banana."

Makes 4 servings

INGREDIENTS

1 cup pearl barley

1 medium tomato, chopped

2 medium carrots, shredded

1 medium red, orange, or yellow bell pepper, seeded and chopped

2 cups chopped fresh spinach

3 tablespoons orange juice

3 tablespoons olive or grapeseed oil

2 tablespoons apple cider vinegar (or any other mild vinegar)

1 teaspoon honey

Salt and freshly ground black pepper

PREPARATION

1. Bring a large pot of water to a boil. Add the barley and cook, uncovered, until tender, about 40 minutes. Transfer to a large bowl. Add the tomato, carrots, bell pepper, and spinach and stir to combine.

2. In a small bowl, whisk together the orange juice, olive or grapeseed oil, vinegar, honey, salt, and pepper. Pour the vinaigrette over the barley salad and mix thoroughly. Refrigerate overnight for best results

294 calories; 5g protein; 44g carbohydrates; 11g fat (1.5g saturated fat); 81mg sodium

K&T'S AMAZING TORTILLA CHICKEN SOUP

INGREDIENTS

2 tablespoons olive oil
1 medium onion, peeled and diced
2 tablespoons minced fresh garlic
2 tablespoons chili powder
1 tablespoon ground cumin
1 whole cooked rotisserie chicken, bones and skin removed and meat cubed, or 4 oven-roasted chicken breasts, cubed
4 (14.5-ounce) cans diced tomatoes
2 (15-ounce) cans black beans, drained and rinsed
1 (15-ounce) can of sweet corn, drained
2 (15-ounce) cans low-sodium chicken broth
Garnish: 2 tomatoes, diced; low-fat shredded cheese; low-fat sour cream or Mexican crema; tortilla chips or whole-wheat rolls; avocado

PREPARATION

In a heavy stock pot, warm the olive oil. Add the onion and sauté over medium heat until soft, about 3 minutes. Add the garlic and sauté for 1 minute, then add the chili powder, cumin, and chicken to the pot.

Cook for 4 minutes, then add the canned tomatoes, black beans, corn, and chicken stock. Bring to a boil, then turn down the heat to low. Simmer for 30 minutes. Serve in bowls with the garnishes of your choice.

Katie Hebdon, age 11 in 2014

"My mom and I were attempting to make a quick, healthy, and easy dinner, and we came up with this recipe," recounts Katie. "Both my brother Timmy and I modified it to make sure it was a complete meal and tasted fabulous!!! We both love to cook! We serve this soup with low-fat sour cream or Mexican crema, low-fat cheese, more fresh chopped tomatoes, yummy avocados, a squeeze of lime or lemon juice, and crushed tortilla chips or a whole-wheat roll to round it out."

Makes 8 servings • 427 calories • 8g fat • 46g carbohydrates • 29g protein

CHEF KATIE

Chef Josie Roll,
age 8 in 2015

"I first made this recipe with my great aunt Maria. My favorite part was pounding out the chicken, because it was fun and it made the chicken tender and juicy," says Josie. "My baby brother likes the carrot noodles best. I decided to use veggies for the noodles so the meal would be healthier. I would serve this meal with a glass of low-fat milk and a spinach salad to complete my plate."

Scrumptious Veggie Noodles with Sun-Dried Tomato Sauce and Chicken

Makes 8 to 10 servings • 465 calories • 18g fat • 39g carbohydrates • 39g protein

---

INGREDIENTS

For the Sauce:

1 tablespoon olive oil
5 garlic cloves, peeled and minced
¼ cup finely chopped fresh basil
1 teaspoon dried oregano
1 ¾ pounds chopped heirloom and cherry tomatoes
1 cup low-sodium chicken broth
½ cup sun-dried tomatoes
½ teaspoon salt
½ teaspoon pepper

For the Chicken:

4 skinless, boneless chicken breasts, quartered
½ cup brown rice flour or whole-wheat flour
Salt and pepper to taste
2 tablespoons olive oil

For the Noodles:

3 carrots, peeled
4 zucchini, ends cut off
3 summer squash, ends cut off
Salt and pepper to taste
1 tablespoon olive oil

For the Bread:

¼ cup olive oil
8 garlic cloves, peeled and minced
1 tablespoon dried oregano
1 tablespoon dried basil
Salt and pepper to taste
1 loaf multigrain bread, cut into 1-inch slices

PREPARATION

1. **To make the Sauce:** In a medium sauté pan heat the olive oil over medium heat. Add the garlic, basil, and oregano and sauté for about 3 minutes, or until fragrant. Add 1 pound of the chopped tomatoes and the broth and bring to a boil. Reduce the heat to a simmer, add the sun-dried tomatoes, salt, and pepper and cook about 20 minutes. About 10 minutes before serving, add the remaining tomatoes and cook until softened.

2. **To make the Chicken:** One at a time, lay the chicken breasts between wax paper and pound out to ¼-inch thickness. On a plate, combine the brown rice flour, salt, and pepper. Lightly dredge the chicken in the flour mixture. In a nonstick sauté pan, heat the olive oil over medium heat. Add the chicken and sauté, flipping, until cooked through and light brown.

3. **To make the Noodles:** Using a mandoline fitted with the appropriate blade attachment, slice the veggies into long thin strips. Season with salt and pepper. In a large nonstick pan, heat the olive oil over medium heat. Add the carrots and sauté for about 4 minutes, or until they start to soften. Add the remaining veggies and sauté 4 minutes more, or until they are all al dente.

4. **To make the Bread:** Preheat the oven to 350°F. In a small bowl, combine the olive oil, garlic, oregano, basil, salt, and pepper. Place the bread slices on a large baking sheet and brush lightly with the olive oil mixture. Toast in the oven for 15 minutes, or until golden.

5. **To serve:** Create a bed of noodles on each plate, top with chicken, and drizzle with sauce. Serve with the garlic bread.

CHEF

Jacob Russell

age 12 in 2016

"I wanted to use Idaho potatoes, as well as create a recipe using super foods for the brain that helps kids with focus and memory," says Jacob. "My mom and I researched the top foods for your brain health. Salmon, found in Idaho's rivers, is one of the best. I came up with an idea to represent the American flag with star-shaped salmon patties and stripes made from vegetables. My parents call me 'The Berry Monster' since I love to pick berries and eat them straight from the vine! Blueberries are also great for the brain. I learned the importance of eating fruits and veggies of all colors." Jacob likes to serve his salmon patty with brown rice and blueberry smoothies.

Super Stars and Stripes Salmon Patty

Makes 4 servings • 374 calories • 16g fat • 28g carbohydrates • 28g protein

INGREDIENTS

1 Yukon Gold potato, peeled and sliced
2 tablespoons grapeseed oil or olive oil
1 garlic clove, peeled and minced
1 shallot, peeled and minced
¼ cup diced red bell pepper
¼ cup diced celery
2 cups cooked, flaked salmon (drained if from a can)
2 eggs
¼ cup parsley
¾ cup whole-grain breadcrumbs
⅛ cup wheat germ
¼ cup grated Parmesan cheese
3 cups fresh spinach
Cut-up strips of jicama, avocado, and red, yellow, and orange bell peppers
Salad dressing of your choice

Optional
Tzatziki sauce, parsley and lemon wedge, for garnish
½ teaspoon lemon pepper
Blackened seasoning
Brown rice

PREPARATION

1. **In a saucepan filled with water,** cook the potato over medium heat for about 8 minutes, or until fork-tender.
2. **Meanwhile, in a nonstick saucepan,** warm 1 tablespoon oil over medium heat. Add the garlic, shallot, red pepper, and celery and cook about 6 minutes, or until golden brown. Let cool.
3. **In a food processor,** combine salmon with eggs, parsley, breadcrumbs, wheat germ, Parmesan, and lemon pepper, if using. Mix together and spoon into a bowl. Wet your hands with water and shape the mixture into 6 patties. (You can cut the patties with a star-shaped cookie cutter.) Sprinkle patties with blackened seasoning, if using.
4. **In a large nonstick skillet,** warm the remaining tablespoon of oil over medium heat, and cook patties for 4 minutes on each side, or until golden brown and firm to touch. Serve with brown rice, spinach, strips of fresh veggies, salad dressing, and fresh Tzatziki sauce, parsley or lemon juice, if desired.

Illinois

Pesto Pasta

Jonah Schaik, age 12 in 2012

"My mom gave me a recipe challenge to come up with a healthy pasta dish that my little brother with food allergies could eat," says Jonah. "This recipe is healthy and inexpensive, especially in the summer, when you could grow fresh basil in your yard or in a potting pot on the back porch." Jonah likes to serve this with a strawberry-banana smoothie made with coconut milk and orange juice.

Makes 6 servings

INGREDIENTS

For the pesto:

4 cups loosely packed fresh basil

5 ounces frozen chopped spinach, defrosted and drained

5 garlic cloves, crushed

2 tablespoons olive oil

Kosher salt

Freshly ground black pepper

For the pasta:

1 pound whole-wheat rotini

2 tablespoons olive oil

1 pound ground turkey breast

½ teaspoon salt

1/2 teaspoon freshly ground black pepper

2 (14-ounce) cans low-fat, low-sodium chicken broth

½ onion, cut into small dice

½ red bell pepper, cut into small dice

3 garlic cloves, minced

¼ cup fresh basil leaves, chopped

¼ teaspoon dried red pepper flakes (optional)

For garnish:

Freshly grated Parmesan cheese

PREPARATION

Make the pesto:

1. In a blender or food processor, combine the basil, spinach, garlic, and olive oil. Blend until smooth. Season to taste with salt and pepper.

Make the pasta:

2. In a large pot of boiling salted water, cook the pasta until al dente, 8 to 10 minutes. Reserve 1 cup of the pasta cooking water, then drain the pasta and return it to the pot.
3. While the pasta is boiling, cook the turkey: In a large, deep skillet over moderate heat, warm the olive oil. Add the ground turkey and cook, stirring to break up the meat, until just starting to brown, about 10 minutes. Season with salt and pepper, then transfer the meat to a plate and reserve.
4. In the same large skillet over low heat, warm 3 tablespoons of the chicken broth. Add the onions and bell pepper, and sauté, stirring occasionally, until softened, 8 to 10 minutes. Add the garlic and sauté, stirring occasionally, 5 minutes. Add the basil and the dried red pepper, and return the cooked turkey to the pan. Add the remaining chicken broth, and simmer over low heat for 10 minutes.
5. Add the pesto to the pasta. Stir well to combine, adding the reserved pasta cooking liquid as necessary to loosen the pesto. Add the turkey sauce to the pasta and cook over low heat, stirring to combine, until heated through. Serve hot, with freshly grated Parmesan on the side.

Black Bean Wrap with Jicama–Grilled Corn Salsa

TADDY PETTIT, age 10 in 2013

"We chose this recipe because the children love bean burritos!" says Taddy's dad, Ryan. "This version is fun for them to build their wraps from the fresh vegetables we grow in our garden. The beans and quinoa are high in nutrients and protein, and there is a nice balance with the yogurt for dessert." Taddy likes to serve it with a nonfat Greek-style yogurt parfait that stars fresh pineapple and strawberries.

Makes 10 servings

INGREDIENTS

For the black bean wraps:

1 cup dried black beans

1 tablespoon olive oil

1/2 medium onion, diced

1 medium carrot, diced

1 rib celery, diced

3 cloves garlic, minced

3 cups water

1/2 cup cooked quinoa

Salt and freshly ground black pepper

For the jicama-grilled corn salsa:

1 cup diced jicama

1 green bell pepper, seeded and diced

1 red bell pepper, seeded and diced

1 jalapeño, seeded and minced

1 cup grilled or boiled corn kernels

1/2 medium red onion, diced (optional)

1/4 cup red wine vinegar

2 tablespoons freshly squeezed lime juice

2 cloves garlic, minced

1 tablespoon Dijon mustard

1 teaspoon salt

1/2 teaspoon freshly ground black pepper

1/2 cup olive oil

To serve:

Whole wheat tortillas

Baby spinach leaves

Avocado

Fresh cilantro

PREPARATION

Make the black bean wraps:

1. Soak the black beans in cold water in the refrigerator overnight. Drain and rinse the soaked beans.

2. In a medium saucepan pan over moderate heat, warm the olive oil. Add the onion, carrot, celery, and garlic and sauté, stirring occasionally, until soft and translucent, about 3 minutes. Add the beans and 3 cups water and bring to a boil. Lower the heat and simmer the beans, stirring occasionally, for 30 minutes. Remove the beans from the heat and cool.

3. Transfer the beans to a food processor and purée until smooth. Transfer to a large bowl, add the cooked quinoa, and stir to combine. Season with salt and pepper.

Make the jicama-grilled corn salsa:

1. In a medium bowl, toss together the jicama, green and red bell peppers, jalapeño, corn, and red onion, if using.

2. In a blender combine the vinegar, lime juice, garlic, mustard, salt, and pepper. Blend well then slowly add the olive oil. Drizzle the vinaigrette over the salsa and stir to combine.

To serve:

1. Warm the tortillas in the oven or microwave. Spread 1 tablespoon of the black bean purée down the middle of each tortilla then top with spinach, avocado, salsa, and cilantro. Roll up and enjoy.

363 calories; 9g protein; 44g carbohydrates; 16g fat (2g saturated fat); 446mg sodium

Tess Boghossian, age 11 in 2014

"We chose to make a soup inspired by Abraham Lincoln's inauguration," says Tess's mom, Deborah. "After some research, we learned a brunoise soup was served for dinner. We wanted to pay tribute to Lincoln's inauguration, but add more nutritional value than the soup originally served by adding whole grains and lean protein. Considering that we are from the Land of Lincoln and Tess is obsessed with Abraham Lincoln, this is the perfect lunch to represent the great state of Illinois."

Makes 4 servings • 371 calories • 13g fat • 29g carbohydrates • 32g protein

CHEF TESS

LINCOLN'S INAUGURAL SOUP

INGREDIENTS

2 tablespoons olive oil
1 small onion, peeled and diced
1 small parsnip, peeled and chopped
½ cup chopped green beans
1 carrot, peeled and chopped
1 quart low-sodium chicken broth
½ cup cooked quinoa
1 cup chopped asparagus (tough ends discarded)
8 ounces canned white beans, rinsed
½ cooked rotisserie chicken, skin removed, and chopped or 2 cups skinless boneless cooked chicken, chopped
¼ teaspoon salt
¼ teaspoon pepper

PREPARATION

In a large pot, warm the olive oil over medium-high heat. Sauté the onion for 4 minutes or until soft. Add parsnips, green beans, and carrots, and continue to cook for 5 minutes, stirring occasionally. Add chicken broth, bring to a boil and then add quinoa. Cover and simmer for 10 minutes. Add asparagus, white beans, and chicken, season with salt and pepper, and cook for 5 minutes more, or until the chicken is heated through.

Garam Masala Quinoa Burger with Raita

Makes 4 Servings • 379 calories • 11g fat • 58g carbohydrates • 15g protein

---

INGREDIENTS

1 cup cooked garbanzo beans
½ cup cooked quinoa
¼ cup chopped kale
¼ cup peeled and chopped onion
1 small boiled potato
½ teaspoon garam masala
½ teaspoon ground cumin
¼ teaspoon peeled and grated fresh ginger
1 garlic clove, peeled and minced
¼ teaspoon grated serrano chile pepper
¼ cup panko breadcrumbs
Salt and pepper to taste
2 tablespoons olive oil
½ cup Greek yogurt
¼ cup grated cucumber
4 whole-wheat buns
Sliced tomatoes
Baby spinach leaves

PREPARATION

1. **Coarsely chop the garbanzo beans** in a food processor or by hand. In a large bowl, combine the chopped garbanzo beans with the quinoa, kale, onion, potato, garam masala, cumin, ginger, garlic, serrano chile pepper, and breadcrumbs. Season to taste with salt and pepper. Stir the mixture thoroughly and form into 4 round patties.
2. **In a large sauté pan,** heat the olive oil over medium heat. Add the patties and cook, flipping once, 5 minutes per side, or until brown and crispy.
3. **Meanwhile, in a small bowl,** combine the yogurt and cucumber. Season to taste with salt and pepper.
4. **To assemble the sandwiches,** place the patties on the whole-wheat buns, and top with the raita, tomato, and spinach leaves.

Chef Shreya Patel,

age 9 in 2015

"I have watched my mom and grandma make all sorts of delicious food in the kitchen with an Indian twist since I was born," says Shreya. "I have been helping them cook since I was three. I love to mix, measure, chop, and even clean up afterwards. My grandma and I came up with this recipe together because we both love sandwiches. We make this recipe often to take to school for lunch or even on picnics with friends."

West Wing Chicken with Secret Service Noodles

Makes 8 servings • 426 calories • 15g fat • 37g carbohydrates • 36g protein

INGREDIENTS

For the West Wing Chicken:

2 eggs
1 teaspoon skim milk
2 cups panko breadcrumbs
8 4-ounce skinless boneless chicken breasts
2 tablespoons olive oil

For the Marinara Sauce:

2 tablespoons olive oil
3 garlic cloves, peeled and minced
½ onion, peeled and chopped
1 carrot, peeled and chopped
2 28-ounce cans crushed or whole plum tomatoes, diced
¼ cup fresh basil, cut into strips
1 bay leaf
Pinch of sea salt
Fresh ground pepper

For the Secret Service Noodles:

6 squash (3 zucchini and 3 yellow squash)
Sea salt and freshly ground black pepper
1 large carrot, peeled
1 bunch asparagus, trimmed and cut into 1-inch pieces
1 tablespoon olive oil
2 garlic cloves, peeled and minced
10 grape tomatoes, halved
¼ cup grated Parmesan cheese
Italian parsley

PREPARATION

1. **To make the West Wing Chicken:** In a medium bowl, whisk together the eggs and milk. Put the breadcrumbs on a plate. Dip the chicken in the egg mixture and then lightly dredge both sides of the chicken in the breadcrumbs. In a large nonstick skillet, warm the olive oil over medium heat. Add the chicken and, cooking in two batches, cook for 6 minutes per side, or until cooked through and golden brown.
2. **To make the Marinara Sauce:** In a large stockpot, heat the olive oil over medium heat. Add the garlic, onion, and carrot and cook for 7 minutes, or until golden brown. Add the remaining ingredients and simmer over low heat for 30 minutes.
3. **To make the Secret Service Noodles:** Spiralize the squash (or you can use a box grater) and put into a colander to drain excess juice. Sprinkle lightly with sea salt and let stand for 15 minutes. Spiralize the carrots. In a large stockpot, bring 8 cups of water to a boil over medium-high heat and add squash, carrots, and asparagus. Cook for 3 minutes, drain into a colander and rinse the vegetables immediately with cold water.
4. **In a nonstick skillet** warm the olive oil over medium heat. Add the garlic, squash, carrots, and asparagus, season with sea salt and pepper to taste, and cook for 1 minute.
5. **To Assemble:** Place serving of noodles on a plate and garnish with tomatoes, Parmesan, and parsley. Place 1 West Wing Chicken breast next to the Secret Service Noodles and top with Marinara Sauce.

CHEF

Maggie Smith

age 11 in 2016

"Last fall, I started to cook different recipes and would change ingredients and measurements to make them healthier and tastier," says Maggie. "My aunt told me that I should enter the Healthy Lunchtime Challenge because I am so interested in cooking. With this recipe, I cooked it three times in order to get it just right. My family enjoyed the meal and commented how yummy and filling it was. My dish includes all food groups, and ingredients that are grown locally. Enjoy!"

Indiana

Vegetable Quinoa Salad with Chicken

Alexander Aylward, age 8 in 2012

"These are my favorite foods, and we came up with this when we put them all together," says Alexander. "This is my actual lunch a lot of the time." While the recipe calls for grilled chicken, you can use any type of cooked chicken or even slices of turkey breast. Alexander likes to have this with milk and some blueberries or raspberries for dessert.

Makes 4 to 6 servings

INGREDIENTS

2 cups cooked quinoa

6 ounces grilled skinless boneless chicken or turkey deli meat, cut into bite-size pieces

2/3 cup chopped fresh spinach

1/2 cup diced tomatoes

1/2 cucumber, peeled and diced

1/2 red pepper, seeded and diced

3 tablespoons homemade or purchased olive-oil vinaigrette

Salt

PREPARATION

In a large bowl, combine the quinoa, chicken or turkey, spinach, tomato, cucumbers, red pepper, and vinaigrette. Toss to combine, and season to taste with salt.

Sneaky Chili Surprise

LYDIA FINKBEINER, age 9 in 2013

"My little brother Ryan doesn't like cooked carrots, so I decided to put them in the recipe to get him to eat cooked carrots," says Lydia. "I like chili so I thought we could use my mom's sweet potato purée to sneak some more vegetables into the recipe and use beans as a lean protein to make it more healthy." She suggests serving it with multigrain tortilla chips, an apple or a bowl of fruit, and a glass of milk.

Makes 10 to 12 servings

INGREDIENTS

4 carrots, diced

1 sweet potato, peeled and diced

1 tablespoon olive or vegetable oil

1/2 large onion, cut into small dice

1 medium red bell pepper, seeded and diced

2 cloves garlic, minced

1/2 tablespoon chili powder

1/2 tablespoon ground cumin

1 teaspoon ground chipotle pepper

1/4 teaspoon salt

1/8 teaspoon freshly ground black pepper

2 (15-ounce) cans tomato purée

2 (15-ounce) cans petite diced tomatoes

2 (15-ounce) cans black beans, drained and rinsed

2 (15-ounce) cans cannellini or other white beans, drained and rinsed

PREPARATION

1. Bring a medium pot of water to a boil. Add half the carrots and potato and boil until soft, about 10 minutes. Mash the carrots and potato by hand or purée them in a blender.

2. In a large stockpot, over moderate heat, warm the olive or vegetable oil. Add the onion, bell pepper, garlic, and the remaining carrots and sweet potato and sauté until soft, about 5 minutes. Add the chili powder, cumin, chipotle pepper, salt, and pepper and cook for 3 minutes. Add the tomato purée and tomatoes, as well as the sweet potato and carrot purée and stir well to combine. Add the black and cannellini beans and simmer, stirring occasionally, for 30 minutes.

181 calories; 8g protein; 32 carbohydrates; 2.5g fat (.25 saturated fat); 863mg sodium

SOPHIE'S HEALTHY COCONUT CHICKEN

INGREDIENTS

3 cups brown rice, rinsed
2 tablespoons olive oil
2 tablespoons minced garlic
1 teaspoon fresh minced ginger
2 (32-ounce) containers of low-sodium chicken stock
2 (13.5-ounce) cans lite coconut milk
2 pounds boneless skinless chicken breast, finely diced
1 pound frozen chopped spinach, thawed and squeezed
1 tablespoon cornstarch
2 pinches salt

PREPARATION

In a rice cooker or covered stockpot, combine rice with 3 cups water. Cook for about 45 minutes or until it's done.

Meanwhile, make the chicken: In a large stockpot, warm the olive oil over medium heat. Add the garlic and ginger and cook for 1 minute. Add the chicken stock and coconut milk, stir and simmer for 5 minutes. Add the chicken and spinach, and simmer for 30 minutes.

In a small bowl, combine the cornstarch with 1 tablespoon water. Add to the chicken and stir well until slightly thickened, season with salt, and serve with the rice.

Sophie McKinney Han, age 10 in 2014

"My dad grew up in Honolulu, so at our house we eat a lot of Asian meals. My parents want me to eat vegetables and try new and different foods; however, when I tried spinach, I wasn't too crazy about it on its own," says Sophie. "My mom and I thought of a creative way to add spinach in this dish because it is so nutritious. The other great thing about my Coconut Chicken dish is it can be eaten as a soup or with rice as a bigger meal."

Makes 12 servings • 367 calories • 11g fat • 38g carbohydrates • 24g protein

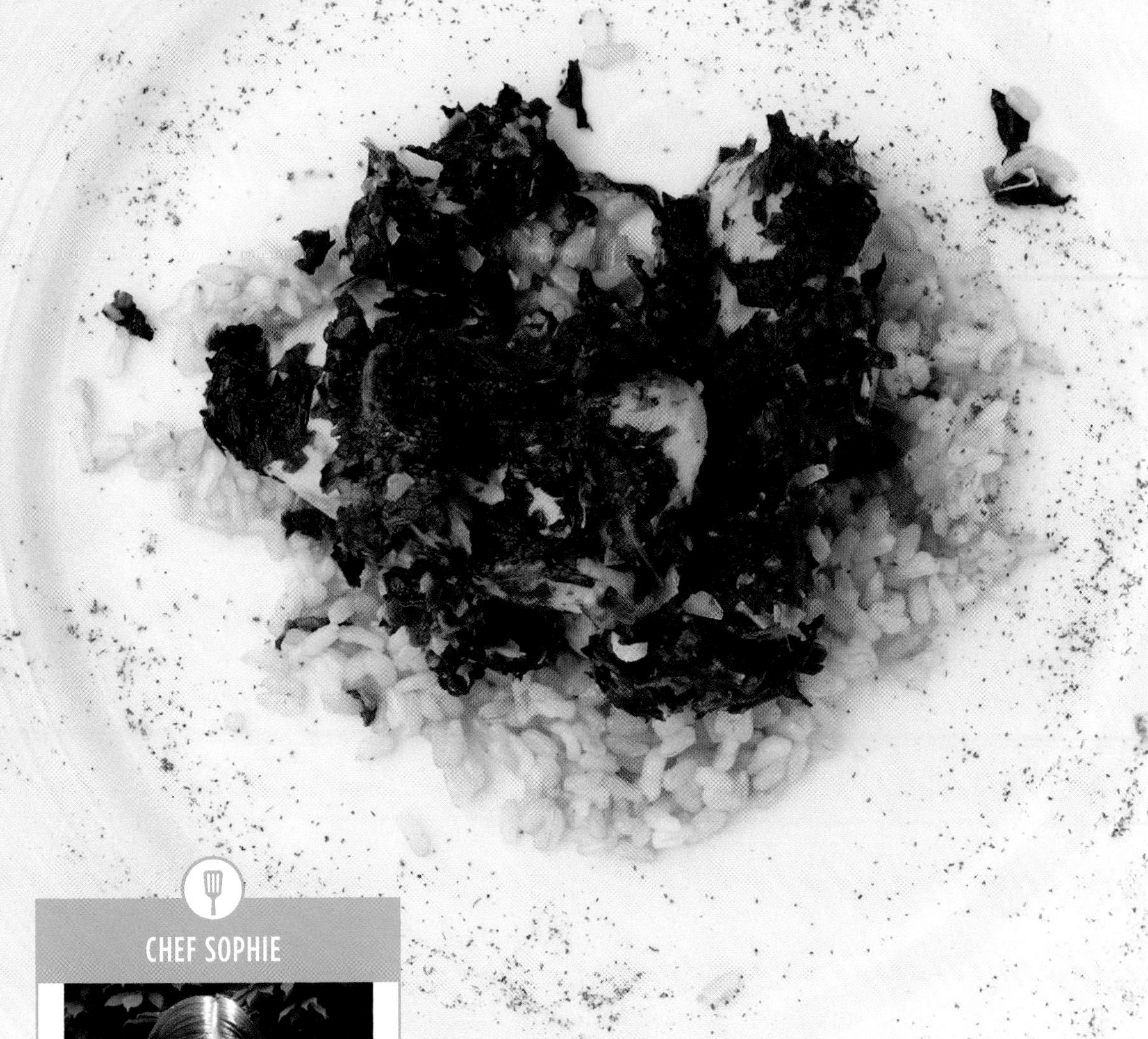

CHEF SOPHIE

Chef Abigail Horne,

age 8 in 2015

"My little brother is sensitive to wheat. Whenever we have sandwiches for lunch he always cries for bread, but we are not allowed to give it to him," says Abigail. "I wanted to come up with a sandwich for him that didn't have wheat bread and was also affordable. My dad loves fried plantains or tostones. I thought it would be a great idea to use the plantains for bread but bake them instead of frying for a healthier option. I ended up with a turkey burger on plantain buns and a fresh jicama and apple slaw. He loved it!"

Little Man Lunch

Makes 8 Servings • 396 calories • 14g fat • 50g carbohydrates • 22g protein

INGREDIENTS

For the Plantain Bread:

2 yellow plantains
1 teaspoon salt
1 cup tapioca flour
1 tablespoon chopped fresh cilantro
2 tablespoons vegetable oil

For the Slaw:

1 large jicama, julienned
2 large Red Delicious apples, julienned
Juice from 2 limes
2 tablespoons agave nectar
2 tablespoons chopped fresh cilantro

For the Burgers:

1 ¼ pounds ground turkey
1 large egg
½ cup old-fashioned rolled oats
2 teaspoons Cajun seasoning
1 teaspoon achiote powder
1 bay leaf, crushed
2 teaspoons dried basil
2 teaspoons salt
1 teaspoon black pepper
½ teaspoon vanilla extract
3 tablespoons olive oil
¾ cup shredded low-fat cheddar cheese
1 large tomato
1 small bunch of kale

PREPARATION

1. **To make the Bread:** Preheat the oven to 375°F. In a food processor or blender, purée the plantains with 2 tablespoons water. In a large bowl, mix the puréed plantains, with the salt, tapioca flour, and cilantro until you have thick smooth dough. Oil a large baking sheet and use a tablespoon to scoop the dough onto the sheet. Use the back of the spoon to flatten the dough into 2-inch-diameter rounds. Bake in the oven for 25 minutes, or until light brown and firm.
2. **To make the Slaw:** Meanwhile, in a large bowl, combine all of the slaw ingredients. Set in the refrigerator to chill.
3. **To make the Burgers:** In a large bowl, mix the ground turkey, egg, rolled oats, seasonings, and vanilla. Using a large spoon, form the mixture into 3-inch-diameter rounds and set aside. In a large sauté pan, heat the olive oil over medium heat. Cook the burgers, flipping once, 6 minutes per side, or until the internal temp reaches 165°F. Remove from the heat and top with some cheddar cheese. Let the burgers rest for 2 minutes, while the cheese is melting, to maintain juiciness.
4. **Top each plantain bun** with a burger, tomato slice, fresh kale leaf, and slaw.

CHEF

Shakthi Ramachandran

age 8 in 2016

"My dad is from India and I like Indian food, especially chicken tikka masala," says Shakthi. "I asked my dad how I can make chicken tikka masala and make it like a sandwich. I love chicken and I also like to eat a lot of vegetables. This recipe combines all these things and is very tasty and delicious. In the summer most of the vegetables we eat are from our garden. The cucumber raita dressing makes it delicious."

Chicken Tikka Pita with Cucumber Raita

Makes 4 servings • 592 calories • 21g fat • 47g carbohydrates • 56g protein

INGREDIENTS

For the Chicken Tikka:

1 pound chicken breast, boneless, skinless, cubed
1 cup low-fat yogurt
1 ½ teaspoon ginger-garlic paste (can use ¾ teaspoon ground ginger and ¾ teaspoon minced garlic)
1 ½ teaspoon cumin powder
1 teaspoon red chili powder
2 teaspoons garam masala (or coriander seed)
Dash to 1 teaspoon salt
1 teaspoon freshly ground black pepper
3 teaspoons tikka masala
1 ½ teaspoons fresh lemon juice
1 tablespoon olive oil

For the Cucumber Raita:

2 hot house/English cucumbers, quartered
3 sprigs mint
20 ounces plain Greek yogurt
10 ounces low-fat sour cream
½ teaspoon roasted ground cumin
1 teaspoon salt

To Assemble:

4 pita breads
1 onion, peeled and chopped
2 carrots, peeled and shredded
2 green bell peppers, seeded and cut lengthwise
1 cucumber slice
1 bunch romaine lettuce, chopped
1 bunch fresh spinach, chopped

PREPARATION

1. **To make the Chicken Tikka:** In a large bowl, combine the chicken with the remaining ingredients and marinate, covered, in the refrigerator, for a minimum of 4 hours or overnight.
2. **Preheat the broiler.** Remove the chicken from the marinade, place it in an oven-safe skillet and broil for about 15 minutes, or until cooked through.
3. **To make the Cucumber Raita:** In a medium bowl, combine the raita ingredients.
4. **To Assemble:** Layer each pita bread pocket with vegetables, chicken, and cucumber raita.

Iowa

Yummy Corn Wraps

Ajani Patton-Imani, age 8 in 2012

"Half of our family is extremely sensitive to sugar. We also have a lot of food allergies among us," reports Ajani's mom, Sandra. As a result, they make a lot of things from scratch, because so many processed foods have added sugar. "We like to stuff our wraps with all kinds of stuff, but one of our favorites is cheese, guacamole, black olives, and tomatoes."

Makes 4 to 6 servings

INGREDIENTS

2 cups masa, plus more for shaping wraps

Salt

1 cup unsweetened soy milk, at room temperature

2 avocados, pitted and mashed

1 garlic clove, minced

Juice of 1/2 lemon

Dash cayenne pepper

2 cups grated Colby or Jack cheese

1 cup sliced olives

1 cup diced tomatoes

PREPARATION

1. In a medium bowl, combine the masa and 1/2 teaspoon salt. Make a well in the center and pour in the soy milk and ¾ cup water, then stir with a wooden spoon until the dough comes together. Turn the dough onto a work surface and knead for 1 minute. Cover with a damp towel or plastic wrap for 30 minutes. After the dough rests, divide it into 12 pieces and roll into Ping-Pong-ball-size balls. Cover the balls with plastic wrap as you work.

2. Heat a dry cast-iron skillet or griddle over moderate heat and dust a work surface with masa. Pat 1 ball of dough flat, then use a rolling pin to roll it into a 6-inch round. (You can also use a tortilla press.) Add to the hot skillet and cook for 30 to 45 seconds on each side, until tiny flecks of black appear and you begin to smell corn. Repeat with the remaining balls of dough. Stack the tortillas and wrap them in a towel to keep warm.

3. In a small bowl, combine the avocado, garlic, lemon juice, and cayenne. Season to taste with salt.

4. In each wrap, spoon guacamole, cheese, olives, and tomatoes. Fold in half, and eat over your plate!

Stone Curry with Brown Rice

CORRINE VANDERGAAST, age 9 in 2013

"My mom runs an in-home day care, and we made this curry with all the kids while acting out the story, Stone Soup," says Corrine. "This curry is served with brown rice, fruit, and a glass of milk. We have a lot of fun making it and learning about the foods we put into it, so we like to eat it. When you taste it, don't forget to say, 'Curry from a stone. Fancy that!'"

Makes 8 servings

INGREDIENTS

3 tablespoons olive oil

1 medium onion, diced

3 cups water

2 (14-ounce) cans chickpeas, drained and rinsed

2 medium red-skinned potatoes, diced

1 medium sweet potato, peeled and diced

1 medium tomato, chopped

4 cups finely chopped spinach

1/2 cup jarred mild curry sauce or 1 tablespoon curry powder

4 cups cooked brown rice

PREPARATION

1. In a large saucepan over moderate heat, warm the olive oil. Add the onion and sauté, stirring occasionally, until soft and translucent, about 4 minutes. Add the water and bring to a boil.

2. Add the chickpeas, red-skinned potatoes, sweet potato, tomato, and spinach, one at a time, while talking about the colors and nutrients in each vegetable and how they keep us healthy.

3. Reduce the heat to low and simmer the vegetables until tender, about 10 minutes. Add the curry sauce or powder and simmer for 5 more minutes. Serve over brown rice.

299 calories; 8g protein; 49g carbohydrates; 8g fat (1g saturated fat); 288mg sodium

Anabel Bradley, age 8 in 2014

"My name is Anabel, and I live on a farm with chickens, turkeys, five acres of asparagus, and two gardens," says Anabel. "I mixed some of my favorite things from our farm, and voilà! The best thing to have with veggie pancakes is blueberries or grapes so you have all the colors of the rainbow on your plate at once. Almost every weekend you will find me in the kitchen because I love to cook. My family gave it the thumbs-up."

Makes 6 servings • 135 calories • 10g fat • 9g carbohydrates • 3g protein

CHEF ANABEL

OVER THE RAINBOW VEGGIE PANCAKES

INGREDIENTS

⅔ cup shredded carrots
⅔ cup chopped yellow sweet bell pepper
⅔ cup diced tomatoes
⅔ cup chopped asparagus (tough ends removed)
¼ cup whole-wheat or all-purpose flour
1 egg
½ teaspoon salt
½ teaspoon dried basil
½ teaspoon garlic powder
Pepper to taste
¼ cup olive oil

PREPARATION

In a large mixing bowl, combine the carrots, yellow pepper, tomatoes, and asparagus. Add flour and stir to coat vegetables. In a small bowl, beat the egg, then add to vegetables. Season with herbs, then mix thoroughly.

In a large skillet, warm the olive oil over medium heat. When it's hot, drop a large serving spoonful of pancake batter into pan in a circle shape. (Depending on the size of your pan, you can probably fit three pancakes at a time.) Cook for 4 minutes on medium heat, flip, and cook until golden brown on each side, about 2 minutes more. Remove from pan with a spatula and set on a plate lined with a paper towel, before serving.

Mary's Garden Farfalle Feast

Makes 4 Servings • 667 calories • 14g fat • 120g carbohydrates • 24g protein

INGREDIENTS

For the Farfalle Feast:

2 cups plain farfalle
or veggie penne pasta
4 ears corn
2 tablespoons olive oil
1 cup cubed extra-firm tofu
½ cup each chopped fresh green beans, Brussels sprouts, and asparagus

For the Fruit Salad:

2 fresh oranges, peeled
1 banana, sliced
1 cup green or red seedless grapes
1 cup mixed berries

For the Kale-Spinach Smoothies:

1 cup fresh kale and spinach
2 cups orange juice
½ cup nonfat plain yogurt
1 cup frozen blueberries
1 ripe peeled banana

PREPARATION

1. **In a pasta pot,** bring 2 cups of water to a boil over high heat. Stir in the pasta and cook for about 10 minutes, or until al dente. Meanwhile, fill another pot with water, add the corn, and bring to a boil over high heat. Drain and set aside.
2. **In a large sauté pan,** heat the olive oil over medium heat. Add the tofu and cook for about 5 minutes. Add the green beans, Brussels sprouts, and asparagus. Cook for about 5 minutes, or until softened. Add the drained pasta and stir to combine.
3. **Arrange the food on the plates** in a butterfly design, with the corn as the body. Arrange the fruit salad in the shapes of little butterflies, placing a red grape between two slices of orange.
4. **In a blender,** combine all the smoothie ingredients and process until well combined.

Chef Mary McFetridge,

age 11 in 2015

"I'm inspired by my sister, who can run as fast as the wind, and my brothers, who taught me basketball. I was also inspired by my coaches on Girls on The Run, who taught me to be the best I can be and much more," says Mary. "Last but not least, I was inspired by my parents. My mom, because she has taught me to be healthy, and because I run with my dad when we do 5Ks and he encourages me all through the race. I'm eating the Farfalle Feast and following MyPlate, so my bones, brain, and muscles will grow strong. I serve this pasta with with Kale-Spinach Smoothies and Fruit Salad."

American Gothic Calzones

Makes 6 servings • 481 calories • 12g fat • 82g carbohydrates • 19g protein

INGREDIENTS

For the Spinach Filling:

½ cup water
½ cup raw unsalted cashew pieces
8 ounces firm tofu, crumbled
Dash to 1 teaspoon salt
1 teaspoon garlic powder
1 teaspoon Italian seasoning
1 teaspoon fresh lemon juice
5 ounces chopped fresh spinach

For the Calzones:

1 ¼ cup warm water
1 package active dry yeast
2 tablespoons unsweetened applesauce
2 tablespoons honey
1 teaspoon salt
2 ½ cups whole-wheat flour

For the 'Food Will Win the War' Medley:

1 tablespoon olive oil
1 15-ounce can corn
1 15-ounce can lima beans (you can substitute with chickpeas)
1 15-ounce can hominy
¼ cup diced red bell pepper
½ cup diced green bell pepper

PREPARATION

1. **To make the Spinach Filling:** In a blender, combine water and cashew pieces. Blend on high for 1 minute until smooth. Pour into a medium bowl. Add tofu, salt, garlic powder, Italian seasoning, lemon juice, and spinach and mix well.
2. **To make the Calzones:** Preheat the oven to 425°F. In a large mixing bowl, combine water and yeast. Let sit for 5 minutes. Add applesauce, honey, salt, and flour and stir well to combine. (You can also use a stand mixer or a food processor.) When dough forms a ball, knead it for 2 minutes on a work surface sprinkled with flour. Divide the bread dough into 6 equal pieces and roll into balls. Flatten dough with a rolling pin to 1/8-inch thickness. Divide the filling among the circles. Lift the edge and stretch the dough over to the opposite edge, enclosing filling, and pressing the edge of the dough gently to seal. Arrange calzones seam-side down on a large baking sheet lined with parchment paper, and bake for 15 minutes or until golden brown.
3. **To make 'Food Will Win the War' Medley:** In a medium saucepan, warm the oil over medium heat. Combine all ingredients, heat for about 15 minutes, until heated through. Serve with American Gothic Calzones.

CHEF

Lola Shorney

age 11 in 2016

"My goal is to be a veterinarian and because I love animals and healthy food, I enjoy inventing recipes that are plant based," says Lola. "Iowa is known for Grant Wood's painting *American Gothic*. My calzones include Iowa grown ingredients. During World War I, when Hoover was appointed U.S. Food Administrator, his slogan was 'Food Will Win the War.' In order to feed our American army overseas, his food conservation campaign successfully reduced domestic food consumption by 15 percent. With my calzones, I serve a 'Food Will Win the War' vegetable medley. Applying Hoover's 'Food Will Win the War' approach to obesity, I vow to be part of the solution." Lola's Go Ride Your Bike dessert has cantaloupe, bananas, and other fruits.

Kansas

Yummy Cabbage Sloppy Joes

Rori Coyne, age 12 in 2012

"We were making dinner one night, and Mom had a lot of cabbage, which I wasn't sure I liked. She also had lean ground beef, which I love," says Rori, who also is a big fan of sloppy joes. "Mom showed me how to make cabbage, beef, and a bunch of other vegetables taste better than a package [of sloppy joes]. She says this is an affordable meal for us, since we can make a pound of beef last several meals. I like mine with fresh fruit."

Makes 8 servings

INGREDIENTS

1 pound lean ground beef

1 medium onion, diced

1 medium zucchini, shredded or diced

2 ribs celery, diced

1/2 cup chopped red pepper

1 1/2 cups finely shredded cabbage

1 cup tomato sauce or crushed tomatoes

1 tablespoon brown sugar

2 tablespoons lemon juice

1 tablespoon white vinegar

1 tablespoon Worcestershire sauce

1 tablespoon mustard

1/2 teaspoon salt

1/4 teaspoon freshly ground black pepper

8 sandwich rolls, split (optional)

PREPARATION

1. In a large skillet, cook the beef until cooked through, about five minutes. Drain the fat from the skillet, and reserve the meat on a plate.
2. In the same pan over moderate heat, cook the onion, zucchini, celery, red pepper, and cabbage until all the vegetables are crisp-tender, about 4 minutes. Add the cooked beef to the pan and stir to combine.
3. In a small bowl, combine the tomato sauce or crushed tomatoes, brown sugar, lemon juice, vinegar, Worcestershire sauce, mustard, salt, and pepper. Pour the sauce into the pan with the beef and vegetables and simmer, stirring occasionally, until thickened, about 8 minutes.
4. While the sloppy joes are simmering, toast the buns in the oven or toaster oven.
5. Evenly divide the mixture among the toasted bun bottoms, top with the other halves, and serve.

Fun Mini Pizzas with Veggies & Cauliflower Crust

OLIVIA NEELY, age 10 in 2013

"Mrs. Obama's focus on healthy eating taught me to look for ways to make healthier choices," says Olivia. "My mom and I came up with a fun team challenge where we earned points for healthy eating, exercise, and choosing to pass up unhealthy treats. We love pizza and made up a delicious gluten-free cauliflower crust with low-fat ground beef packed with zucchini and squash as toppings. The result is a crazy-good pizza with tons of veggies. We even make our pizzas in fun shapes, including our state—Kansas!" She suggests rounding the meal out with apple slices and a Greek-style yogurt smoothie with strawberries, blueberries, and flaxseed.

Makes 4 servings (2 mini pizzas per person)

INGREDIENTS

For the cauliflower crusts:

1 medium head cauliflower, chopped

1 cup shredded part-skim mozzarella cheese

1 large egg

1/2 teaspoon garlic powder

1/2 teaspoon dried oregano

1/4 teaspoon salt

For the pizza topping:

1/2 pound lean ground beef

1/4 cup shredded yellow squash

1/4 cup shredded zucchini

1 clove garlic, minced

1/4 teaspoon dried oregano

Salt and freshly ground black pepper to taste

1/2 cup tomato sauce

1 cup shredded part-skim mozzarella cheese

Optional toppings:

16 cherry tomatoes (halved), 3 tablespoons sliced almonds, 1/2 cup chopped broccoli florets, 1/2 cup sliced mushrooms, several leaves baby spinach

PREPARATION

Make the cauliflower crusts:

1. Preheat the oven to 400°F and line a large baking sheet with parchment paper.

2. In a food processor, pulse the cauliflower until it's in very small pieces. Transfer to a microwave-safe bowl and microwave until tender, about 4 minutes. Let the cauliflower cool for several minutes. Wrap the cooled cauliflower in a kitchen towel and squeeze out any excess liquid.

3. In a medium bowl, combine the cauliflower, mozzarella cheese, egg, garlic powder, oregano, and salt and stir to combine. Divide the mixture into 8 equal parts and form each one into a ball. Press and flatten the balls into circles or fun shapes, and place them onto the prepared baking sheet. Bake the pizza crusts for 15 minutes then flip them over and continue baking until firm and light golden brown, about 15 minutes. Leave the oven on.

While the crusts are baking, make the pizza topping:

1. In a large sauté pan over moderate heat, cook the ground beef, yellow squash, zucchini, garlic, oregano, salt, and pepper, stirring to break up the beef, until the beef is cooked through, about 8 minutes. Drain any excess liquid.

Assemble and bake the pizzas:

1. Spread the tomato sauce on the crusts. Top the pizzas with the beef mixture, cheese, and your favorite toppings as desired. Bake until the cheese bubbles, about 6 minutes. (Or for a delicious smoky taste, heat pizzas on a wood-fire or charcoal grill.) Serve with additional toppings.

336 calories; 33g protein; 17g carbohydrates; 16g fat (7.5g saturated fat); 754mg sodium

Jasmy Mavilla, age 8 in 2014

"I love to help my dad grow vegetable and fruits in our home garden, and I love to help my mom use those veggies in different ways with our cooking," recounts Jasmy. "My favorite dish is this spaghetti with lots of vegetables and shrimp cooked in lemony sauce. I like to eat this with fresh fruit or a fruit smoothie."

Makes 4-6 servings • 467 calories • 10g fat • 43g carbohydrates • 32g protein

CHEF JASMY

TANGY VEGGY SPRINGETTY

INGREDIENTS

♥ For the Pasta:

1 pound whole-wheat spaghetti or angel hair pasta

3 cups fresh or frozen mixed vegetables

Parmesan cheese, for garnish

♥ For the Sauce:

2 tablespoons olive oil

1 pound of 20 count shrimp, peeled and deveined

1 tablespoon minced garlic

Salt and pepper to taste

½ cup fresh lemon juice (from about 2 lemons)

½ teaspoon white wine vinegar, optional

1 tablespoon lemon zest, optional

1 cup canned garbanzo beans, optional

PREPARATION

Bring a large pot of salted water to a boil. Add the pasta and cook until almost al dente, about 6 minutes. Add in the vegetables and cook about 3 minutes more. Drain, reserving 1 cup of the cooking liquid.

In a large sauté pan, warm the olive oil over medium heat. When the oil is hot add the shrimp and cook until the shrimp are pink, about 4 minutes. Add the garlic and season with salt and pepper. Transfer the shrimp to a separate bowl. Turn the heat to low and add lemon juice, white wine vinegar, and reserved cooking liquid (¼ cup at a time). Whisk until the sauce is well mixed and reduced by one third.

Add the pasta to the pan along with the shrimp, lemon zest, and garbanzos, if using, and mix to combine. Serve with Parmesan.

Black Bean Burger with Kale Chips and Jasmine's Freeze Out Smoothie

Makes 6 Servings • 404 calories • 9g fat • 68g carbohydrates • 17g protein

---

INGREDIENTS

For the Burgers:

2 (15-ounce) cans low-sodium black beans, drained and rinsed
1 ripe banana, mashed
1 cup breadcrumbs
3 tablespoons chopped fresh basil
1 teaspoon dried oregano
1 ½ teaspoons ground cumin
Pinch sea salt and pepper
Nonstick cooking spray
6 whole-wheat hamburger buns
Optional topping: 1 avocado, sliced

For the Kale Chips:

10 ounces kale, chopped
2 teaspoons olive oil
¼ teaspoon sea salt

For Jasmine's Freeze Out Smoothie:

1 cup organic 1% milk
1 cup frozen mixed berries
1 handful spinach

PREPARATION

1. **To make the Burger:** In a large bowl, mash the black beans, banana, breadcrumbs, basil, oregano, and cumin. Season to taste with salt and pepper and mix well. Form the mixture into 6 patties.
2. **Heat a large nonstick skillet over medium heat.** Spray the pan with cooking spray, then add the patties and cook, flipping once, for about 4 minutes per side, or until heated through. Place on whole-wheat buns, and top with avocado, if desired.
3. **To make the Kale Chips:** Preheat the oven to 400°F. In a large bowl, combine the kale with the olive oil and salt and toss thoroughly to coat the kale. Place on a nonstick baking sheet and bake for about 12 minutes, or until the kale is crispy.
4. **To make Jasmine's Freeze Out Smoothie:** In a blender, blend the ingredients together and enjoy!

Chef Jasmine Dulan,

age 11 in 2015

"First, I really want to be a nutritionist like my mommy when I grow up, and help others eat healthy," says Jasmine. "I developed my black bean burger recipe for this challenge for a healthier and more affordable option than a regular hamburger. Black beans are so yummy and eating plant-based recipes more often is good for the earth, too. I included my kale recipe as I LOVE kale chips. I also included my favorite smoothie recipe with my secret ingredient—spinach."

Lentil Tacos with Cilantro-Avocado Drizzle

Makes 4 servings • 347 calories • 11g fat • 48g carbohydrates • 19g protein

INGREDIENTS

For the Lentil Tacos:

1 ¼ cup water
½ cup green lentils
1 teaspoon extra-virgin olive oil
1 garlic clove, peeled and minced
½ teaspoon salt
½ teaspoon dried oregano
1 teaspoon cumin
1 teaspoon ground ancho chili pepper
4 whole-grain tortillas
1 cup shredded purple cabbage
½ cup canned pineapple, drained
½ fresh lime, quartered

For the Cilantro-Avocado Drizzle:

1 small ripe avocado, peeled, pitted, and thinly sliced
½ cup non-fat plain Greek yogurt
¼ teaspoon salt
1 garlic clove, peeled and minced
¼ cup fresh cilantro, chopped

For the Mango-Peach Smoothie: *(not pictured)*

½ cup sliced peaches
½ cup frozen mango chunks
½ cup low-fat milk
½ cup non-fat plain Greek yogurt

PREPARATION

1. **To make the Lentil Tacos:** In a large stockpot, bring 1 cup of water to a boil over medium heat. Add lentils, return to boiling, reduce heat, partially cover, and simmer for 25 minutes, or until al dente. Remove from heat and drain. In a small nonstick skillet, warm the olive oil on medium heat and add the garlic. Cook for 1 minute then add the lentils, salt, oregano, cumin, chili pepper, and remaining ¼ cup water. Reduce the heat to low and simmer for about 5 minutes or until most of the water evaporates.
2. **To make Cilantro-Avocado Drizzle:** In a food processor, combine all ingredients and pulse until smooth. Transfer to a small bowl for serving.
3. **To Assemble:** Divide lentil mixture amongst the tortillas and top with cabbage, pineapple, fresh lime, and Cilantro-Avocado Drizzle.
4. **To make Mango-Peach Smoothie:** Combine all ingredients in a blender and blend until smooth.

CHEF
Joey Heidari
age 12 in 2016

"This recipe includes a number of colorful ingredients such as corn, lentils, peaches, cabbage, cilantro, and garlic, all of which are grown in Kansas," says Joey. "My recipe has many healthy ingredients from each food group on MyPlate, such as whole grains in the tortillas; vegetables like purple cabbage and garlic; fruits like pineapple tidbits and avocado; lentils, for protein; and dairy from the Greek yogurt. I also made a Mango-Peach Smoothie to add more fruit and dairy. My family enjoyed eating this meal, so I hope you enjoy it, too."

Kentucky

Perfect Curry Chicken Wraps

Myka Smith-Jackson, age 8 in 2012

"I was on the Internet, and was thinking, *You know, anything can be made into a wrap.* So I decided that I'd make a curry chicken wrap," says Myka. "For a side: sliced strawberries and a fruit and yogurt smoothie." Myka's recipe calls for grilled chicken, but you can use any kind of cooked chicken.

Makes 2 to 4 servings

INGREDIENTS

2 grilled skinless boneless chicken breasts, cut into bite-size pieces

2 stalks celery, chopped

1 red apple, peeled and diced

1/4 cup raisins

1/2 cup mayonnaise

1/4 teaspoon curry powder

Salt and pepper

2 (10-inch) whole-wheat tortillas

PREPARATION

1. In a large bowl, combine the chicken, celery, apple, raisins, mayonnaise, and curry powder. Stir to combine, and season to taste with salt and pepper.
2. Divide the mixture between the tortillas, and wrap tightly around the filling from bottom to top, overlapping one end, burrito style. Cut the wraps in half to serve.

Raisin Bran Muffins

REGAN STREHL, age 11 in 2013

"My mom and I came up with this recipe when I was very young and it has always been one of my favorites. I eat the muffins various times during the day with a big glass of fat-free milk," says Regan. "Last November I was diagnosed with type 1 diabetes and Mom and I had to go back and work on the recipe to get the carbohydrate count down. You could take out the walnuts, but there goes your protein. I have learned that protein is very important in your diet!" Combined with a salad with lean protein, this makes for a great lunch. (You can make two dozen muffins by halving the ingredients.)

Makes 48 muffins

INGREDIENTS

3 cups unbleached all-purpose flour

2 cups whole wheat flour

1/2 cup sugar substitute (baking blend)

1/2 cup brown sugar substitute (baking blend)

1 tablespoon baking soda

1 tablespoon ground cinnamon

2 teaspoons salt

5 large eggs, slightly beaten

1 quart low-fat buttermilk

1 cup canola oil

1 cup unsweetened applesauce

1 (17.3-ounce) box bran flakes cereal

2 large carrots, grated

1 cup raisins

1 cup chopped walnuts

PREPARATION

1. Preheat the oven to 375°F and line 2 (12-cup) cupcake pans with liners.

2. In a large bowl, whisk together the all-purpose and whole wheat flours, along with the sugar substitute and brown sugar substitute, baking soda, cinnamon, and salt.

3. In a second large bowl, whisk together the eggs, buttermilk, oil, and applesauce. Gradually fold the dry ingredients into the wet ingredients then add the bran flakes cereal, carrots, raisins, and walnuts and gently stir until incorporated. Divide the batter in half. Fill the 2 pans with half the batter and bake the muffins until a toothpick inserted in the center of a muffin comes out clean, 15 to 20 minutes. Once the pans are cool, remove the muffins and line both pans with new liners. Fill the muffin cups with the remaining batter and bake the muffins until a toothpick inserted in the center of a muffin comes out clean, 15 to 20 minutes.

170 calories; 4g protein; 24g carbohydrates; 7g fat (.8g saturated fat); 335mg sodium

AROUND THE WORLD IN ONE BITE

INGREDIENTS

1 tablespoon vegetable oil
1 scallion, chopped
½ cup finely diced red bell pepper
4 cups chopped kale
3 cups shredded or grated sweet potato
½ cup crushed pineapple in juice, not drained
2 cups shredded cooked chicken
½ cup cooked brown rice
⅛ teaspoon cayenne pepper
½ teaspoon salt
2 tablespoons chopped cilantro
1 package 6-inch egg roll wrappers
⅓ cup plain yogurt
2 tablespoons lime juice
2 teaspoons honey

PREPARATION

In a large sauté pan, warm the oil over medium heat. Add the scallions and peppers and cook for about 2 minutes. Add kale and sweet potato and cook for 5 minutes more, stirring often. Add the pineapple and its juice, chicken, rice, cayenne, and salt and cook until vegetables are soft, about 5 minutes. Remove from heat and add cilantro.

Preheat the oven to 400°F. Fill each egg roll wrapper with approximately 3 tablespoons filling in the center of the roll. Fold in both sides and tightly roll closed according to egg roll package instructions. Bake on a cookie sheet for 10 minutes or until lightly golden. While the pockets cook, whisk together the yogurt, lime juice, and honey for a dipping sauce.

Lucy Fairhead Hickerson, age 8 in 2014

"My mom and I went to an event called The Taste of Diversity. I tasted three different kinds of pockets from different places in the world," says Lucy. "I decided to make a pocket. We talked about different kinds of filling, and we decided to start with some of my favorite vegetables, sweet potatoes and kale. I said that our recipe was like an Indian samosa, a Spanish empanada, and an Asian spring roll all at the same time. It's like going around the world in one bite."

Makes 10 servings • 289 calories • 5g fat • 37g carbohydrates • 14g protein

CHEF LUCY

Chef Izzy Washburn,

age 9 in 2015

"I presented to the school board my suggestions to help students identify what makes a lunch healthy. This recipe is one of my favorites," says Izzy. "I saw in my experiment that pre-packaged food and fruit snacks/ chips and other unhealthy foods were in my friends' lunch boxes. It is important to teach my friends what good choices look like and how what FUEL they choose for their bodies affects how they perform throughout their day."

Shake It Off with a Turkey Roll

Makes 1 Serving • 501 calories • 22g fat • 39g carbohydrates • 35g protein

---

INGREDIENTS

Fresh blueberries
Fresh strawberries, sliced
Fresh spinach, torn into bite-sized pieces
Fresh romaine lettuce, torn into bite-sized pieces
Carrot slivers
1 tablespoon ranch dressing
1 soft tortilla
¼ teaspoon mayonnaise
2 slices turkey breast
1 slice Colby Jack cheese

PREPARATION

1. **Place the blueberries** and strawberries in a small container together.
2. **Place the spinach,** romaine, and carrots in a small container together. Place the lid on the container and shake.
3. **Place the ranch dressing** in a small container (I like mine separate so my salad isn't soggy by lunchtime).
4. **Place the tortilla** on the cutting board. Spread mayonnaise on the tortilla, add the turkey, veggies, and cheese, roll the tortilla up, and cut it into 1-inch sections.

CHEF

Will Bingham

age 10 in 2016

"My family likes to go camping and hiking a lot," says Will. "My mom and I were trying to think of some healthy choices for lunch instead of hotdogs and hamburgers on the grill. So we came up with this one-bag bake that included seasonal veggies and local fish. We used an aluminum foil pouch and placed it in our campfire. It was a hit with our whole family! All we needed was our one bag and a fork! Now we make it at home all the time! Super yummy!!!"

One Bag Bluegrass Bake!

Makes 1 serving • 459 calories • 26g fat • 28g carbohydrates • 30g protein

INGREDIENTS

4 ounces trout fillets
or any local flaky fish, like salmon
1 tablespoon grated lemon zest
½ lemon, thinly sliced
1 tablespoon lemon juice
1 tablespoon extra-virgin olive oil
Kosher salt and freshly grated pepper
½ red or yellow bell pepper, julienned
½ cup zucchini, peeled and julienned
1 garlic clove, peeled and minced
2 sprigs thyme
½ cup navy or white beans,
rinsed and drained
Plain Greek yogurt as topping (optional)
Cooked brown rice (optional)

PREPARATION

1. **Preheat oven to 400°F.** In a large mixing bowl, gently toss all ingredients except navy beans, yogurt, and rice. On a large piece of parchment paper or aluminum foil, add the fish and beans. Fold the parchment or foil over and crimp and fold so it's sealed. Bake in the oven for 25 minutes. Let bag sit for 5 minutes before opening. Serve with yogurt and cooked brown rice.

Louisiana

Fish Tacos

Michael Prados, age 12 in 2012

"I am the JR. Food Critic from Louisiana," says Michael. "I love to cook with my family and go on food adventures. We made up this fish taco recipe. You can see my other dishes at jrfoodcritic.com."

Makes 4 to 8 servings

INGREDIENTS

2 pounds fresh mahimahi or other white flaky fish, cut into 8 pieces

2 tablespoons low-sodium soy sauce

1 (14- to 16-ounce) bag shredded cabbage slaw

1/4 cup plus 1 tablespoon olive oil

1 tablespoon freshly squeezed lime juice

1 tablespoon orange juice

1 tablespoon rice-wine vinegar

Freshly ground black pepper

8 whole-wheat tortillas

For garnish: Sliced green apple, guacamole, and salsa

PREPARATION

1. In a large bowl, combine the fish and soy sauce, and stir to completely coat the fish in soy sauce. Cover and refrigerate at least 1 hour and up to 3 hours.
2. Place the shredded cabbage slaw in a large bowl.
3. In a small bowl, whisk the 1/4 cup of olive oil with the lime juice, orange juice, and rice-wine vinegar. Pour the dressing over the shredded cabbage slaw and toss to combine.
4. In a large saute; pan over moderately high heat, warm the remaining 1 tablespoon olive oil. Sprinkle the fish lightly with black pepper and sear, turning once, until cooked through, about 2 minutes per side.
5. While the fish is cooking, warm the tortillas in the microwave.
6. On a work surface or individual plates, divide the fish among the 8 tortillas. Top each taco with slaw, and fold or roll up the tacos. Serve with sliced green apple, guacamole, salsa, or other fresh toppings.

Sweet and Spicy Stir-Fry

BRYNNA ROBERT, age 12 in 2013

"I started with a recipe my mother made—I didn't enjoy it as it was too bland," says Brynna. "It got me wondering if I could change it so it could be something I liked, so I brainstormed. I came up with a new twist on Mom's recipe. The spicy chili-garlic sauce kicks up the sweet pineapples and orange juice, creating an explosion of flavors that are absolutely savory. I would serve it with a tall glass of skim milk because it makes a complete serving from every food group."

Makes 4 servings

INGREDIENTS

1 tablespoon canola oil

1/2 fresh pineapple, peeled and sliced

2 medium carrots, sliced on the diagonal

1/2 cup broccoli florets

1 red bell pepper, seeded and sliced into thin rings

4 cloves garlic, minced

2 teaspoons grated fresh ginger

2 cups cooked brown rice

1 (15-ounce) can chickpeas, rinsed and drained

3 scallions, thinly sliced

3 tablespoons reduced-sodium soy sauce

1 tablespoon chili-garlic sauce (optional)

1/2 cup coarsely chopped fresh parsley leaves

1 orange, separated into sections

PREPARATION

1. In a medium sauté pan over moderate heat, warm 2 teaspoons of the canola oil. Add the pineapple slices and cook until golden and softened, about 3 minutes. Transfer the pineapple to a plate and set aside. Do not clean the pan.

2. In the same pan, warm the remaining 1 teaspoon of oil. Add the carrots and cook for 3 minutes. Add the broccoli, red bell pepper, garlic, and ginger and sauté, stirring occasionally, until the vegetables are tender and brown, 3 to 4 minutes.

3. Add the cooked brown rice, chickpeas, scallions, soy sauce, and chili-garlic sauce, if using. Stir and continue cooking for 4 more minutes. Add the parsley and the reserved pineapple and stir to combine. Serve the stir-fry with orange wedges to squeeze juice on top.

286 calories; 8g protein; 53g carbohydrates; 5.7g fat (.46g saturated fat); 519mg sodium

Moira Doran, age 10 in 2014

"My Dad and I came up with this idea. We often have lunch or brunch at friends' houses or at our house," says Moira. "They are good for lunch, breakfast, or a snack! I'd serve them with fresh salsa. They fit easily in a lunch box, and travel well. Every time you make a frittata, you can change the ingredients and that will change the flavor. My favorite is when we make it with cooked onions, low-fat feta cheese, and chopped spinach!" *(Please note: Recipe pictured was not cooked in a muffin tin.)*

Makes 12 servings • 81 calories • 4g fat • 3g carbohydrates • 7g protein

CHEF MOIRA

MUFFIN TIN EGG WHITE FRITTATAS

INGREDIENTS

1 yellow onion, peeled and chopped
2 teaspoons olive oil
1 package frozen chopped spinach, thawed
Cooking oil spray
6 ounces feta cheese
1 tomato, chopped
Salt and pepper
1 pint of egg whites or whites from 8 eggs

PREPARATION

Preheat oven to 300°F. Grease a 12-muffin tin with cooking spray. In a large sauté pan, warm the oil over medium-low heat. Add the onion and cook until soft, about 3 minutes.

Squeeze the water out of the spinach and add to the cooked onion. Add the feta cheese and tomatoes, and season with salt and pepper to taste. Using a large spoon, divide this mixture into each muffin cup in the tin. Carefully pour the egg whites into each, leaving a little space, about ¼ inch, for it to rise. Bake for 15 to 20 minutes, or until the frittatas have risen and feel set. Place on a cooling rack for 10 minutes, then remove from the cups.

Chef Samuel Davis,

age 11 in 2015

"At first, my parents promised to get me a dog if I took care of the garden... so I was excited to be in charge of watering and gathering the harvest each day," says Samuel. "Since I love science and math, I created this mouthwatering dish which uses every fresh-grown vegetable in my family's garden, plus my favorite meat, salmon. It has become a family favorite. I'm the new chef in the house! I'm just a southern boy who loves to eat healthy!"

Sam's Southern Savoring Salmon Supreme (S to the 5th power)

Makes 4 Servings • 443 calories • 20g fat • 46g carbohydrates • 22g protein

---

INGREDIENTS

1 cup brown rice
2 (6-ounce) salmon fillets
¼ teaspoon salt
¼ teaspoon pepper
¼ cup olive oil
2 cups okra, chopped
½ cup red bell pepper, chopped
½ cup green bell pepper, chopped
1 tablespoon green onion (scallion), chopped
1 teaspoon diced jalapeño
2 cups diced tomatoes
¼ cup feta cheese crumbles
1 lemon, halved

PREPARATION

1. **In a saucepan,** combine 1 ½ cups water with the rice, and bring to a boil over high heat. Cover, reduce the heat, and simmer for 20 minutes, or until tender. Set aside.
2. **Sprinkle the salmon with salt and pepper.** In a sauté pan, heat 2 tablespoons of the olive oil over medium-high heat. Add the salmon, and cook, flipping once, for about 5 minutes per side, or until opaque. Transfer the salmon to a plate using a wide spatula. Cut each fillet into 2 pieces and keep warm.
3. **In the same pan,** heat the remaining 2 tablespoons olive oil over medium-high heat. Add the okra, red and green bell peppers, green onion, and jalapeño, and sauté for about 5 minutes, or until the vegetables are softened. Add the diced tomatoes, stir well, and cook for 10 minutes.
4. **On each plate,** spoon rice and salmon, and top with vegetables. Sprinkle lightly with feta cheese. Squeeze lemon on top of salmon and serve.

CHEF

Owen Osborne

age 8 in 2016

"Owen's severe food allergies mean that he will never be able to eat from his school cafeteria menu, or from most prepackaged lunch meals," says Owen's mom, Jeanae. "He, like most kids, loves fun lunches, with loads of colors, and ways to dip them. He picked his favorite foods and created this meal to rival all prepackaged and cafeteria offerings. The ingredients are all locally sourced, and the dessert was inspired by the Louisiana Peach Festival."

Sweet Savory Dip-tastic Louisiana Power Lunch

Makes 6 servings • 656 calories • 15g fat • 77g carbohydrates • 53g protein

INGREDIENTS

For the Chicken:

1 ¾ cup vegetable broth
1 cup brown rice
2 medium sweet potatoes, peeled and chopped
2 tablespoons extra-virgin olive oil, plus more as needed
Dried basil, oregano, thyme, Creole seasoning, salt, and freshly ground black pepper (optional)
1 pound fresh broccoli florets
1 tablespoon fresh lemon juice
4 skinless, boneless chicken breasts, cut into bite-sized pieces
Barbecue sauce, soy sauce, or salsa, for dipping

For the Fruit Salsa & Cinnamon Tortilla Crisps:

1 apple, peeled, cored, and coarsely chopped
2 tablespoons fresh lemon juice
2 cups strawberries, stemmed and chopped
2 cups peaches, peeled, pitted, and chopped
4 large whole-wheat tortillas
1 tablespoon cinnamon
1 tablespoon brown sugar

PREPARATION

1. **Preheat the oven to 375°F.** In a large stockpot, bring broth to a boil over medium heat. Add in the rice, stir and cover, reduce heat to low. Cook for 25 minutes, or until tender.
2. **Meanwhile, on a large baking sheet,** coat sweet potatoes lightly with 1 tablespoon olive oil, sprinkle with any seasoning you like, and bake for 30 minutes, or until tender. On a second large baking sheet, lightly season broccoli with lemon juice, salt, pepper, thyme, or any other seasonings you like. Bake on the other oven shelf for 30 minutes, alongside the sweet potatoes.
3. **In a large nonstick skillet,** warm remaining tablespoon olive oil over medium heat. Add the chicken and cook 6 minutes on each side, or until golden brown.
4. **To make the Fruit Salsa & Cinnamon Tortilla Chips:** In a large bowl, toss apples with lemon juice. Add remainder of fruit and stir. Place tortillas on nonstick baking tray, sprinkle with cinnamon and brown sugar, and place in the warm oven until slightly crisp. Remove from oven and cut into triangles or strips.
5. **To Assemble:** Divide the rice, broccoli, sweet potatoes, and chicken amongst the plates. Serve with the Fruit Salsa and Cinnamon Tortilla Crisps.

Maine

Turkey Dumplings

Annalee Carroll, age 12 in 2012

Annalee's family are big fans of sushi and dumplings, and decided to make them at home. "We make a large batch of dumplings and freeze them on trays so that they are a fast meal choice," says Annalee's mom, Marydale. They also make veggie sushi with carrots, cucumbers, and avocados.

Makes 6 to 8 servings

INGREDIENTS

2 tablespoons vegetable oil

1 tablespoon minced fresh ginger

2 scallions, white and light green parts only, thinly sliced

1 small garlic clove, minced

2 cups shredded green cabbage

1/2 cup mung bean sprouts (optional)

¼ cup plus 2 tablespoons low-sodium soy sauce

½ pound ground turkey or chicken

About 32 (3 ½-inch-diameter) wonton skins

Rice vinegar

Sesame oil

PREPARATION

1. In a large nonstick skillet over moderate heat, warm 1 tablespoon vegetable oil. Add the ginger, scallions, and garlic, and sauté, stirring occasionally, until fragrant, about 2 minutes. Add the cabbage and sauté, stirring occasionally, until wilted, about 4 minutes. Stir in the bean sprouts, if using, then remove from the heat and stir in 2 tablespoons of soy sauce. Let cool, then transfer to a bowl, add the meat, and mix with hands until blended. Wash the skillet.

2. Lay 4 wontons skins on a work surface. Add a scant tablespoon of the filling in the center of each. Brush around the edge of the wrappers with water and then fold the wrappers in half, pinching to seal. Place dumplings, pinched-edge-up, on a wax-paper-lined baking sheet and cover with a damp towel. Continue making dumplings with the remaining wonton skins and filling.

3. Add ½ inch of water and the remaining 1 tablespoon vegetable oil to the same large skillet and bring to a simmer over moderately high heat. Add about half the dumplings, cover and cook until the wrappers are tender and the meat is cooked through, about 8 minutes. Repeat with the remaining dumplings, adding more water and oil as necessary.

4. In a small bowl, combine the remaining ¼ cup soy sauce with 1 tablespoon water, a dash of rice vinegar, and sesame oil. Whisk together and serve with the dumplings.

Vegan Powerhouse Pesto Pasta

NOAH KOCH, age 9 in 2013

"Noah's younger brother has serious health issues and making food that everyone can eat can be challenging," says Noah's mom, Hilary. "This recipe is gluten-free and vegan, things that many people often think mean sacrificing favorite comfort foods or flavor. It took us a while to create a pesto recipe that was tasty, super healthy, and easy to make. We finally created one that is packed with just about everything a growing body needs. Noah likes this with Red, White, and Blue Salad—strawberries, peeled and diced apples, and Maine blueberries, served with a glass of soy milk."

Makes 8 servings

INGREDIENTS

1 pound quinoa pasta (we like macaroni)

2 ripe avocados, pitted and flesh scooped out

1 cup fresh baby spinach leaves

4 cups fresh basil leaves, plus a few leaves reserved for garnish

1/2 cup walnuts

1 (15-ounce) can cannellini beans, drained and rinsed

2 tablespoons freshly squeezed lemon juice

1 clove garlic, minced

1/8 teaspoon freshly ground black pepper

1/4 cup olive oil

1 cup grape tomatoes, cut in half

PREPARATION

1. Bring a large pot of salted water to a boil. Add the pasta and boil until al dente, about 10 minutes. Drain the pasta and return it to the pot.

2. While the pasta is boiling, combine the avocados and spinach in a food processor and pulse briefly (about 6 times). Add the basil, walnuts, 1/4 cup cannellini beans, lemon juice, garlic, and pepper and pulse about 6 more times. With the food processor on, gradually add the olive oil in a slow, steady stream.

3. Add 3/4 of the sauce to the cooked pasta, tossing gently to coat the noodles. Add the remaining sauce, as desired, and stir to coat the noodles evenly.

4. To serve, transfer the pasta to a big pasta bowl (family-style) and top with the remaining cannellini beans and grape tomatoes. Garnish with the reserved basil.

431 calories; 8g protein; 58g carbohydrates; 20g fat (2.5g saturated fat); 83mg sodium

Sienna Mazone, age 12 in 2014

"Cooking is one of my passions! I like my mom to give me ingredients and time me while I create my own unusual dishes," says Sienna. "I asked my mom to give me three ingredients to start the process: She gave me a sweet potato, a red Fresno chile pepper, and an avocado. I used these as a starting point and then added other ingredients. I just went to the Boston Museum of Science to see an exhibit about chef Ferran Adrià. I was inspired by his creativity for presenting food and flavors, and tried to think of a clever way to combine colors and textures in a healthy one-dish meal."

Makes 6 servings • 298 calories • 10g fat • 36g carbohydrates • 9g protein

CHEF SIENNA

MEXICAN HAYSTACK

INGREDIENTS

6 whole-grain flour tortillas
1 cup cherry tomatoes, sliced thin
1 red Fresno chile pepper, seeded and chopped
½ red onion, chopped
2 tablespoons chopped fresh cilantro
Juice of one lemon or lime
2 tablespoons chopped fresh cilantro
1½ teaspoons salt
1 avocado, seeded and mashed
2½ teaspoons ground cumin
1 large sweet potato, peeled, baked, and mashed
1 (15-ounce) can of vegetarian refried beans

PREPARATION

Preheat the oven to 400°F. Cut the flour tortillas in strips and place them on a baking sheet. Bake for about 10 minutes, or until the strips are crispy and slightly brown.

To make the salsa: In a medium bowl, combine the tomatoes, pepper, onion, cilantro, two tablespoons of the lemon or lime juice, and 1 teaspoon of salt.

In a separate bowl, combine the remaining 2 tablespoons lemon juice and the avocado along with ½ teaspoon each of cumin and salt. Set aside.

In a separate bowl, add the remaining 2 teaspoons cumin to the mashed sweet potato. In the microwave, warm the sweet potato and the beans in two separate bowls for 1 minute.

To make the haystack: First place a few tablespoons of refried beans on the plate, then sweet potato, salsa, and avocado. Place the baked tortilla strips around the haystack and use for dipping.

Chef Leo Koch,

age 8 in 2015

"My name is Leo and I am a Superhero! Well, at least that is what my mama and papa tell me. I have Type 1 Diabetes and Hydrocephalus," says Leo. "So eating healthy foods helps me to stay as strong as I possibly can. I like to eat this soup the night before one of my 5K races. Beans are already a super food, but we packed a few more secret ingredients into our soup! My parents say that desserts are "sometimes" foods, so I helped them come up with an "everyday" dessert! Now, my brother can't stop thanking me!"

Vegan Superhero Soup

Makes 8 Servings • 526 calories • 9g fat • 91g carbohydrates • 23g protein

INGREDIENTS

For the Soup:

½ head cauliflower, cut into bite-sized pieces
2 tablespoons olive oil
¾ cup peeled and diced sweet onion
2 carrots, peeled and diced
1 red bell pepper, diced
2 garlic cloves, peeled and minced
2 teaspoons chili powder
½ teaspoon ground cumin
½ teaspoon salt
4 cups vegetable broth
2 (29-ounce) cans black beans, drained and rinsed
2 cups baby spinach
3 tablespoons apple cider vinegar
2 cups brown rice
Bunch of fresh cilantro
1 lime, halved
½ ripe avocado, diced

PREPARATION

1. **To make the Soup:** In a large stockpot, steam or boil the cauliflower until very tender. Set aside.
2. **In a large stockpot,** heat the olive oil over medium heat. Add the onion, carrots, and red bell pepper and sauté for 3-4 minutes, or until the onions are translucent. Add the garlic, chili powder, cumin, and salt and stir for 1 minute. Add 3 cups of the vegetable broth.
3. **In a blender or food processor,** combine 3 cups of the black beans with the remaining 1 cup broth, the cauliflower, and spinach and blend until smooth. Add the puréed mixture and the remaining beans to the soup. Stir in the apple cider vinegar. Increase the heat to medium high and bring to a boil. Reduce the heat to low, and simmer, stirring frequently, for 40 minutes, or until soup is thick.
4. **Meanwhile,** combine 5 cups of water with the brown rice. Bring to a boil over medium heat, then reduce the heat to low, and cook, covered, for 30 minutes, or until tender. Serve the soup over the brown rice with cilantro and a squeeze of lime. Top with diced avocado.

CHEF

Scout Bookham

age 8 in 2016

"Scout began her brainstorming session by listing ingredients native to Maine," says Scout's mom, Jessie. "Her list included lobster, blueberries and potatoes. Given the health and affordability requirements of the challenge, she chose to highlight our delicious Maine blueberries in her side salad! We had so much fun collaborating on this project, and it was great to see how enthusiastic she was while fine-tuning her recipe, especially as she worked to get the salad dressing's oil-to-vinegar ratio."

Quinoa Chickpea Salmon Rolls with Salad

Makes 4 servings • 377 calories • 15g fat • 38g carbohydrates • 22g protein

INGREDIENTS

For the Quinoa Chickpea Salmon Rolls:

1 cup vegetable broth
½ cup quinoa
½ pound salmon fillets
Salt and freshly ground black pepper
1 15-ounce can chickpeas, rinsed and drained
Juice from ½ fresh lemon
½ teaspoon garlic powder
½ teaspoon paprika
4 sheets nori or seaweed paper
½ cucumber, thinly sliced
Ponzu, for sprinkling (optional)

For the Salad:

1 tablespoon blueberry jam
1 tablespoon extra-virgin olive oil
Dash champagne vinegar, or any vinegar
2 cups baby spinach, chopped
4 ounces blueberries
3 tablespoons goat cheese, crumbled

PREPARATION

1. **To make the Quinoa Chickpea Salmon Rolls:** In a large stockpot, bring the broth to a boil over medium heat, then add quinoa, cover, reduce heat to low, and simmer for 15 minutes, or until tender.
2. **Meanwhile, preheat oven to 450°F.** Line large baking sheet with parchment paper, place salmon fillets skin side down, and sprinkle with salt and pepper, to taste. Bake for about 10 minutes, depending on thickness, or until it flakes easily with a fork.
3. **In a medium mixing bowl,** combine chickpeas, lemon juice, salt, pepper, garlic powder, and paprika, and mash until chunky. Add in quinoa and stir to combine.
4. **To Assemble:** On a nori sheet, spread ¼ of the chickpea-quinoa mash, sprinkle with ponzu if using, then add cucumber and salmon pieces to the edge closest to you. Tightly roll nori sheet away from you. With warm water, moisten top edge like an envelope to seal the roll. (The rolling action can be done freestyle, or with the help of a bamboo rolling mat and clean dish towel.) Cut each maki roll into six pieces with a serrated knife.
5. **To make Salad:** In a large salad bowl, combine blueberry jam, oil, and vinegar and whisk. Add spinach and toss. Portion dressed spinach equally onto 4 plates and top with fresh blueberries and crumbled goat cheese.

Maryland

Sizzling Tofu with Green Onions and Sugar Snap Peas

Samuel Hightower, age 10 in 2012

"Well, I don't really eat sandwiches very well, so my mom has to find other things for me to eat for lunch," says Samuel. "One day I tried tofu and I liked it, so my mom got it. Then my mom was asking me what I wanted for lunch, and I asked her for the tofu. She made it and put it in a thermos. My friends wondered what it was, and a couple of them tried it and really liked it too!"

Makes 1 serving

INGREDIENTS

2 tablespoons vegetable or olive oil

¼ pound firm tofu, cut into small cubes

1 garlic clove, minced

2 scallions, white and light green parts only, chopped

1 cup sugar snap peas, cut into thirds

½ cup cooked brown rice

PREPARATION

1. In a large sauté pan over moderate heat, warm the oil. Add the tofu and cook, stirring often, until golden brown, about 15 minutes. Add the garlic, scallions, and sugar snap peas, and cook 5 more minutes.
2. While the vegetables are cooking, warm the rice in the microwave for 1 minute on high, then serve the sizzling tofu on top.

Chicken Masala Wrap

EMMA SCIELZO, age 10 in 2013

"My Nani (grandmother) cooks healthy and delicious Indian food for us whenever we visit. (I am Indian-American.) She inspires me to try different flavors, spices, and herbs in the food I eat," says Emma. "Many of the ingredients found in Indian cooking are very healthy for our bodies, such as garlic, ginger, turmeric, and cumin. Also, Indian cooking uses a lot of vegetables that are good for you, such as tomatoes, onions, and peppers. I don't like a lot of spice in my food, but I do like a lot of flavor!! My dish is a chicken masala wrap, paired with a refreshing raita and fresh mango slices."

Makes 4 servings

INGREDIENTS

1 sweet potato, peeled and 1 tablespoon vegetable oil

2 to 3 red, yellow, green, or orange bell peppers, seeded and sliced

1 medium tomato, chopped

1 sweet onion, sliced

1/2 teaspoon ginger paste or 1 teaspoon freshly grated ginger

1/2 teaspoon garlic paste or 1 clove garlic, minced

1/8 teaspoon crushed red pepper or paprika

1/4 teaspoon ground cumin

1/8 teaspoon ground cinnamon

1/8 teaspoon ground turmeric

1 teaspoon salt

1/4 teaspoon freshly ground black pepper

1/4 cup water

4 medium grilled or cooked boneless, skinless chicken breasts, thinly sliced

1 cup plain nonfat yogurt

1/3 medium cucumber, peeled and grated

Fresh mint leaves for garnish (optional)

1 cup chopped lettuce

4 whole wheat tortillas or flatbread, warmed

Fresh mango slices

PREPARATION

1. In a medium sauté pan over moderate heat, warm the oil. Add the bell peppers, tomato, onion, ginger, garlic, crushed red pepper, cumin, cinnamon, turmeric, 1/2 teaspoon salt, and 1/8 teaspoon pepper and cook until slightly tender, about 10 minutes. Add 3 tablespoons water and chicken and continue to cook for several more minutes.

2. In a medium bowl, stir together the yogurt, cucumber, and the remaining 1 tablespoon water. Sprinkle with the remaining 1/2 teaspoon salt and 1/8 teaspoon pepper and garnish with fresh mint leaves.

3. To serve: Place lettuce and a scoop of chicken masala mixture in the center of each tortilla or roll. Add a spoonful of the raita to each wrap, or serve it on the side, along with fresh mango slices.

330 calories; 21g protein; 42g carbohydrates; 8g fat (1g saturated fat); 415mg sodium

CHESAPEAKE FISH TACOS

INGREDIENTS

♥ For the Salsas:
1 onion, chopped
1 jalapeño, chopped
2 tablespoons chopped cilantro
1 mango, pitted and chopped
1 small cucumber, chopped
1 tomato, chopped
Juice of 1 lime
Olive oil

♥ For the Tacos:
2 tablespoons all-purpose flour
Salt and pepper, to taste
6 ounces rockfish or any firm fish
2 tablespoons olive oil
8 whole-wheat tortillas
2 cups shredded cabbage

♥ For the Lemon-Basil Sorbet:
Juice from 3 lemons
24 basil leaves
¾ cup sugar
1 pint raspberries

PREPARATION

To make the Salsas: In one bowl, combine onion, jalapeño, and cilantro. Place half of that into another bowl and add the mango and cucumber. Add the tomato to the other bowl. Squeeze lime and drizzle olive oil over each and stir.

To make the Tacos: On a plate, combine the flour with salt and pepper. Lightly roll the fish in the flour. In a medium sauté pan, warm the olive oil over moderate heat. Add the fish and cook until lightly browned and firm, about 3 minutes per side. Remove and flake into small pieces. Warm tortillas in microwave. Put fish on warmed tortillas and top with cabbage and salsas.

To make the Sorbet: In a medium bowl, stir together lemon juice, basil, sugar, and 1 cup water. Chill until cold, about 4 hours.

Esther Matheny, age 10 in 2014

"My family believes in making things from scratch and not using canned or preserved food," says Esther. "It is healthier and tastier to use nutritious ingredients and make it yourself. Plus, it's much more fun to do! It is also a good idea to use local ingredients, which is why I chose a Maryland fish. This is because it prevents pollution and the great use of fuel. I have tried a variety of fish taco recipes, but this was an opportunity to try making my own recipe." She serves this with a corn, avocado, and tomato salad and a Lemon-Basil Sorbet.

Makes 4 servings • 439 calories • 15g fat • 42g carbohydrates • 19g protein

CHEF ESTHER

Quinoa Crusted Spinach Tofu Pie

Makes 4 Servings • 280 calories • 13g fat • 29g carbohydrates • 12g protein

---

INGREDIENTS

For the Spinach Pie Filling:

⅓ cup tofu, cut into small cubes
Salt and pepper to taste
1 tablespoon coconut oil
½ white onion, peeled and diced
½ cup peeled and shredded carrots
1 garlic clove, peeled and minced
½ tablespoon maple syrup
8 ounces fresh baby spinach
1 teaspoon dried thyme
2 large eggs
2 tablespoons of your favorite non-dairy milk

For the Crust:

¾ cup cooked red quinoa, drained well
2 tablespoons buckwheat flour
1 large egg
1 tablespoon olive oil
½ teaspoon baking powder
¼ teaspoon of salt

PREPARATION

1. **To make the Spinach Pie Filling:** Preheat the oven to 425°F. Place the tofu on a paper towel-lined plate and press with another paper towel to squeeze excess water out of the tofu. Place the tofu on a baking sheet in a single layer and sprinkle with salt. Bake for 10 minutes, or until light brown. Don't turn off the oven.
2. **Meanwhile, in a medium sauté pan,** heat the coconut oil over medium heat. Add the onion and sauté for 2 minutes. Add the carrots, garlic and maple syrup and sauté for 2 minutes. Add the spinach and sauté until wilted and there is no extra liquid in your pan. Add the thyme and season to taste with salt and pepper. Cook for another 30 seconds and set aside in a bowl to cool. Add the tofu and mix to combine. Cover and let cool in the refrigerator.
3. **To make the Crust:** In a small bowl, combine the cooked quinoa, buckwheat flour, egg, olive oil, baking powder, and salt and mix well. Press into 4 mini quiche dishes and bake for 10 minutes.
4. **To finish the Spinach Pie Filling:** Whip the eggs in a small bowl. Remove the spinach filling from refrigerator and add the eggs and non-dairy milk. Stir quickly for another 1 minute.
5. **Remove the quinoa crusts from oven.** Pour the spinach pie mixture into the four mini crusts. Reduce the oven temperature to 400°F and bake for about 15 minutes, or until golden brown.

Chef Braxton Young,

age 8 in 2015

"I created this recipe for kids like me who are allergic to dairy, nuts, and gluten. But, even if you don't have an allergy, you'll love it too," says Braxton. "I started cooking with my mom when I was two. But, then I stopped cooking, because food started to make my stomach hurt. I used to have seizures and bad asthma, but now that I'm not eating gluten, my seizures and asthma are gone. Now I love to cook and eat healthy food. A lot of other kids don't eat very healthy lunches in my school and unless I have smelly eggs in my lunchbox, they want my healthy food."

Maryland Crab Lettuce Cups

Makes 8 servings • 143 calories • 8g fat • 11g carbohydrates • 8g protein

---

INGREDIENTS

2 tablespoons unsalted butter
½ pound Maryland blue crabmeat (lump or backfin)
3 fresh limes, zested and juiced
1 cup frozen corn
½ red bell pepper, seeded and chopped
¼ teaspoon smoked paprika
¼ teaspoon cumin
Sea salt and freshly ground black pepper
1 tablespoon grapeseed oil or olive oil
2 fresh oranges, juiced
1 head of Bibb lettuce
½ cup micro greens or salad greens
1 avocado, pitted, peeled, and cut into thin slices
½ cup low-fat Jack cheese, shredded

PREPARATION

1. **In a large nonstick skillet,** melt 1 tablespoon butter over medium heat. Add the crabmeat and zest of 1 lime and cook for 3 minutes, or until crab turns light brown. Remove crab to separate bowl and set aside.
2. **In the same pan,** melt remaining tablespoon butter over medium heat, add the corn, red pepper, smoked paprika, cumin, and 1 tablespoon lime juice. Cook until kernels start to turn golden-brown, about 5 minutes. Season with salt and pepper, to taste. Set aside.
3. **To make citrus dressing,** in a small bowl, whisk together oil, remaining lime juice and zest, and all of the orange juice. Add salt and pepper to taste.
4. **To Assemble:** Set out 8 plates and place two Bibb lettuce leaves on each plate, so that each leaf forms a cup shape. To each lettuce cup, add: 1 tablespoon micro greens, 2 tablespoons corn mixture, 2 tablespoons crab meat, and 1 tablespoon Jack cheese. Drizzle 2 teaspoons citrus dressing over each lettuce cup. Serve with avocado slices (not shown).

CHEF

Colby Trenor

age 9 in 2016

"Feeling blue or crabby? This tasty pick-me-up highlights Maryland blue crab meat, which is with other ingredients in a Bibb lettuce cup that can be rolled up for fun eating," says Colby. "Working with my mom, we nixed some ingredients and reduced others. We also reworked proportions and used fresh-frozen foods in place of some items not in season right now, to save money. I then presented two options to three tough critics: my preschool siblings, including a very picky eater. This dish got smiles and clean plates all around, so it's a hands-down winner." Colby serves this treat with Delmarva Chips—baked whole-wheat tortillas dusted with seasonings and sea salt—and an Apple-Tomatillo Green Salsa.

Massachusetts

Tapenade and Goat Cheese Sandwich

Rachel Goldsmith-Levitt, age 11 in 2012

"I had a sandwich at a restaurant similar to this and I loved it. However, I thought it could be healthier, so I kept on changing the ingredients and amounts till I got the perfect sandwich," says Rachel. "My dad introduced me to tapenade at a young age, and both my parents are lactose-intolerant, so we have goat cheese at home a lot." Rachel likes to eat this with strawberries and carrots.

Makes 1 serving

INGREDIENTS

10 kalamata olives, pitted

1 clove garlic, minced

1 tablespoon lemon juice

1 teaspoon olive oil

Salt and pepper

2 tablespoons goat cheese

2 pieces of whole-wheat bread

1/2 cup fresh baby spinach

1/2 cucumber, peeled and thinly sliced

PREPARATION

1. In a food processor or blender, combine the olives, garlic, lemon juice, and olive oil. Process until a thick paste forms. Season to taste with salt and pepper.
2. Spread the goat cheese on the bread, and top with the olive tapenade, spinach, and cucumber slices.

Shefali's Scrumptious Spring Rolls

SHEFALI SINGH, age 12 in 2013

"My mom really loves noodles and she is always looking for different things to go with them," Shefali recalls. "So when we found the recipe for spring rolls, we decided to give it a try. They turned out better than we expected, and were very easy to make as well. The peanut sauce was also an experiment that went the right way. Now we have spring rolls with peanut sauce all the time for lunch and dinner. Sometimes we have noodles on the side, along with a glass of milk."

Makes 2 to 4 servings

INGREDIENTS

For the spring rolls:

8 brown rice paper rounds

1 medium carrot, finely chopped

1 medium cucumber, finely diced

1/2 cup tofu, thinly sliced

1 cup shredded lettuce

1 cup bean sprouts

8 to 10 fresh mint leaves

For the sauce:

1/4 cup peanut butter

1 tablespoon hot water

1 teaspoon vinegar

1 teaspoon sugar

1 teaspoon reduced-sodium soy sauce

PREPARATION

Make the spring rolls:

1. Fill a pie dish with warm water. Immerse 1 rice paper round in the water until pliable, about 15 seconds, then transfer to a cutting board. Place some carrot, cucumber, tofu, lettuce, and bean sprouts in the center of the rice paper round. Each filling should amount to about 2 tablespoons. Add a mint leaf on top. Fold the bottom of the wrapper over the filling then fold both sides into the center, and roll the wrapper up tightly to form a spring roll. Transfer the spring roll to a plate and keep covered with a damp paper towel. Repeat with the remaining rice paper rounds and filling.

Make the sauce:

1. In a small bowl, whisk together the peanut butter, hot water, vinegar, sugar, and soy sauce. Add more hot water, if needed, to thin the sauce to the desired consistency. Serve the sauce with the spring rolls.

335 calories; 17g protein; 33g carbohydrates; 18g fat (3.5g saturated fat); 552mg sodium

Yonah Kalikow, age 10 in 2014

"My family and I were cleaning out our house for Passover," says Yonah, "and I wanted to give myself a challenge. I used ingredients that we needed to get rid of for Passover for the burger. Then I thought, kale is a very big power food, and I have it a lot and enjoy it, so why don't I make a salad with it? I was thinking that most burgers come with coleslaw, so I made a kale slaw instead."

Makes 4-8 servings • 431 calories • 13g fat • 36 carbohydrates • 14g protein

CHEF YONAH

QUINOA LENTIL BURGERS WITH KALE SALAD

INGREDIENTS

♥ For the Burgers:

½ cup quinoa

1 cup dried green or brown lentils

3 bay leaves

¼ cup olive oil

1 large tomato, finely diced

1 medium yellow onion, peeled and grated or chopped

2 tablespoons low-sodium soy sauce

½ cup BBQ sauce

1 cup wasabi peas

Hamburger rolls

Garnish: Tomato and onion slices, lettuce leaves

♥ For the Kale Slaw:

1 bunch kale, chopped

2 carrots, peeled and grated

¼ cup dried cranberries

Juice of ½ lemon

♥ For the Dressing:

½ lemon

2 tablespoons mustard

2 tablespoons raw agave syrup or honey

♥ For the Sauce:

2 tablespoons Sriracha

2 tablespoons mayonnaise

2 tablespoons mustard

1 tablespoon raw agave syrup or honey

PREPARATION

To cook the quinoa/lentils for the Burgers: In a large pot, combine quinoa and lentils. Add 3 cups of water and bay leaves, bring to a boil over moderate heat, cover, and cook on low for about 30 minutes, or until quinoa and lentils are tender. Remove from the heat and discard the bay leaves.

In a wok or sauté pan, warm 2 tablespoons olive oil over moderate heat. Add the tomato and onion and sauté for 5 minutes or until soft. Add the lentil/quinoa mix, soy sauce and BBQ sauce, and stir for 2 minutes.

To make the Kale Slaw and Dressing: In a large bowl, combine the kale, carrots, and cranberries. Squeeze lemon over slaw, add mustard and agave, and stir well to combine.

Put the wasabi peas into a blender and coarsely grind. Add two-thirds of the lentil/quinoa mixture and pulse until smooth, then return to pan, mix thoroughly and let cool. Once cool, shape into 4 large patties or 8 small ones.

In a large sauté pan, warm the remaining olive oil and cook patties over moderate heat for 3 minutes on each side, or until lightly golden. Meantime, in a small bowl, combine all of the sauce ingredients. Serve on rolls with sauce and slaw.

Melting Pot Soup

Makes 6 Servings • 421 calories • 9g fat • 53g carbohydrates • 37g protein

---

INGREDIENTS

For the Turkey Meatballs:

1 pound ground turkey
¼ cup grated Parmesan cheese
½ cup cooked quinoa
1 large egg
4 teaspoons dried parsley or ¼ cup fresh parsley

For the Soup:

1 cup whole-wheat pasta, such as rotini or farfalle
1 tablespoon olive oil
1 medium onion, peeled and diced
2 cloves garlic, peeled and minced
2 carrots, peeled and diced
2 celery stalks, diced
1 medium sweet potato, peeled and cut into small cubes
1 cup green beans, cut or broken into 1-inch pieces
Salt and pepper to taste
6 cups low-sodium chicken broth
1 (14.5-ounce) can diced tomatoes
1 box frozen spinach (or 16 ounces fresh spinach)
1 (15-ounce) can red kidney beans
Parmesan cheese

PREPARATION

1. **To make the Turkey Meatballs:** In a large mixing bowl, combine all of the meatball ingredients. Mix well, form into 1-inch balls, and refrigerate until ready to use.
2. **Fill a large pasta pot with water** and bring water to a boil. Add the pasta and cook about 8 minutes, or until al dente. Drain and set aside.
3. **In a large stockpot,** heat the olive oil over medium heat. Add the onions and sauté for 2 minutes, then add the garlic and sauté for 2 minutes. Add the carrots and celery and sauté for about 7 minutes, or until the vegetables are soft. Add the sweet potatoes and green beans, season to taste with salt and pepper, and stir. Add the broth and tomatoes, cover, and bring to a boil. Add the meatballs and return to a boil. Reduce the heat to low, then simmer for 20 minutes, stirring occasionally. Add spinach and kidney beans, cover, and simmer for 10 minutes.
4. **To serve,** spoon ⅓ cup cooked pasta into each bowl, then ladle the soup over the pasta. Sprinkle with Parmesan cheese and serve.

Chef Aster Toole,

age 10 in 2015

"I lived in Ethiopia until my sister and I were adopted by my mother. In Ethiopia many families do not have enough food to eat," says Aster. "I like to cook and have learned to make healthy and delicious foods. I now live in New England and when the weather is cold our family makes soup together. We first made this soup on a cold snowy Sunday. We chopped many different vegetables, made turkey meatballs, and added beans and pasta. All of the flavors go really well together. This soup has many different ingredients mixed together so I call it Melting Pot Soup."

Fit to Run Boston Marathon Cod-Potato Cake

Makes 6 servings • 410 calories • 15g fat • 44g carbohydrates • 28g protein

INGREDIENTS

For the Cod-Potato Cakes:

2 large russet potatoes, peeled and sliced
1 tablespoon olive oil
1 ½ pounds fresh cod, or any flaky white fish
¼ cup rolled oats
2 eggs
¼ cup low-fat milk
Salt and freshly ground black pepper
2 tablespoons canola oil

For the Salad:

4 cups fresh spinach, chopped
2 apples, peeled, cored, and chopped
½ cup strawberries, stemmed and sliced
2 clementines, peeled and sectioned
¼ cup dried cranberries
3 tablespoons toasted almonds

For the Vinaigrette:

¼ cup fresh strawberries
1 tablespoon olive oil
2 teaspoons local honey
2 teaspoons mustard
Juice from ½ large lemon
Salt and freshly ground black pepper

PREPARATION

1. **To make the Cod-Potato Cakes:** In a large stockpot, boil water over high heat. Add the potatoes and cook for 10 minutes, or until potatoes are tender. Mash with a masher or fork. Let cool. Meantime, in a large nonstick skillet, warm the olive oil over medium heat. Add the cod and cook for 4 minutes per side, or until flaky and cooked through. Let cool. In a large mixing bowl, combine mashed potatoes, oats, cod fish, eggs, milk, salt, and pepper. Mix well. In a large cast iron skillet or nonstick skillet, warm the oil on medium heat and cook 4 cod cakes at a time, turning over after 4 minutes or until crisp on both sides and hot throughout.
2. **To make the Salad:** In a large salad bowl, combine all of the ingredients together. In a small bowl, whisk together the vinaigrette ingredients.
3. **To Assemble:** Divide the Salad and Cod-Potato Cakes amongst the plates, drizzle with the Vinaigrette, and garnish with toasted almonds.

CHEF

Abby Newman

age 10 in 2016

"We live at the start of the Boston Marathon. Our school and community become one soul during marathon season as we are a runners' town," says Abby. "We used local ingredients in our recipe plus what our state is known for. We created a healthy and balanced dish packed with protein and fresh ingredients that will bring the marathon spirit to the schools during lunch time. Our town is still healing after the Boston Marathon bombing, and this project gave us an opportunity to see the goodness and unity of our town. Eating healthy helps us stay alert and participate in school activities and extracurricular events as well."

Michigan

Apple Oat Balls!

Avery McNew, age 8 in 2012

"We were inspired to make these by one of our equestrian 'neigh'bors," says Avery's mom, Carrie. "My daughter asked her what we could bring her horses for a reward after competing in the horse show, and she told us to ball up some raw oats, apples, and carrots with a dash of brown sugar, and the horses would be thrilled! We rushed home, and our Apple Oat Balls were born when my 2-year-old tried one and exclaimed 'Yum!'" The family loves to pair these with yogurt. Peanut butter was added to the recipe to make the balls hold together tightly, but you can make it without it.

Makes about 30 (1-inch) balls

INGREDIENTS

6 cups old-fashioned rolled oats

1 carrot, peeled and shredded, or ½ cup shredded carrots (optional)

½ cup pecans, toasted and chopped (optional)

2 tablespoons sugar

2 tablespoons packed light or dark brown sugar

¼ teaspoon ground cinnamon

2 organic apples, peeled

Juice of 1 lemon

½ to ¾ cup creamy peanut butter

3 tablespoons raisins

2 tablespoons dried cranberries

PREPARATION

1. In a large bowl, stir together the oats, carrot, pecans, sugar, brown sugar, and cinnamon.
2. Cut the apples in half and remove the cores. Chop the apples into very small pieces and place in a small bowl. Add the lemon juice and toss to coat the apples. Add the apples to the oats and stir to combine.
3. Add ¾ cup water and stir to wet the ingredients. Add ½ cup peanut butter and stir to thoroughly combine.
4. Using damp hands, form the mixture into 1-inch balls. If the mixture isn't sticky enough to form balls, add additional peanut butter. Press 2 raisins and 1 dried cranberry into each ball to create a face. Store Apple Oat Balls in an airtight container in the refrigerator.

Picky-Eater Pita Pizza Pockets

JACOB HIRSCH, age 8 in 2013

"Like many kids, Jacob is a very picky eater! Pizza is one of his favorite foods, but he's well aware that the pizza we buy is generally not a nutritionally wise choice. Together we discussed ways to make a healthier version of pizza that he could enjoy for lunch," says Karen Ann, Jacob's mom. "We decided on using whole wheat pita pockets; a healthy, veggie-filled tomato sauce; chicken for protein; and mozzarella cheese. We would serve these pita pizza pockets with some fruit (his favorites are apples, bananas, and watermelon) to complete his plate for a healthy, well-rounded meal!"

Makes 4 servings

INGREDIENTS

2 tablespoons olive oil

2 medium onions, chopped

4 cloves garlic, minced

1 (28-ounce) can whole tomatoes

2 medium carrots, shredded

1 red bell pepper, seeded and chopped

1 medium zucchini, shredded

1 teaspoon dried oregano

1/4 cup baby spinach leaves

2 cooked boneless, skinless chicken breasts, cut into cubes

4 whole wheat pitas

1 cup shredded part-skim mozzarella cheese

PREPARATION

1. Preheat the oven to 350°F.

2. In a medium saucepan over moderate heat, warm the oil. Add the onions and garlic and sauté until they begin to soften and caramelize, about 5 minutes. Add the tomatoes, carrots, bell pepper, zucchini, and oregano, and simmer for 20 minutes. Add the spinach, stir to combine, and continue simmering to wilt the spinach, about 1 minute. Remove the vegetables from the heat and let cool. Purée the vegetables with an immersion or regular blender, leaving the vegetables chunky, or simply leave the vegetables whole.

3. Open the pita pockets and place a quarter of the chicken cubes inside each one. Add a few tablespoons of sauce to each pita and sprinkle with mozzarella cheese. Arrange the pita pizza pockets on a large baking sheet and bake until the cheese is melted, 8 to 10 minutes.

512 calories; 54g protein; 53g carbohydrates; 20g fat (7g saturated fat); 520mg sodium

BARACK-OLI & MICH-ROOM OBAMA-LET

INGREDIENTS

1 tablespoon olive oil
½ onion, sliced and carMALIAized
2 cloves garlic, peeled and chopped
½ tablespoon sage, chopped
¼ cup butternut SquASHA (squash)
peeled, seeded, and chopped
¼ cup BARACKoli (broccoli)
¼ cup MICHrooms (mushrooms)
¼ cup goat cheese, crumbled
2-3 egg whites, lightly beaten,
or egg substitute

PREPARATION

In a large sauté pan, warm the oil over moderate-low heat. Add the onion and cook until soft, about 5 minutes. Add the garlic and sage and sauté until fragrant, 1 minute. Add the butternut squash, broccoli, and mushrooms and cook until tender, about 8 minutes. Lower the heat, sprinkle the goat cheese on top, and let melt slightly.

Pour the egg whites or egg substitute into the pan and let them cook without touching the eggs until they have set, about 3 minutes. Fold over, cut in half, and slide the omelet onto a plate.

Elena Hirsch, age 11 in 2014

"We love to eat omelets, and we love to try new vegetable combinations in our omelets," says Elena. "We decided to create an omelet for the First Family to enjoy, using veggies to represent each of them—BARACKoli, MICHrooms, CarMALIAized Onions, and Butternut SquASHA. We hope they enjoy this creation as much as we do!"

Makes 2 servings • 157 calories • 12g fat • 6g carbohydrates • 7g protein

CHEF ELENA

Chef Eva Paschke,

age 12 in 2015

"I first encountered stir-fry in my seventh grade foods and nutrition class during our Asian unit. I loved it right away," says Eva. "Therefore, I decided to create my own stir-fry recipe. I did loads of research and found out some pretty cool stuff. This has been a great experience for me. Who knew eating healthy could taste so good...or be so fun!"

Fizzle Sizzle Stir Fry

Makes 6 Servings • 540 calories • 19g fat• 51g carbohydrates • 41g protein

---

INGREDIENTS

1 cup dry brown rice
3 tablespoons canola oil
1 ½ pounds boneless, skinless chicken breast, cut into bite-sized pieces
3 cups kale, stems removed and leaves torn into bite-sized pieces
1 cup edamame, shelled
2 cups frozen California medley or any frozen mixed veggies
½ cup peas
1 can sliced water chestnuts
½ red bell pepper, sliced into bite-sized pieces
1 (2-inch) piece fresh ginger, peeled and minced
4 garlic cloves, peeled and minced
6 green onions (scallions), chopped into ½-inch lengths
Pinch crushed red pepper flakes
½ cup tamari
¼ cup sweet Asian chile sauce
½ cup chopped peanuts (optional)

PREPARATION

1. **In a medium stockpot,** combine 1 ½ cups water with the rice and bring to a boil over medium-high heat. Reduce the heat to low, cover, and simmer for 20 to 30 minutes, or until tender. Set aside.
2. **Meanwhile, in a wok or large sauté pan,** heat the canola oil over medium-high heat. Add the chicken, and sauté, turning, for about 6 minutes, or until cooked through. Add the kale and cook for about 2 minutes, or until the kale is cooked down. Add the edamame, California medley, peas, water chestnuts, bell pepper, ginger, garlic, and green onions, and cook for 3 minutes. Add the cooked rice, red pepper flakes, tamari, and chile sauce and mix thoroughly. Sprinkle on chopped peanuts as a garnish (optional). Serve with a smile.

CHEF

Ethan Yodzevicis

age 10 in 2016

"Ethan created this recipe specifically for this contest," says Ethan's mom, Shannon. "Since Ethan recently discovered he liked acorn squash and is not a big fan of the purple carrots, he decided to make the squash the star of his dish. He also knew he wanted to use one of his favorite seasonings, smoked paprika. He thought about how his ingredients would go together, brainstormed ideas with his mom and grandma, and shopped for ideas and locally available ingredients that would go with the squash and pork." He serves his Squash with a Maple-Granola Yogurt Parfait on the side.

Super Stuffed Squash

Makes 4 servings • 631 calories • 30g fat • 66g carbohydrates • 26g protein

INGREDIENTS

2 acorn squash
2 ½ cups water
1 cup brown rice
1 pound ground pork
1 medium onion,
peeled and chopped
3 garlic cloves,
peeled and minced
1 medium sweet apple,
peeled, cored, and diced
1 teaspoon smoked paprika
Dash of cayenne, salt
and freshly ground pepper
4 teaspoons olive oil
Chopped fresh parsley

PREPARATION

1. **Preheat the oven to 350°F.** On a large baking sheet, place the squash in the oven for 30 minutes, remove, cut in half and remove and discard the seeds. (Cooking it whole makes it much easier and safer to cut in half.) Put squash, cut-side down, back on the baking sheet with ¼ cup water, for another 20 minutes or until soft.
2. **Meanwhile, in a large stockpot,** bring the water and the rice to a boil on medium-high heat, about 4 minutes. Cover, reduce the heat to low, and simmer for about 40 minutes, or until tender and liquid has been absorbed.
3. **In a large nonstick skillet,** warm 3 teaspoons of olive oil over medium heat and add the pork. Cook until lightly browned, about 6 minutes, then add onions, garlic, apples, smoked paprika, cayenne, salt, and pepper. Cook another 6 minutes, or until onion is soft. Add the brown rice, mix well.
4. **When squash is done,** turn cut-side up in the baking dish. Add a teaspoon of olive oil to the center of each squash half and season with salt and pepper, to taste. Divide the meat and rice mixture amongst the four squashes and fill the centers. Return to the oven for 10 minutes. Garnish with fresh chopped parsley and serve. (If your squashes are big, you may want to cut into quarters to serve.)

Minnesota

Stuffed Red Peppers

Riley Sorensen, age 12 in 2012

"This lunch is so yummy. My mom and I mixed chicken with tomato sauce, and we added spinach and garlic to make it healthy. We thought it would be good to put it in a red pepper for flavor and more nutrients, also to make it fun to eat," says Riley. She likes to eat this with her famous Banana and Oat Stacks, which combine banana slices topped with a mixture of oats, almonds, flax, coconut, and peanut butter.

Makes 1 serving

INGREDIENTS

1 medium red bell pepper, stem and seeds removed

1 scallion, chopped

1 clove garlic, minced

1 cup fresh baby spinach

1/2 cup tomato sauce

1 grilled or broiled skinless chicken breast, cut into bite-size pieces

2 tablespoons freshly grated Parmesan cheese

1/2 cup hot cooked brown rice

PREPARATION

1. Preheat the oven to 375F.
2. In a pot of boiling salted water, cook the red pepper until slightly soft, about 5 minutes. Drain and let dry.
3. In a sauté pan over moderate heat, cook the scallion, garlic, spinach, and tomato sauce for 5 minutes. Add the chicken and cook, stirring occasionally, until it is heated through, about 3 minutes.
4. Fill the red pepper half way with the chicken-spinach mixture, then add a layer of Parmesan. Fill the pepper with the remaining chicken-spinach mixture and top with the remaining Parmesan. Bake, in an ovenproof dish, until the red pepper is soft, about 15 minutes. Serve atop hot brown rice.

Garden Stir-Fry

KAITLYN KIRCHNER, age 9 in 2013

"This is my favorite recipe because it tastes great and it is fun to make! My mom, sisters, and I grow all the vegetables in our garden," says Kaitlyn. "We pick the vegetables in the morning, wash and cut them, and have them ready for our dad to stir-fry when he arrives home for lunch. We serve the recipe with cooked quinoa and a glass of soy milk."

Makes 4 servings

INGREDIENTS

1/2 cup low-sodium chicken broth

1/2 tablespoon cornstarch

1 teaspoon reduced-sodium wheat-free soy sauce

1 tablespoon sesame oil

2 cloves garlic, minced

1 teaspoon freshly grated ginger

2 cups chopped broccoli

1 1/4 cups chopped yellow squash

1 1/4 cups carrots, cut into matchsticks

1 1/4 cups sugar snap peas

1 cup sliced onion

1 cup sliced red bell pepper

PREPARATION

1. In a medium bowl, whisk together the chicken broth, cornstarch, and soy sauce. Set aside.

2. In a wok or sauté pan over moderately high heat, warm the sesame oil. Add the garlic and ginger and cook for 1 minute. Add the broccoli, squash, carrots, sugar snap peas, onion, and bell pepper and cook until tender, 7 to 10 minutes. Add the soy sauce mixture, reduce the heat to moderate, and continue cooking until the sauce is thickened.

100 calories; 3g protein; 15g carbohydrates; 4g fat (1g saturated fat); 215mg sodium

QUINOA & BLACK BEANS

INGREDIENTS

1 teaspoon olive oil
1 cup chopped celery
2 teaspoons chopped garlic
¾ cup uncooked quinoa
1½ cups low-sodium vegetable broth
1 teaspoon ground cumin
1 teaspoon chili powder
1 cup frozen mixed vegetables
1 (15-ounce) can of black beans,
rinsed and drained
½ cup low-fat cheese, optional
Salt and pepper to taste

PREPARATION

In a medium saucepan, warm the olive oil over medium heat. Stir in the celery and garlic, and sauté until lightly browned, about 3 minutes. Add the quinoa and vegetable broth. Season with cumin, chili powder, and salt and pepper to taste, and bring the mixture to a boil. Cover, reduce heat to low, and simmer 20 minutes.

Add the vegetables and black beans into the saucepan and simmer for 5 minutes. Top with cheese, if using, season with salt and pepper to taste, and serve.

Sophia Webster, age 12 in 2014

"My family loves quinoa, and I love black beans, so we mixed the two together and voilà," notes Sophia. "We serve it with a fresh fruit salad. It is gluten-free and nut-free, and you can make it lactose-free by omitting the cheese."

Makes 4 servings • 408 calories • 14g fat • 32g carbohydrates • 23g protein

CHEF SOPHIA

Secret Service Pizza Delight

Makes 4 Servings • 393 calories • 19g fat • 45g carbohydrates • 12g protein

INGREDIENTS

For the Crust:

1 ½ cups almond flour
¼ cup tapioca flour
¼ teaspoon baking soda
½ teaspoon cream of tartar
⅛ teaspoon salt
⅓ cup flax seed meal
½ cup warm water
½ tablespoon butter
or grapeseed oil

For the Sauce:

¾ cup tomato sauce
1 tablespoon basil pesto
or grapeseed oil
1 tablespoon hot sauce
1 tablespoon pizza seasoning

For the Toppings:

¼ cup diced red bell peppers
1 cup spinach
½ cup diced zucchini
¼ cup dairy-free cheese,
or regular cheese if you can have dairy
Drizzle of hot sauce
(shhh, that's the secret ingredient)

PREPARATION

1. **To make the Crust:** Preheat the oven to 375°F. In a large mixer bowl, thoroughly combine the crust ingredients with a mixer paddle or a wooden spoon. Line a large baking sheet with a piece of parchment paper, and place the dough on top. Place another piece of parchment paper on top and roll the dough out with a rolling pin until it's a thin even circular crust. Take off the top piece of parchment paper and bake the crust for 20 minutes. Meanwhile, mix the sauce ingredients in a small bowl.

2. **Once the pizza crust is light brown,** remove it from the oven and raise the oven temperature to 400°F. Remove the bottom piece of parchment paper, and place the crust back on the baking sheet. Evenly spread the sauce on the pizza crust, and put the diced red bell peppers on top of the sauce. Place the spinach on next and then sprinkle the cheese over the spinach. Finally, evenly place the zucchini on top of the pizza and drizzle some hot sauce on top if you like spicy food. Put the pizza back in the oven for 10 to 12 minutes, or until the cheese has melted. Remove from oven, and enjoy! I hope you liked the secret ingredient.

Chef Ava Nebben,

age 9 in 2015

"Recently, I have had to change my diet because of tummy troubles. So, for the last month, we have been eating 'clean' and gluten, dairy, and corn free," says Ava. "My favorite foods are veggies and pizza, so we decided to make a pizza I could eat. It's really yummy and healthy, and I hope you love it as much as my mom and I do...and I really hope you love the secret ingredient as much as we do, too!"

Alexandra's Refreshing Watermelon Salad

Makes 4 servings • 215 calories • 11g fat • 27g carbohydrates • 6g protein

INGREDIENTS

1 cup fresh spring greens
1 cup fresh cilantro
1 cup fresh watermelon, cubed
½ cup red grapes, halved
¼ cup walnuts, chopped
¼ cup Feta cheese
4 whole-grain dinner rolls
2 teaspoons butter

PREPARATION

1. **In a large salad bowl,** mix all ingredients together. Arrange the salad mixture on a platter and serve with whole-grain dinner rolls spread with grass-fed butter, if possible. Enjoy!!!

CHEF

Alexandra Steele

age 9 in 2016

"Alexandra was given a gift of a cast iron skillet," says Alexandra's mom, Brianna. "Upon the realization that anything is possible with cooking and understanding the limitless potential of creating healthy foods that are fulfilling to the senses and the soul, she has expanded her cooking talents to include the artistic, nutritious creation of salads! Alexandra's salad was created the day that her grandmother gave her a fresh watermelon. She quickly got busy creating this tantalizing salad that got rave reviews from her family!"

Mississippi

Mississippi Tacos

Linda Martinez, age 12 in 2012

"This recipe is a mixture of my heritage and where I live," says Linda. "I wanted to combine Mexican food and blend in the culture of the South together." To include all of the major food groups, Linda serves this with carrots and applesauce. "This recipe has an immense amount of nutrients in it. That is why this meal will help kids to be healthy."

Makes 4 servings

INGREDIENTS

1/2 pound ground turkey

2 teaspoons fresh flat-leaf parsley

1 teaspoon fresh oregano

1 teaspoon cumin

Salt and pepper

4 (10-inch) corn or whole-wheat tortillas

1/4 cup crumbled Feta or shredded mozzarella, plus more if desired

1/4 cup barbecue or tomato sauce (optional)

PREPARATION

1. In a large saute pan over moderate heat, cook the turkey until well browned, about 10 minutes.
2. Drain the fat from the pan and add the parsley, oregano, and cumin. Cook, stirring occasionally, for 5 minutes. Season to taste with salt and pepper.
3. While the turkey is cooking, warm each tortilla in the microwave for 10 to 20 seconds. Place the tortillas on individual plates and place 1/4 cup of the cooked turkey in the middle of each. Top each taco with 1 tablespoon Feta or mozzarella and 1 tablespoon barbecue or tomato sauce, if desired. Fold the tortillas in half and warm each one in microwave for 20 seconds to melt the cheese. Serve with carrots and applesauce on the side.

Pan-Seared Mississippi Catfish on a Bed of River Rice

REED LINDSEY, age 10 in 2013

"My favorite thing to do is go to the catfish pond behind my house. I feed the fish, the ducks, and make sure all is in order at my little cabin," says Reed. "The next stop is usually through the pine trees and to my aunt and uncle's garden. I have a bucket of fresh vegetables when I arrive home. Fishing and gardening in our own backyard inspired our recipe. A quick swim in the pond after fishing makes the food go down even better!" Reed's family uses sautéed zucchini, broccoli, and carrots to create a steamship shape on the plate alongside the catfish.

Makes 2 servings

INGREDIENTS

1/4 cup olive oil

1/4 cup diced red bell pepper

1/4 cup diced yellow bell pepper

2 cups cooked brown rice

2 (4-ounce) catfish fillets

1 1/2 teaspoons Creole seasoning

1/2 teaspoon freshly ground black pepper

PREPARATION

1. In a medium sauté pan over moderate heat, warm 2 tablespoons of the oil. Add the red and yellow bell peppers and cook, stirring occasionally, until softened, about 5 minutes. Add the cooked brown rice and stir to combine. Arrange half the rice mixture in the center of each plate.

2. In the same sauté pan over moderately high heat, warm the remaining 2 tablespoons oil. Using a paper towel, pat both sides of the catfish dry. Sprinkle both sides of the catfish with Creole seasoning and pepper. Add the catfish to the pan and cook until the bottom is golden brown, about 3 minutes. Flip the catfish over and continue cooking until the other side is golden brown and the fish is fork tender, about 3 minutes. Arrange the catfish atop the rice and garnish with additional vegetables, if desired.

589 calories; 23g protein; 48g carbohydrates; 33g fat (5g saturated fat); 504mg sodium

Devlyn Williams, age 10 in 2014

"I came up with this because my family and I decided to give up meat for Lent, but we needed protein," says Devlyn. "I studied black beans in health class along with quinoa. My mom had some sweet potatoes left over, so I thought I should experiment. And I love South American food mixed with my heritage, and I channeled that."

Makes 6 servings • 456 calories • 10g fat • 36g carbohydrates • 20g protein

CHEF DEVLYN

QUINOA SWEET POTATO BOAT

INGREDIENTS

4 medium sweet potatoes, rinsed and punctured with fork
1 cup uncooked quinoa
1¾ cups low-sodium chicken broth
1 tablespoon extra virgin olive
1 cup chopped yellow onion
1 minced garlic clove
1 (15-ounce) can black beans, drained and rinsed
1½ cups frozen corn
½ teaspoon ground cumin
½ teaspoon ground red pepper
½ teaspoon ground paprika
½ teaspoon ground coriander
⅛ teaspoon ground cayenne
2 tablespoons honey
Juice of 3 limes
1/3 cup chopped cilantro
½ cup shredded low-fat pepper Jack cheese
Low-fat sour cream, for serving

PREPARATION

Preheat oven 400°F. Place sweet potatoes on a baking sheet and bake for 40 minutes, or until tender.

While potatoes bake, in a large stockpot, bring quinoa and chicken broth to a boil over high heat. Reduce heat, cover, and simmer for 15 minutes.

In a large skillet, warm the oil on medium heat. Add onion and sauté until tender, about 5 minutes. Add garlic, quinoa, black beans, corn, cumin, red pepper, paprika, coriander, cayenne, honey, lime, and 3 tablespoons of cilantro. Cook, stirring, for about 5 minutes before removing from heat.

Remove potatoes from oven and let cool. Cut potatoes in half and scoop out some of the potato in each half to make boats. Divide the quinoa among the boats and sprinkle with cheese. Place boats in oven and broil until cheese melts, about 5 minutes. Remove from oven and serve warm. Garnish with leftover cilantro and sour cream.

Chef Bre Donald,

age 11 in 2015

"I was inspired to create something that was healthy, creative, and attractive," says Bre. "There are too many people in my state who are overweight. I want my school to start making meals that children like to eat and that are healthy so that we will not grow up to be overweight and unhealthy."

Ground Turkey Flower

Makes 6 servings • 157 calories • 5g fat • 9g carbohydrates • 20g protein

---

INGREDIENTS

1 pound ground turkey
1 small onion, peeled and finely chopped
1 garlic clove, peeled and minced
½ cup red bell pepper, seeded and finely chopped
½ cup yellow bell pepper, seeded and finely chopped
Pinch chicken seasoning
¼ cup seasoned breadcrumbs
1 tablespoon coconut oil
1 pint cherry tomatoes, halved
1 hard-boiled egg, sliced
1 cup spinach

PREPARATION

1. **In a large bowl,** thoroughly combine the ground turkey, onion, garlic, red and yellow bell peppers, and chicken seasoning. On a platter, form the turkey mixture into the shape of a flower. Sprinkle breadcrumbs over the sculpture front and back.
2. **In a large sauté pan,** heat the coconut oil over medium-high heat. Using a large spatula, transfer the turkey flower to the pan, and cook, turning once, for about 12 minutes total, or until done on both sides. Arrange the cooked flower on a platter with cherry tomato halves accenting the petals. Put a slice of hard-boiled egg in the middle. Place spinach as grass at the base of the flower.

CHEF

Aniya Madkin

age 10 in 2016

"I was inspired to make Kickin' Cauliflower Shrimp and Grits, because a lot of the people in Mississippi love shrimp and grits," says Aniya. "Sadly, some of my fellow Mississippians add pounds of butter and salt to their shrimp and grits. So this is my version of healthy shrimp and grits, dedicated to the state of Mississippi."

Kickin' Cauliflower Shrimp and Grits

Makes 4 servings • 232 calories • 14g fat • 16g carbohydrates • 14g protein

INGREDIENTS

3 tablespoons olive oil
¼ onion, peeled and chopped
2 garlic cloves, peeled and minced
1 bunch collard greens, chopped
½ cup water
Dash of balsamic vinegar
Salt and freshly ground pepper
1 head cauliflower,
  stem removed and chopped
Zest and juice of 1 fresh lemon
½ cup lite coconut milk
10 ounces fresh shrimp,
  peeled, tails removed, deveined
1 ear corn, kernels removed (or ½ cup kernels)
1 teaspoon fresh chives
1 teaspoon chili powder
Red pepper flakes (optional)

PREPARATION

1. **In a large stockpot,** warm 1 tablespoon of oil over medium heat, add the onion and garlic and cook for 1 minute. Add the collard greens, water, balsamic, salt, and pepper. Cook for 25 minutes on low heat, or until greens are tender.
2. **Meanwhile, in a food processor,** add cauliflower and pulse until it's rice-like in consistency. In a large saucepan, cook the cauliflower over medium heat until it releases some water, about 3 minutes. Add ¾ of the zest and juice of lemon, the coconut milk, and 1 tablespoon of olive oil. Reduce heat to low, add the corn, and cook for 5 minutes, or until cauliflower and corn are cooked through.
3. **In a large nonstick skillet,** warm remaining tablespoon of olive oil on medium heat. Add the shrimp, chives, salt, pepper, chili powder, and red pepper flakes, if using, and cook about 5 minutes or until shrimp are pink and cooked through.
4. **To Assemble:** Plate the cauliflower grits topped with greens and shrimp and squeeze a little lemon juice on top before serving.

Missouri

Chicken Spinach Pasta

Kyle Moore, age 12 in 2012

"I was trying to think of something for lunch, and I found these [ingredients] in the fridge and spice cabinets," says Kyle, who recommends serving this pasta with a small fruit salad on the side.

Makes 6 servings

INGREDIENTS

1 pound linguine

3 tablespoons olive oil

2 garlic cloves, minced

2 large tomatoes, diced

2 grilled or cooked skinless chicken breasts, cut into small pieces

3 cups fresh spinach

1/4 teaspoon dried oregano

1/4 teaspoon dried basil

1/4 cup freshly grated Parmesan cheese

Salt and pepper

PREPARATION

1. In a large pot of boiling salted water, cook the linguine until al dente, 8 to 10 minutes. Drain the linguine and place it in a large serving bowl.
2. While the linguine is cooking, in a large sauté pan over moderate heat, warm the oil. Add the garlic and sauté, stirring occasionally, until softened, about 3 minutes. Add the tomatoes, chicken, spinach, oregano, and basil, and sauté, stirring occasionally, until the tomato has softened and chicken is warmed through, about 2 minutes.
3. Add the chicken-tomato mixture to the bowl with the linguine and stir to combine. Sprinkle with Parmesan cheese, season to taste with salt and pepper, and serve.

Confetti Peanut-Ginger Party Pasta

HENRY OATES, age 8 in 2013

"My mom and I came up with this recipe last year when we had lots of fresh vegetables in our garden," notes Henry. "She has a summer Garden Day Camp and we were learning to cook but had no stove. So, she made the pasta in the morning and took it to camp. All of us kids harvested veggies from our garden, chopped them up, blended the sauce, and had a picnic. I would serve this with fresh watermelon slices or a simple fruit salad on the side."

Makes 4 servings

INGREDIENTS

2 cups whole wheat bow tie pasta

1 large carrot, cut into thin rounds

1 medium zucchini, thinly sliced

1 red or yellow bell pepper, seeded and diced

1/2 cup snow peas

1/2 cup chopped spinach

1/4 cup diced sweet onion

1/2 cup natural peanut butter

1/4 cup freshly squeezed orange juice

2 tablespoons soy sauce or tamari sauce

1 tablespoon honey

2 teaspoons sesame oil

1 clove garlic, minced

1 (1-inch) piece fresh ginger, peeled and minced

1/2 teaspoon crushed red pepper

1 cup cooked, diced chicken (optional)

Optional garnish: 1/4 cup chopped peanuts, 1/4 cup fresh cilantro leaves

PREPARATION

1. In a large pot of boiling water, cook the pasta until al dente, about 8 minutes.

2. While the pasta is boiling, in a large bowl, toss together the carrot, zucchini, bell pepper, snow peas, spinach, and onion.

3. Drain the pasta and add it to the bowl of vegetables.

4. In a medium bowl, whisk together the peanut butter, orange juice, soy sauce, honey, sesame oil, garlic, ginger, and crushed red pepper. If necessary, add a little water, one tablespoon at a time, to make a smooth sauce. Pour over the pasta, add the chicken (if using), and stir to combine. Garnish with peanuts and cilantro, if using.

557 calories; 29g protein; 59g carbohydrates; 25g fat (3g saturated fat); 828mg sodium

ASIAN CHICKEN MEATBALL & CAULIFLOWER RICE TORTILLA

INGREDIENTS

♥ For the Meatballs:
1 pound ground chicken
1 teaspoon sesame oil
1 garlic clove, peeled and crushed
2 tablespoons almond flour or all-purpose flour
3 tablespoons panko breadcrumbs
1 egg
3 tablespoons finely chopped scallions
½ teaspoon sea salt
1 teaspoon Sriracha
6 whole-wheat tortillas

♥ For the Sauce:
1 teaspoon sesame oil
¼ cup seasoned rice vinegar
2 teaspoons Sriracha
2 tablespoons honey

♥ For the Cauliflower Rice:
1 head broccoli, finely chopped and steamed
1 head cauliflower, trimmed
1 tablespoon olive oil
2 tablespoons sesame seeds
Pinch minced garlic
Pinch salt and pepper
½ cup low-fat shredded cheddar cheese

PREPARATION

To make the Meatballs: Turn on the oven to 375°F. In a large bowl mix together all meatball ingredients and form into balls. Bake on a baking sheet for about 20 minutes or until meatballs are browned and cooked through.

To make the Sauce: While the meatballs are baking, add all of the sauce ingredients into a saucepan and heat over low heat, stirring often, until warm.

To make the Cauliflower Rice: Place the cooked broccoli in a large skillet. Use a cheese grater and grate the head of the cauliflower into the pan with the broccoli and then add the sesame seeds. Put the pan over medium heat and cook, until cauliflower is lightly toasted. Season with garlic, salt and pepper.

Spoon the broccoli and cauliflower rice onto tortillas, top with meatballs, sauce, cheese and fold!

Joshua Murphy, age 10 in 2014

"I love Chinese food and tortillas like at Chipotle, so I decided to create my own with two of my favorite types of foods," says Joshua. "My mom was diagnosed with breast cancer a few years ago, so she is trying to teach me about using healthy ingredients and why it is important to know what I put in my body. She said that vegetables like cauliflower and broccoli have a lot of cancer-fighting power. I think that it is pretty cool that food can be powerful!"

Makes 6 servings • 489 calories • 21g fat • 40g carbohydrates • 30g protein

CHEF JOSHUA

Gateway Crescent

Makes 4 Servings • 301 calories • 17g fat • 32g carbohydrates • 8g protein

---

INGREDIENTS

¼ cup quinoa, rinsed
½ cup low-sodium chicken broth
¼ cup olive oil
1 green onion (scallion), chopped
¼ orange bell pepper, seeded and chopped
½ zucchini, chopped
2 tablespoons spinach, chopped
¼ jalapeño pepper, minced
4 whole-wheat tortillas
¼ cup feta cheese
Red pepper flakes to taste
¼ cup plain yogurt
½ teaspoon lemon juice
½ teaspoon honey

PREPARATION

1. **Preheat the oven to 350°F.** In a large saucepan, combine the quinoa and chicken broth and bring to a boil over medium-high heat. Reduce the heat to medium and cook for 15 minutes, or until the quinoa is tender.
2. **In a large sauté pan,** heat 2 tablespoons of the olive oil over medium heat. Add the green onion, bell pepper, zucchini, spinach, and jalapeño, and cook about 5 minutes, or until soft and lightly brown.
3. **On a large baking sheet,** brush the remaining 2 tablespoons olive oil on 1 side of each tortilla, then flip over the tortillas. Fill each tortilla with 2 tablespoons cooked quinoa, ¼ cup veggies, 1 tablespoon feta, and a sprinkle of red pepper flakes. Brush the edges of each tortilla with water. Fold each tortilla in half and press with a fork to seal the edges. Bake for 10 minutes.
4. **Meanwhile, in a small bowl,** combine the yogurt, lemon juice, and honey. Serve the tortillas with the sauce. Enjoy!

Chef Blake Koehr,

age 12 in 2015

"I like to be creative with combinations of ingredients and sauces and try different tastes together to see what goes best," says Blake. "My first idea for a fun lunch recipe included wontons. My mom and I tried several different combinations and determined we needed a bigger shell. We replaced the wontons with whole-wheat tortillas. I tried various ingredients on the inside and decided on this recipe. Add a side of nectarines or peaches and you have a meal following MyPlate guidelines."

Tropical Vacation with Catfish and Quinoa

Makes 4 servings • 443 calories • 12g fat • 65g carbohydrate • 21g protein

---

INGREDIENTS

For the Catfish:

8 ounces boneless, skinless catfish, cut into small chunks
¼ teaspoon turmeric
½ teaspoon paprika
½ teaspoon fennel
½ teaspoon fresh lemon juice
Salt and freshly ground black pepper

For the Veggies:

1 red bell pepper, seeded and chopped
1 yellow bell pepper, seeded and chopped
1 red onion, peeled and chopped
1 small zucchini, chopped
½ green papaya, seeded and chopped
1 tablespoon olive oil
Salt and freshly ground black pepper

For Quinoa:

1 ½ cups quinoa
1 tablespoon olive oil
1 ounce raisins
4 cloves
½ teaspoon chopped fresh ginger
1 bay leaf
1 garlic clove, peeled and minced
1 small cinnamon stick
Salt to taste
4 cardamom pods
¼ red onion, peeled and sliced
¼ cauliflower, chopped
1 tablespoon cilantro, chopped

For the Sauce:

½ cup fat-free plain yogurt
1 tomato, chopped
1 teaspoon cilantro, chopped
Salt

PREPARATION

1. **To make the Catfish:** In a bowl, combine the fish with the remaining ingredients and refrigerate for 20 minutes. Preheat oven to 375°F; bake fish for 25 minutes, or until flaky and cooked through.
2. **To make the Veggies:** Meanwhile, in a large bowl, combine the vegetables and seasonings and mix well. Bake in the oven at the same time as the fish, for 25 minutes, or until tender and golden.
3. **To make the Quinoa:** In a medium saucepan, cook the quinoa according to package instructions. In a nonstick skillet, warm the olive oil over medium heat. Add all of the ingredients and cook for 7 minutes, or until cauliflower and onions are golden brown and tender. Add cooked quinoa, catfish and stir gently to combine.
4. **To make the Sauce:** In a medium mixing bowl, combine all ingredients together.
5. **To Assemble:** Pack Catfish into a small bowl. Flip bowl over onto plate to make quinoa dome. Place Veggies on side and serve with Sauce in separate bowl.

CHEF

Abhijith Jenkins

age 11 in 2016

"I was inspired to make this dish because I love the beach!" Abhijith says. "I used mangoes, pineapple, and home-grown papaya to make it feel tropical. I wanted to keep the recipe simple and healthy, so I chose the quinoa, something my mom likes, especially since she is a cardiac patient. Lastly, I used fresh, local farm-raised catfish because you don't always have to be at the beach to feel like you're there!" Abhijith likes to serve this dish with a Pineapple-Banana-Spinach Smoothie.

Montana

Garden Chicken Pizza

Kayla Wayman, age 9 in 2012

"I do a lot of cooking with my family, and we do homemade pizza a lot. It's fun, since everyone can choose what they would like on their own pizza," says Kayla. "I always like to use things from my own garden, such as the spinach, basil, and cherry tomatoes." She enjoys this with milk and an apple with cinnamon.

Makes 1 to 2 servings

INGREDIENTS

Whole-Wheat Pizza Crust:

1/3 cup all-purpose flour

¼ cup whole-wheat flour

¾ teaspoon rapid-rise yeast (from a ¼-ounce packet)

¼ teaspoon salt

¼ teaspoon sugar

½ teaspoon olive oil

¼ cup warm water (105-115°F)

Toppings:

2 tablespoons pizza or tomato sauce

6 fresh spinach leaves

¼ cup sliced leftover grilled chicken breast

¼ cup shredded part-skim mozzarella

4 cherry tomatoes, sliced

2 fresh basil leaves, chopped

PREPARATION

1. In a medium bowl, whisk together the all-purpose flour, whole-wheat flour, yeast, salt, and sugar. Add the oil and warm water, and stir with a wooden spoon to form a sticky ball. On a lightly floured work surface, knead the dough, dusting with flour as needed, until smooth and elastic, about 4 minutes. Transfer to a medium bowl, cover with plastic wrap, and let rise in a warm place until nearly doubled, about 25 minutes.
2. Arrange a rack in the bottom of the oven and preheat to 500°F, or preheat a gas grill.
3. Stretch dough to about 9 inches, or in whatever shape you want, and place on a lightly oiled baking sheet.
4. Spoon the tomato sauce on top and, using the back of a spoon and leaving a border of at least ½ inch, spread it over the dough. Top with the spinach, chicken, cheese, and fresh tomato. Cook the pizza on the pan in the oven or on the grill, covered, until the crust is crisp and golden and the cheese is bubbly, about 7 minutes. Sprinkle with fresh basil and serve.

Healthy Vegetable Fried Quinoa

JOSHUA GARRIGUES, age 8 in 2013

"One night at dinner we had leftover quinoa and a garden full of vegetables and came up with this dinner. I liked it so much that I wanted the leftovers in my lunch the next day and even requested it for my birthday dinner," says Joshua. "I would serve orange slices with mango Greek yogurt to have all the food groups represented from ChooseMyPlate."

Makes 4 servings

INGREDIENTS

2 cups quinoa, rinsed

1 tablespoon safflower oil

1 tablespoon grated fresh ginger

1 clove garlic, minced

1 cup diced carrots

6 snow peas

1 cup baby bok choy

2 cups kale, stems removed, and torn into small pieces

1/4 cup minced fresh chives

2 large eggs or ½ cup egg substitute

1 tablespoon reduced-sodium soy sauce

PREPARATION

1. In a medium saucepan, cook the quinoa according to the package directions.

2. While the quinoa is cooking, in a large sauté pan or wok over moderately high heat, warm the oil. Add the ginger and garlic and sauté, stirring, for 1 minute. Add the carrots, snow peas, bok choy, kale, and chives and continue cooking, stirring occasionally, until tender, about 5 minutes. Add the cooked quinoa and stir to combine. Add the eggs and continue to cook, stirring, until scrambled, about 3 minutes. Add the soy sauce and continue to cook, stirring, for 1 minute. Serve hot.

333 calories; 16g protein; 51g carbohydrates; 9g fat (1.5g saturated fat); 319mg sodium

Chloe Long, age 10 in 2014

"Mealtimes in my house are always a debate. My dad eats meat, and my mom is a vegetarian," says Chloe. "One day, my mom bought tofu and my dad said, 'But, I do not like tofu.' So my mom and I created a tofu meal that he liked. Tofu is very bland when eaten alone, but it absorbs all the flavors that you add to it. We serve it over brown rice to add a whole grain."

Makes 4 servings • 383 calories • 22g fat • 30g carbohydrates • 24g protein

"WHAT! YOU DON'T LIKE TOFU?" STIR-FRY

INGREDIENTS

♥ For the Tofu Marinade:

1 tablespoon low-sodium soy sauce
1 tablespoon teriyaki sauce
1 tablespoon rice vinegar
1 tablespoon cornstarch
14 ounces extra-firm tofu, drained and cubed

♥ For the Sauce:

2 tablespoons oyster sauce
1 tablespoon low-sodium soy sauce
1 tablespoon teriyaki sauce
1 tablespoon rice vinegar
1 tablespoon cornstarch

♥ For the Stir Fry:

½ head of broccoli, florets cut and stalks sliced
1 tablespoon peanut oil or canola oil
3 scallions, peeled and minced
1 teaspoon minced garlic
1 tablespoon minced fresh ginger
1 red bell pepper, seeded and sliced into sticks
7 button mushrooms, sliced
Steamed brown rice, optional
½ bunch of cilantro, minced
1 avocado, pitted and sliced into lengths
1 tablespoon sesame seeds
1 lime, cut into wedges

PREPARATION

To make the Marinade and Sauce: In a medium bowl, whisk the marinade ingredients together with 2 tablespoons of water. Add the tofu, stir, and refrigerate for one hour, stirring once or twice. In a small bowl, whisk the sauce ingredients together and set aside.

In a large pot of boiling water, cook the broccoli for 2 minutes. Rinse under cold water and set aside.

In a large skillet or wok, warm the oil over moderate heat. Add the scallions, garlic, and ginger and cook for about 3 minutes, stirring constantly. Add the pepper and mushrooms and cook until slightly soft, about 3 minutes. Add the broccoli, tofu, and sauce and simmer about 7 minutes, so the flavors will blend.

To serve, put some rice on a plate, if using, then the tofu stir-fry. Top with cilantro, avocado, sesame seeds, and a squirt of lime juice.

Hungry Brother's Stew

Makes 8 Servings • 402 calories • 8g fat • 71g carbohydrates • 18g protein

---

INGREDIENTS

1 large butternut squash, peeled
3 tablespoons extra-virgin olive oil
1 onion, peeled and chopped
6 garlic cloves, peeled and minced
1 large red bell pepper, seeded and cut into strips
1 (28-ounce) can fire roasted diced tomatoes
1 (15-ounce) can white beans, drained and rinsed
1 (15-ounce) can pinto beans, drained and rinsed
2 ½ cups fresh or frozen corn
32 ounces low-sodium chicken broth
1 (4-ounce) can green chile peppers
1 tablespoon ground cumin
2 teaspoons chili powder
1 teaspoon dried oregano
Pinch crushed red pepper flakes
½ teaspoon salt
½ teaspoon black pepper
1 cup cooked quinoa
¼ cup fresh cilantro, for garnish

PREPARATION

1. **Preheat the oven to 375°F.** Cut the squash in half and remove the seeds. Fill a large shallow baking pan with 2 inches of water. Place squash halves, cut sides up, in the pan and cover with aluminum foil. Bake for 40 minutes, or until the squash is tender when pierced with a fork. Let the squash cool, then cut into cubes.

2. **In a large stockpot,** heat the olive oil over medium-high heat. Add the onion and cook for 3 minutes. Add remaining ingredients, except the squash, quinoa and cilantro, and bring to simmer. Reduce the heat to medium and cook for 20 minutes. Add the cooked squash and quinoa and cook for 5 minutes more. Spoon into bowls, top with cilantro, and serve.

Chef Colton Kuka,

age 9 in 2015

"My grandma told me about this contest and I thought it would be fun to create a recipe and to have the opportunity to dine with the First Lady at the Kids' "State Dinner," says Colton. "I read a story about the Native American "Three Sisters." I liked how the boy in the story came and picked the "Three Sisters" and how the corn supports the beans, and the squash helps support and protect the corn and beans, just like a family. We altered this recipe to match My Plate requirements. I first made this recipe with my grandma at my grandparents' house."

Bison in a Field

Makes 4 servings • 592 calories • 30g fat • 42g carbohydrates • 38g protein

INGREDIENTS

For the Mini Meat Loaves:

1 tablespoon olive oil
½ cup sweet onion, peeled and diced
1 pound ground bison (you can substitute with ground turkey)
1 cup seasoned breadcrumbs (you can substitute with plain breadcrumbs and 1 tablespoon Italian seasoning)
1 garlic clove, peeled and minced
½ cup grated Parmesan
½ cup nonfat milk
1 egg, beaten
¼ teaspoon salt
⅛ teaspoon freshly ground black pepper
Dash of ground sage (optional)

For the Salad:

8 ounces mixed greens and spinach
4 ounces crumbled goat cheese
¼ cup dried cherries or dried cranberries
11 ounces mandarin orange segments, packed in juice
Raspberry vinaigrette salad dressing or balsamic vinaigrette

PREPARATION

1. **To make the Mini Meat Loaves:** In a medium nonstick skillet, warm the olive oil over medium heat, add the onion and cook for 2 minutes, or until soft. Set aside.
2. **Preheat the oven to 375°F.** In a large bowl, mix all the remaining Mini Meat Loaf ingredients, including the sautéed onions. Combine well using your hands. Line a 9 x 11-inch glass baking dish with parchment paper, or grease with oil or nonstick cooking spray. Place cookie cutter on paper or pan and fill with meat loaf mixture. Remove cookie cutter and repeat. Bake meat loaves for 30 minutes, or until cooked through.
3. **To make the Salad:** In a large bowl, combine all of the ingredients and toss well.
4. **To Assemble:** On each serving plate, arrange salad and place the Mini Meat Loaf in "the field" (on the salad).

CHEF

Brooke DuCharme

age 8 in 2016

"I love to go hunting with my dad. One of my favorite meals to help make is mini meat loaves with ground venison," says Brooke. "For this recipe, we decided to use ground bison, which is raised here in Montana, and is healthy. I had an image of a mini bison in a field of green. If you don't have a bison cookie cutter like we do, you can use any shape—we also like to use heart shapes. I also used cherries, goat cheese, sage, and whole wheat, which are all ingredients from Montana." Brooke serves this with salad and toasty dinner rolls.

Nebraska

Apple Alien

Aaron Beckman, age 8 in 2012

Dad Kenneth writes: "Operation Apple Alien Status Report. Mission: Make and eat an out-of-this-world lunch that is fun and nutritious:

1. *Assemble Apple Alien and place it on launch pad (plate).*
2. *Remove Apple Alien's antennas and prepare for take-off.*
3. *Launch a flying object (flying disk wrap, fruit meteor, or veggie asteroid) from antenna and fly it to the mother ship (a hungry tummy).*

Final Report: Mission accomplished! Kids had fun flying (eating) the Apple Alien, are reenergized with healthy food and ready for more adventures."

Makes 1 serving

INGREDIENTS

1 (10-inch) whole-wheat wrap

¼ cup plus 1 tablespoon ranch dressing or your favorite homemade dressing

1 1/2 tablespoons cottage cheese

2 slices smoked turkey breast

1 1/2 slices Cheddar or your favorite cheese

1/4 cup fresh baby spinach

4 baby carrots, cut into slices

6 snap peas, cut in ¼-inch-thick slices

6 grape tomatoes

4 grapes, halved

2 large strawberries, halved

1 large apple

1 teaspoon creamy peanut butter

1 cashew, sliced horizontally in half

¼ cup low-fat vanilla yogurt

SPECIAL EQUIPMENT

3 long wooden skewers, 1 short plastic cup (2 1/2 inches diameter, 1 inch high)

PREPARATION

1. Place the wrap on a plate and spread 1 tablespoon of the ranch dressing in the center, then add the cottage cheese, turkey, Cheddar, and spinach. Tightly roll the wrap into a cylinder, and cut into ¾-inch-thick slices.
2. Thread 8 to 10 pieces of fruit and vegetables (reserving 2 carrot slices), along with the wrap slices, in the desired order on each of 3 wooden skewers, keeping the skewer base empty.
3. Place the base of the apple in the opening of a short plastic cup and push the filled skewers into the top part of the apple to create the alien's antennas.
4. Spread peanut butter on 1 side of each of the 2 reserved carrot slices and the flat side of both cashew halves. Using the peanut butter as "glue," attach the carrot slices as eyes and the cashews as a smile for the apple alien. Serve with the remaining ¼ cup of ranch dressing and the yogurt, for dipping the fruits and veggies in.

Terrific Tuna Casserole

BENCE BROWN, age 9 in 2013

"This is an all-time go-to dish for our family. My mom learned to make it from my grandma as a kid and would make it for her family," says Bence. "As a quick, family favorite on a weeknight, it's always requested. It includes items we have in our pantry and costs very little to make. We serve it with baby carrots, apple slices, and a glass of milk for wholesome comfort food."

Makes 6 to 8 servings

INGREDIENTS

8 ounces whole wheat pasta (rotini or shells work best)

1 (10-ounce) can fat-free cream of chicken soup

2 (6-ounce) cans tuna packed in water

1 cup shredded cheddar cheese

1 cup frozen peas

1/2 cup fat-free milk

3 tablespoons margarine

1 tablespoon onion powder

1 teaspoon garlic powder

Salt and freshly ground black pepper to taste

1 slice whole wheat bread, torn into pieces

PREPARATION

1. In a large pot of boiling water, cook the pasta until al dente, about 7 minutes.

2. While the pasta is boiling, in a large casserole dish, combine the cream of chicken soup, tuna, cheese, peas, milk, 2 tablespoons margarine, onion and garlic powders, salt, and pepper.

3. Drain the pasta, add it to the casserole dish, and stir to combine.

4. In a small saucepan over moderate heat, melt the remaining 1 tablespoon margarine. Add the bread pieces and cook, stirring, until lightly toasted, about 2 minutes. Add the toasted bread to the top of the casserole and microwave on high power until heated through, about 6 minutes.

352 calories; 23g protein; 37g carbohydrates; 13g fat (5g saturated fat); 409mg sodium

TERRIFIC TURKEY TACOS

INGREDIENTS

1 tablespoon vegetable oil
1 pound ground turkey
2 teaspoons chili powder
1½ teaspoons paprika
½ teaspoon sea salt
½ teaspoon ground cumin
½ teaspoon oregano
¼ teaspoon black pepper
Pinch cayenne pepper
6 whole-wheat soft tortillas
Garnish: Shredded low-fat Colby Jack cheese, romaine lettuce, diced tomatoes, and avocados

PREPARATION

In a large sauté pan, warm the oil over moderate heat. Add the turkey and cook for 5 minutes, breaking up with a wooden spoon until crumbly. In a small bowl, mix all of the seasonings and ½ cup water. Add to the turkey and simmer for 10 minutes, or until the turkey is cooked through.

Warm tortillas in microwave. Serve with turkey and all of the garnishes. Roll up and enjoy!

Zienna Peterson, age 10 in 2014

"We love tacos at our house! We have them once a week, on taco Tuesdays!" says Zienna. "We wanted to find a healthier way to make them. Something we all love, and simple for our fun family of seven! We love to serve them with different fruits on the side."

Makes 6 servings • 286 calories • 12g fat • 26g carbohydrates • 19g protein

CHEF ZIENNA

Chef Grace Brown,

age 8 in 2015

"My family loves spending time together outdoors camping and fishing. We have lots of fresh produce in our garden and our dad is a really good fisherman," says Grace. "The best thing about these fabulous fish tacos is they use all the food groups. We use whole-wheat tortillas as a grain, the fruit and vegetables add lots of nutrients, and the Greek yogurt is a great source of calcium. We've tried the recipe many times, adjusting the peppers to suit everyone."

Fabulous Fish Tacos

Makes 8 servings • 233 calories • 4g fat • 35g carbohydrates • 17g protein

---

INGREDIENTS

For the Salsa:

1 green onion (scallion), peeled and sliced
¼ cup chopped yellow bell pepper
¼ cup chopped red bell pepper
½ chopped seedless jalapeño
1 garlic clove, peeled and minced
½ chopped avocado
½ cup chopped mango
¼ cup chopped fresh cilantro
⅛ cup orange juice

For the Garlic-Lime Sauce:

¼ cup plain Greek yogurt
½ teaspoon lime juice
1 garlic clove, peeled and minced

For the Quinoa and Fish:

⅓ cup quinoa, rinsed
¼ cup lime juice
¼ cup chopped red bell pepper
¼ cup chopped yellow bell pepper
1 garlic clove, peeled and minced
1 pound fish fillets
1 teaspoon ground cumin
1 finely chopped green onion (scallion)
½ teaspoon chili powder
8 whole-wheat tortillas

PREPARATION

1. **To make the Salsa and Sauce:** In a medium bowl, combine all the salsa ingredients. Cover and chill. In a small bowl, combine all of the sauce ingredients. Cover and chill.
2. **In a medium saucepan,** combine ⅔ cup water with the quinoa and bring to a boil over medium-high heat. Reduce the heat to low, cover, and simmer for about 15 minutes, or until the quinoa is tender. Set aside.
3. **In a large nonstick sauté pan,** heat 2 tablespoons of the lime juice over medium heat. Add the red and yellow bell peppers and garlic and cook for about 4 minutes. Sprinkle the fish fillets on both sides with cumin and add to the pan with the peppers. Add the remaining 2 tablespoons lime juice and cook, turning once, for 5 minutes per side, or until the fish flakes easily. Gently tear the fish into bite-sized pieces. Add the green onion and chili powder to the quinoa, then gently add the quinoa to the fish, and stir to combine.
4. **To assemble tacos,** warm the tortillas in the microwave. On a plate, spread 1 tablespoon of the garlic-lime sauce on each warm tortilla, and top with approximately ½ cup spinach. Arrange ¼ cup of the quinoa-fish mixture down the center of each tortilla and top with salsa. Tightly wrap the tortillas and cut in half to serve.

CHEF

Lauren Hinrichs

age 10 in 2016

"In Nebraska we are fortunate to have access to delicious fresh and garden-raised vegetables," says Lauren. "It hit me that we can make foods that we already love, into healthier but yummy foods. That inspired me to whip up something that utilized vegetables for more than just the toppings. Cauliflower creates a twist on taco shells and is the foundation of a new take on tacos. I hope you enjoy this new take on tacos!"

Tasty Veggie Tacos

Makes 4 servings • 435 calories • 15g fat • 56g carbohydrates • 24g protein

INGREDIENTS

For the Cauliflower Tortillas:

1 head cauliflower, chopped
2 large eggs
¼ cup chopped fresh cilantro
Juice of ½ fresh lime
Salt and freshly ground black pepper

For the Corn Salad:

2 ears of corn, kernels removed (about 1 cup fresh corn kernels)
¼ cup chopped cilantro
1 teaspoon zest and juice of ½ fresh lime
1 tablespoon olive oil
¼ teaspoon sea salt
½ cup crumbled queso fresco

For the Black Beans:

1 tablespoon olive oil
1 yellow onion, peeled and chopped
Salt and freshly ground black pepper
1 tablespoon ground cumin
2 15-ounce cans black beans, rinsed and drained
¼ cup water

Garnish:

1 large avocado, sliced into thin strips
Pickled jalapeños
Salsa and/or fresh tomatoes

PREPARATION

1. **To make the Cauliflower Tortillas:** Preheat the oven to 375°F. Line a large baking sheet with parchment paper or grease with oil or nonstick cooking spray. In a food processor, add cauliflower and pulse until it becomes rice-like consistency. Place in a microwave-safe bowl and microwave for 2 minutes, then stir and microwave again for another 2 minutes. Place in a thin dish towel, let cool for several minutes and then squeeze out as much liquid as possible. In a medium bowl, whisk the eggs. Add in cauliflower, cilantro, lime, salt, and pepper and mix until well combined. Use your hands to shape 4 "tortillas" on the parchment paper. Bake for 10 minutes, carefully flip each tortilla, and return to the oven for an additional 7 minutes, or until completely set and light golden. Place tortillas on a wire rack to cool slightly.
2. **To make the Corn Salad:** In a microwave-safe bowl, cook the corn for 2 minutes. In a medium-sized mixing bowl, combine the corn with the remaining ingredients and set aside to marinate.
3. **To make the Black Beans:** In a large nonstick skillet, warm the olive oil over medium heat, add the onions and salt, to taste. Cook, stirring occasionally, about 5 minutes, or until the onions have softened. Add the cumin and cook for about 30 seconds, add the beans and water. Stir, cover, reduce heat to low, and simmer for 5 minutes. Mash half of the beans with the back of a fork or a masher. Remove from heat, season with salt and pepper to taste.
4. **To Assemble:** Place 2 tablespoons of the bean mixture into each cauliflower taco shell, top with corn salad, and enjoy with optional garnish.

Nevada

Vegan Sloppy Joes

Alexea Wagner, age 9 in 2012

"I saw sloppy joes at school, but I wanted to make sure they were cruelty-free," says Alexea, who serves this with kale salad that has shredded carrot, spicy pecans, and sliced strawberries, and a big glass of soy milk.

Makes 4 servings

INGREDIENTS

1 tablespoon olive oil

1 (8-ounce) package tempeh, sliced

1 tablespoon low-sodium soy sauce

½ onion, diced

2 garlic cloves, peeled and mashed

1 tablespoon diced and seeded jalapeño

1 (14-ounce) can diced tomatoes

¼ cup apple-cider vinegar

1 tablespoon mustard

1 tablespoon maple syrup

½ tablespoon molasses

4 whole-wheat buns

For garnish: Lettuce and slices of avocado

PREPARATION

1. In a large sauté pan over moderate heat, warm the olive oil. Add the tempeh, soy sauce, and ¼ cup water, and cook for 8 minutes, breaking up the tempeh. Add the onion, garlic, jalapeño, tomatoes, apple-cider vinegar, mustard, maple syrup, and molasses, and cook, stirring often, for 10 minutes.
2. While the sloppy joe mixture is cooking, toast the buns in the oven or toaster oven. Divide the sloppy joe mixture among the 4 buns, top with lettuce and avocado, and serve.

Chex Chicken and Bellaberry Smoothie

ISABELLA GROSS, age 11 in 2013

"In April 2012 I got diagnosed with type 1 diabetes. Followed along with that, I have been diagnosed with celiac, so I am working on a gluten-free diet," says Isabella. "When my mom told me about this challenge, I thought, why not make something sweet, and gluten-free? So I came up with the nutty Chex Chicken. It is served with a side of fresh veggies and a fresh-fruit smoothie that I call the Bellaberry Smoothie." Her signature drink includes 1 cup of berries, low-fat milk, and Boston cream pie yogurt.

Makes 2 servings

INGREDIENTS

1 cup gluten-free corn cereal, such as Chex

1/4 cup gluten-free baked veggie chips with chili lemon

1/4 cup pecans

1 teaspoon ground lemon pepper

3 large egg whites

8 ounces boneless, skinless chicken breast, halved

1 medium yellow squash, cut into half moons

1 medium zucchini, cut into half moons

PREPARATION

1. Preheat the oven to 350°F.

2. In a large bowl, stir together the cereal, veggie chips, pecans, and lemon pepper. Smash and combine the cereal mixture.

3. Place the egg whites in a small bowl.

4. Working with 1 piece at a time, dip the chicken into the cereal mixture then dip it into the egg whites then back into the cereal mixture, making sure all of the chicken is covered. Transfer the "breaded" chicken to a baking dish and repeat with the remaining chicken, cereal mixture, and egg whites.

5. Bake the chicken until golden brown, about 30 minutes

6. While the chicken is baking, bring a small saucepan of water to a boil. Add the squash and zucchini and simmer, lowering the heat if necessary, until tender, about 7 minutes. Serve the squash and zucchini with the chicken.

530 calories; 38g protein; 54g carbohydrates; 19g fat (2g saturated fat); 598mg sodium (does not include smoothie)

Grace Keating, age 11 in 2014

"My grandma started making this recipe for my dad when he was little. My mom and I took the original recipe and made it healthier," says Grace. "I love to adapt recipes and make them healthy. I would serve the Chicken and Grape Salad Lettuce Wraps with a fresh quinoa salad. When I grow up, I want to be a nutritionist, to make a change in people's lives, and to go further with helping children and families eat healthy."

Makes 4-6 servings • 429 calories • 25g fat • 37g carbohydrates • 19g protein

CHEF GRACE

CHICKEN & GRAPE SALAD LETTUCE WRAPS

INGREDIENTS

1 pound boneless, skinless chicken breasts
1 cup red or green grapes, halved
2 tablespoons minced onion
2 tablespoons diced red bell pepper
½ cup plain nonfat Greek yogurt
½ cup nonfat sour cream
1¼ teaspoons fresh lemon juice
½ teaspoon curry powder
Salt and pepper, to taste
Whole lettuce leaves
Dried cranberries, for garnish

PREPARATION

Preheat the grill. Cook the chicken for about 10 minutes on each side, until cooked through. Let cool then dice into 1-inch cubes. In a large bowl, mix the chicken with grapes, onion, and red pepper.

In a separate bowl, whisk together the yogurt, sour cream, lemon juice, curry powder, salt, and pepper. Pour over the chicken-grape salad and mix thoroughly.

On top of lettuce leaves, scoop ¼-cup servings of chicken and grape salad. Garnish with dried cranberries. Enjoy!

Eggplant "Obama"san

Makes 4 Servings • 362 calories • 7g fat • 22g carbohydrates • 30g protein

---

INGREDIENTS

2 eggplants, peeled and cut lengthwise
1 tablespoon olive oil
1 medium onion, peeled and diced
3 garlic cloves, peeled and minced
1 pound spicy or sweet turkey sausage, casings removed
2 cups crushed tomatoes
½ cup panko breadcrumbs
Salt and pepper to taste
½ cup shredded low-fat mozzarella cheese
¼ cup grated Parmesan cheese
4 fresh basil leaves, thinly sliced

PREPARATION

1. **Preheat the oven to 400°F.** Using a melon baller, remove the meat of the eggplant. Reserve the hollowed out eggplants. In a large pot of boiling water, cook the eggplant balls for 5 minutes. Remove from the water and set aside on paper towels to drain.
2. **In a large sauté pan,** heat the olive oil over medium heat. Add the onion, garlic, and eggplant balls and sauté for about 3 minutes. Add the sausage and cook, breaking the meat up with a wooden spoon, for about 7 minutes, or until lightly brown. Add 1 ½ cups of the crushed tomatoes, and the breadcrumbs. Season to taste with salt and pepper, and cook for 5 more minutes.
3. **In a large baking dish,** spread the remaining ½ cup of crushed tomatoes, and then top with the hollowed out eggplant. Scoop the cooked sausage mixture into the eggplants, and top with the mozzarella and Parmesan cheese. Sprinkle with the basil leaves. Cover the dish with foil and bake about 25 minutes, or until the cheese is melted. Remove from the oven and enjoy!

Chef Jack Newkirk,

age 9 in 2015

"My dad is my favorite person in the world. This year he is not only my dad but also my 4th grade teacher," says Jack. "A few years ago my dad was diagnosed with Type II diabetes. Since then we have tried to change our eating habits and embrace a healthier lifestyle. Before his diagnosis, one of his favorite dishes was always Eggplant Parmesan. My mom and I decided to try to make a healthier version of this dish that we all could enjoy without feeling an ounce of guilt."

Veggie-Packed Indian Lentils

Makes 6 servings • 325 calories • 5g fat • 58g carbohydrates • 16g protein

INGREDIENTS

For the Veggie-Packed Indian Lentils:

1 tablespoon canola oil
¼ cup yellow onion, peeled and chopped
3 garlic cloves, peeled and minced
4 cups vegetable broth, plus 2 cups water
2 cups peeled and diced carrots
2 cups chopped cauliflower
2 cup lentils, rinsed and drained
1 15-ounce can kidney beans, rinsed and drained
1 6-ounce can tomato paste
1 bay leaf
1 tablespoon fresh ginger, grated
2 tablespoons curry powder
1 teaspoon cumin
1 teaspoon salt
½ teaspoon freshly ground black pepper
¼ teaspoon cinnamon
⅛ teaspoon ground cloves
½ teaspoon coriander
1 tablespoon chili powder
½ cup lite coconut milk
4 cups fresh spinach, chopped
Cooked brown rice (optional)

For the Mango Lassi ***(not pictured)*****:**

1 cup frozen mango chunks
1 cup nonfat plain yogurt
¼ cup milk (or soy, almond or coconut milk)
¼ teaspoon cardamom powder
¼ cup maple syrup

PREPARATION

1. **In a large stockpot,** warm oil over medium heat, add onion and cook about 4 minutes, or until slightly tender. Add garlic and cook 1 minute, then add all of the other ingredients except the spinach and rice, and bring to a boil. Reduce the heat to low and simmer for 40 minutes, or until lentils are tender. Add spinach and simmer for 5 minutes more, or until heated through. Serve with brown rice.
2. **To make Mango Lassi:** In a blender, thoroughly blend all the ingredients. Serve chilled.

CHEF

Skylar McGough

age 8 in 2016

"My mom inspires me to eat healthy. She encourages me to eat fresh fruits and vegetables," says Skylar. "Our family recently became vegan. For this recipe we recreated my favorite store-bought boxed Indian lentils, and made it full of veggies. Vegan food can be healthy and full of flavor. I love this recipe served with brown rice and a Mango Lassi. I hope you enjoy."

New Hampshire

Black Bean and Avocado Burrito with Pineapple Salsa

Ella Barrett, age 8 in 2012

"I came up with this lunch because I like to eat burritos, and sometimes my Mom packs them for my lunch at school. I serve homemade pineapple salsa with the burrito," says Ella. She likes to have this with a berry smoothie made with Greek yogurt, as well as a side salad.

Makes 4 servings

INGREDIENTS

For the pineapple salsa:

1 pineapple, peeled, cored, and cut into small pieces

1/2 red onion, thinly sliced

1 1/2 red, green, yellow, or orange bell peppers, stemmed and sliced

1 jalapeño, seeded and sliced

Fresh cilantro leaves from 6 sprigs

¼ cup freshly squeezed lime juice

½ teaspoon packed brown sugar

1/2 teaspoon salt

For the burrito:

1 tablespoon olive oil

1 (15-ounce) can black beans, drained and rinsed

Salt

4 (10-inch) whole-wheat tortillas

½ cup grated or shredded cheese of your choice

1 avocado, pitted, peeled, and sliced

Fresh cilantro, chopped (optional)

PREPARATION

Make the pineapple salsa:

1. In a food processor or blender, combine the pineapple, red onion, bell peppers, jalapeño, and cilantro. Blend just until chunky, then transfer to a bowl.
2. In a small bowl, whisk together the lime juice, brown sugar, and salt. Drizzle the lime-juice mixture over the salsa, and stir to combine.

Make the burrito:

3. In a small saucepan over moderate heat, warm the olive oil. Add the beans and cook, mashing gently with a wooden spoon, until heated through, about 3 minutes. Season to taste with salt.
4. Warm the tortillas in the microwave, then place them on individual plates. Evenly divide the beans among the tortillas, then top each with cheese; microwave to melt the cheese, about 20 seconds each. Divide the avocado slices among the burritos, then tightly roll each tortilla around its filling from bottom to top, overlapping one end, burrito style. Serve with the Pineapple Salsa and additional cilantro, if desired.

Liv's Curry Chicken Salad Sandwich

OLIVIA BEAUCHESNE, age 12 in 2013

"I wanted to make a dish that is healthy, delicious, and inspires children all around the country to have healthy eating habits," says Olivia. "I am including a strawberry and banana smoothie with low-fat yogurt to add dairy to my recipe. My recipe has slivered almonds in it for texture, but the almonds can be taken out for a nut-free family."

Makes 6 servings

INGREDIENTS

For the curry chicken salad sandwich:

3/4 cup light mayonnaise

2 tablespoons mild curry powder

Salt and freshly ground black pepper to taste

4 cups cooked shredded boneless, skinless chicken

1/2 cup diced celery

2 tablespoons finely chopped onion

1/2 cup toasted sliced almonds

1 1/2 cups grapes, cut in half

6 mini whole wheat pitas

Lettuce leaves (optional)

For the strawberry-banana smoothie:

1 frozen banana

1 cup whole strawberries, stems removed

3/4 cup low-fat vanilla yogurt

1/2 cup freshly squeezed orange juice

PREPARATION

Make the curry chicken salad sandwich:

1. In a medium bowl, whisk together the mayonnaise, curry powder, salt, and pepper. Add the chicken, celery, onion, almonds, and grapes and stir, being careful not to crush the grapes. Fill each pita with about 1/2 cup chicken salad and garnish with lettuce leaves, if using.

Make the strawberry-banana smoothie:

1. In a blender, combine the banana, strawberries, yogurt, and orange juice and blend until smooth. (You will need to make two batches of the smoothie for 6 servings.)

391 calories; 34g protein; 30g carbohydrates; 15g fat (2g saturated fat); 269mg sodium (includes both sandwich and smoothie)

PAN-SEARED SALMON WITH VEGETABLES & TRICOLOR SALAD

INGREDIENTS

♥ For the Tricolor Salad:
2 ounces buffalo mozzarella cheese, thinly sliced
1 plum tomato, thinly sliced
¼ teaspoon oregano
¼ teaspoon pepper
½ teaspoon olive oil
¼ teaspoon balsamic vinegar
1 small avocado, diced
1 whole-wheat wrap, warmed and cut into rectangles

♥ For the Salmon:
1 6-ounce salmon fillet
⅛ teaspoon Greek seasoning
¼ teaspoon pepper
1 teaspoon butter

♥ For the Cream Sauce:
¼ teaspoon butter
2 teaspoons half-and-half
4 ounces broccoli florets
½ portobello mushroom
5 sprigs fresh parsley

PREPARATION

To make the Tricolor Salad: Arrange alternating layers of cheese and tomato, season with oregano, black pepper, olive oil, and balsamic vinegar, and top with avocado and warm tortilla rectangles.

To make the Salmon: Rub salmon with Greek seasoning and black pepper. In a large pan, melt the butter over moderate heat. Sear the salmon and cook until firm, about 3 minutes per side. Transfer to a plate.

To make the Cream Sauce: In the same saucepan that you used for the salmon, melt the butter over moderate heat. Add half-and-half and ¼ cup water. Cook for 1 minute, then add the broccoli and portobello mushroom and cook for 3 minutes, until vegetables are tender. Pour the sauce and veggies over the salmon, garnish with fresh parsley, and serve.

Jessica Bakas, age 12 in 2014

"I always try to eat healthy every day, and I think everyone should too," says Jessica. "I know that some kids think that healthy foods do not taste good, and I hope to turn that around with my dish. I included all of my favorite foods in the dish that are low on calories and have good flavors. Kids, including myself, eat with their eyes, so when I created this recipe I wanted to make the dish look fresh, delicious, and have lots of colors. Know that you can still have something delicious that's good for you!"

Makes 2 servings • 453 calories • 27g fat • 25g carbohydrates• 23g protein

CHEF JESSICA

Chef Ana Bernazzani,

age 8 in 2015

"When my mom immigrated to the U.S. from Venezuela with her parents, they had little money and making healthy meals for not too much money was hard. So my mom told me that they always ate beans—black beans and lentils were her favorites. And that is why I want to show you how to make our own special lentil soup—it is one of my favorite ones to make with my mom and it has a special meaning to me as well. It reminds me (and my mom) of all we, as a family, have accomplished in the U.S. and it tastes yummy too!"

Corn and Turkey Meatball Lentil Soup with Whole-Wheat Pita Chips

Makes 6 Servings • 621 calories • 22g fat • 71g carbohydrates • 42g protein

---

INGREDIENTS

For the Meatballs:

Nonstick cooking spray
2 slices whole-wheat bread
¾ pound lean ground turkey
2 large eggs
1 tablespoon fresh basil leaves

For the Lentil Soup Base:

2 tablespoons olive oil
8 garlic cloves, peeled and crushed
2 ½ cups sweet kernel corn
1 ½ cups carrots, peeled and diced into ¼-inch pieces
1 cup celery, chopped
2 ½ cups tomatoes, diced
1 ½ cups lentils, rinsed
11 cups fat-free reduced-sodium chicken broth
1 ½ teaspoons chili powder
1 tablespoon ground cumin
Salt and pepper to taste
Low-fat shredded mozzarella cheese for topping
Whole-wheat pita chips

PREPARATION

1. **To make the Meatballs:** Preheat the oven to 375°F. Spray a large baking sheet with nonstick cooking spray. In a food processor, make breadcrumbs from the bread. In a large bowl, combine the breadcrumbs with the turkey, eggs, and basil and mix thoroughly. Roll into 1-inch meatballs and place on a baking sheet. Bake, turning the meatballs every 3-5 minutes to prevent them overly browning, for about 25 minutes.
2. **To make the Lentil Soup Base:** In a large sauté pan, heat the olive oil over medium heat. Add the garlic, corn, carrots, celery, and tomatoes and cook for about 20 minutes, or until the vegetables are soft and the tomatoes are reduced.
3. **Add the lentils and stir,** then add the chicken broth, chili powder and cumin. Increase the heat to high and bring to a boil. Stir one more time, then reduce the heat to a simmer, cover, and cook for about 45 minutes, or until the lentils are tender. Season to taste with salt and pepper.
4. **Stir in the turkey meatballs,** being careful not to break them when you stir. For the best-tasting soup and a little more thickness, let it simmer all together for an additional hour. Serve hot with mozzarella on top. Enjoy with a side of pita chips for dipping!

CHEF

Jude VanderHooven

age 8 in 2016

"Here in New Hampshire, there is a big push to support local farmers and to urge our community to buy local," says Jude. "My family likes to grow food in our backyard garden. In August we usually get lots and lots of zucchini. My grandpa says 'you need to have a lot of friends and neighbors if you grow zucchini so you can give it away to them.' I like to pick the zucchini (and other yummy vegetables) and fill a few boxes and bring it to our local food pantry and soup kitchen. I enjoyed creating and eating this recipe with my mom and it is part of our monthly menu rotation."

Teeny Zucchini Triangular Panini

Makes 6 servings • 342 calories • 16g fat • 40g carbohydrates • 12g protein

INGREDIENTS

2 cups grated zucchini
2 eggs, lightly beaten
½ cup crumbled low-fat feta cheese
¼ cup diced sweet peppers (red, orange, yellow or green)
¼ cup mashed chickpeas (from ½ cup whole chickpeas)
¼ cup diced green onions
1 garlic clove, peeled and minced
Salt and freshly ground black pepper
½ cup breadcrumbs
¼ cup chopped fresh parsley or 1 teaspoon dried parsley
¼ cup olive oil
6 whole-wheat pitas
Heirloom or beefsteak tomato slices
Baby Lettuce
1 cup hot marinara sauce

PREPARATION

1. **Place the zucchini** into a clean dish towel, and tightly squeeze the water out into the sink. In a large mixing bowl, add all of the ingredients up to the olive oil. and mix together well. Using your hands, create 6 patties about the size of the pita bread.
2. **In a large nonstick skillet,** warm the olive oil over medium heat and cook the patties, about 4 minutes per side, or until golden brown on each side and heated through. Place the patties on the pita bread and top with tomato slices and lettuce. Then grill the sandwich on a panini press, indoor electric grill, or even a waffle maker until the bread is crispy. Cut into small triangles on a cutting board. Enjoy with marinara sauce for dipping, a glass of milk and, if in season, a McIntosh apple.

New Jersey

The Golden Plate

Tarteel Idais, age 9 in 2012

"I first made this recipe when I was about 4 years old," says Tarteel. "What inspired me to create it is that me and my whole family always loved salmon as our fish of the month. One story I can tell you about this wonderful recipe is that salmon was the first type of fish I ever had." Tarteel serves this with a berry smoothie.

Makes 4 Servings

INGREDIENTS

1 pound salmon, divided into 4 (4-ounce) fillets

1 1/2 cups broccoli

1 garlic clove, peeled

1 medium onion, thinly sliced

1 scallion, white and light green parts only, chopped

1 tablespoon olive oil

1/3 cup barbecue sauce

1 cup brown rice

PREPARATION

1. Preheat the oven to 400°F. Place the salmon, broccoli, garlic, onion, and scallions in a greased baking dish. Brush with oil, drizzle with barbecue sauce, and bake until the salmon is cooked through and crispy and the vegetables are soft, about 20 minutes. (You can also grill or broil the salmon.)
2. While the salmon is baking, cook the rice in 2 cups of water. Serve the salmon and veggies atop the rice.

Hawaiian Turkey Sliders with Mango-Pineapple Salsa

GOLDIE SIEGEL, age 8 in 2013

"My family has to be creative when it comes to preparing tasty and healthy food. I have celiac disease, and one of my sisters is allergic to eggs, dairy, nuts, and more!" says Goldie. "I wanted to make a dish that used ingredients from Hawaii because the President was born there and the Obamas like to visit there. My dad doesn't like red meat, so we use ground turkey instead. Served with a smoothie, this 'burger and shake' lunch fits perfectly within the MyPlate guidelines."

Makes 12 servings

INGREDIENTS

For the mango-pineapple salsa:

1 ripe mango, peeled and diced

1 cup diced fresh (or canned in own juice) pineapple

1 to 2 small jalapeños, finely diced (optional)

3 tablespoons diced Bermuda or Vidalia onion

Juice of 1 medium lime

Pinch of sea salt

Freshly ground black pepper

For the Hawaiian turkey sliders:

2 pounds ground turkey

1 clove garlic, peeled and crushed

3 tablespoons ketchup

1 tablespoon extra-virgin olive oil

1 tablespoon gluten-free soy sauce

1 tablespoon dried cilantro

1 teaspoon onion powder

1/2 teaspoon dried oregano

Salt

1/4 teaspoon freshly ground black pepper

12 romaine or Bibb lettuce leaves

12 gluten-free rolls or whole-grain dinner rolls

PREPARATION

Make the mango-pineapple salsa:

1. In medium, non-metallic bowl, stir together the mango, pineapple, jalapeños, onion, lime juice, salt, and pepper. Cover and chill in the refrigerator until ready to use. (The salsa is best when made several hours to one day in advance.)

Make the Hawaiian turkey sliders:

1. In a large bowl, combine the turkey, garlic, ketchup, olive oil, soy sauce, cilantro, onion powder, oregano, salt, and pepper. Gently mix the ingredients until they are thoroughly combined. Divide the mixture into 12 equal parts and shape each one into a ball that is slightly smaller than a tennis ball. Using the palm of your hand, gently flatten each into a patty.

2. Heat a grill or barbecue to medium-high heat. Grill the turkey sliders until cooked through, about 5 minutes per side. Place one lettuce leaf on the bottom of each roll. Serve the sliders on the rolls, topped with a dollop of mango-pineapple salsa.

194 calories; 22g protein; 21g carbohydrates; 4g fat (1g saturated fat); 401mg sodium

SWEET-POTATO-CRUSTED TURKEY & VEGGIE PIZZA

INGREDIENTS

♥ For the Crust:

1½ cups cooked or microwaved sweet potato (1 large sweet potato)

1½ cups almond flour or all-purpose flour

¾ cup egg substitute

½ cup low-fat shredded mozzarella cheese

1 teaspoon gluten-free baking powder

2 teaspoons garlic powder

1 teaspoon oregano

¼ teaspoon chipotle chili powder

½ teaspoon sweet paprika

¼ teaspoon cinnamon

♥ For the Toppings:

1 tablespoon canola oil

2 ounces ground turkey

½ red onion, peeled and sliced

½ small eggplant, peeled and chopped

½ zucchini, chopped

3 portobello mushrooms, sliced

½ yellow bell pepper, sliced

½ orange bell pepper, sliced

¾ cup tomato sauce

½ cup low-fat mozzarella cheese

PREPARATION

Preheat oven to 375°F. In a large bowl, combine all of the crust ingredients and mix thoroughly. Spray a 9-inch round springform pan or pizza pan with cooking spray. Spread the dough into a circle, to cover the pan. Bake the dough for 25 minutes or until the center is firm and the edges are browned. Remove from the oven and let cool.

Meanwhile, in a large sauté pan, warm the oil over moderate heat. Add the turkey and onion, and cook about 5 minutes, or until turkey is cooked through and onions are tender. Add the eggplant, zucchini, mushrooms, and bell peppers and cook for about 5 minutes, until they are soft. Remove from heat.

To assemble: Spread the sauce on the pre-baked crust, top with the turkey-vegetable mix and cheese. Bake for about 10 minutes, or until cheese is melted.

Jacob Cook, age 9 in 2014

"I love pizza! I can eat it every meal and every day!" admits Jacob. "My Mom and I came up with this low-fat option, which lets us enjoy what we like, while it's healthier for us. It is gluten-free and low-carb, which allows my Mom to eat it too. I would serve this pizza with a berry smoothie, made with fresh berries and yogurt!"

Makes 6 servings • 429 calories • 25g fat • 33 carbohydrates • 19g protein

CHEF JACOB

Crispy-Skin Salmon Over Pasta with Garbanzo Bean Sauce

Makes 1 Serving • 519 calories • 21g fat • 51g carbohydrates • 34g protein

---

INGREDIENTS

2 tablespoons acini di pepe pasta
1 tablespoon olive oil
1 (2 ½-ounce) piece salmon, with skin on
½ cup canned garbanzo beans (chickpeas), rinsed and drained
1 garlic clove, peeled and minced
3 ounces plain nonfat yogurt
Pinch oregano
Pinch salt
Juice of ½ lime
9 fresh cilantro leaves

PREPARATION

1. **Fill a medium stockpot with water** and bring to a boil. Add the acini di pepe pasta and cook for 7 minutes, or until al dente. Drain and set aside.
2. **In a large sauté pan,** heat ½ tablespoon of the olive oil over medium-high heat. Add the salmon, skin-side down, and cook until the skin is blackened and the salmon is almost cooked through. Flip onto the flesh side and cook approximately 1 minute, or until browned. Remove the salmon from the pan and let it cool enough to be handled. Cut off the skin and cut it into small pieces. Set the salmon and cut up skin aside.
3. **In the same pan,** heat the remaining ½ tablespoon of the olive oil over medium heat. Add the garbanzo beans and garlic and cook for 2-3 minutes, or until the garbanzo beans are slightly browned. Drain. In a small bowl, blend the garbanzo beans, yogurt, oregano, salt, and lime juice until smooth.
4. **Place the cooked pasta** in a square in the center of a plate. Gently place the salmon on top of the pasta. Add the garbanzo bean sauce to the side. Sprinkle the salmon skin and cilantro on top of salmon and serve.

Chef Emma Schramm,

age 9 in 2015

"I made this recipe because I L-O-V-E, love, pasta, and salmon is my favorite fish," says Emma. "I made the garbanzo bean sauce because my dad used to make garbanzo beans frequently when I was four. I am always open to trying new things." Emma serves this with a banana-strawberry smoothie.

Gianna's Salmon Paradise

Makes 4 servings • 433 calories • 24g fat • 23g carbohydrates • 30g protein

INGREDIENTS

For the Salmon Marinade:

1 cup fresh orange juice
¼ cup fresh lemon juice
1 tablespoon low-sodium soy sauce
2 tablespoons extra-virgin olive oil
2 tablespoons minced garlic
1 teaspoon chopped parsley
1 pound salmon fillet, skin removed

For the Salmon Cakes:

½ cup whole-grain seasoned breadcrumbs
2 medium eggs
1 ½ tablespoons Pecorino Romano or Parmesan grated cheese
6 basil leaves, finely chopped
1 tablespoon fresh lemon juice
½ teaspoon lemon zest
¼ cup chopped fresh spinach
¼ teaspoon salt
⅛ teaspoon ground black pepper
1 teaspoon Dijon mustard
1 teaspoon minced garlic
¼ cup shredded carrots

For the Pickle Sauce:

2 tablespoons dill pickle, diced
1 tablespoon pickle juice
1 tablespoon low-fat mayonnaise
¼ cup low-fat plain Greek yogurt
½ tablespoon fresh lemon juice

PREPARATION

1. **To make the Marinade:** In a large bowl, whisk together all of the ingredients and add the salmon last. Marinate up to 1 hour in the refrigerator.

2. **To make the Salmon Cakes:** Preheat the oven to 400°F. In a nonstick skillet over medium heat, cook salmon with ¼ cup of marinade, about 6 minutes per side or until both sides are slightly opaque. Let cool. On a large nonstick baking sheet, or one lined with parchment or greased with oil or nonstick cooking spray, pull apart cooled salmon using 2 forks. Add in all ingredients and mix with your hands, forming 4 cakes. Bake about 10 minutes, or until golden brown on the bottom, and then carefully flip to cook the other side, about 10 minutes.

3. **To make Pickle Sauce:** In a medium mixing bowl, combine all the ingredients. Top cooked Salmon Cakes with 2 teaspoons Pickle Sauce and serve with salad.

CHEF

Gianna Malecki

age 8 in 2016

"At dinner one night, my mom made salmon cakes with leftover salmon," says Gianna. "They were crispy and yummy. After I met with a worker from my town's farm and learned all about New Jersey's state fruits and vegetables, I decided to make my own recipe, but with healthier foods. Many of the fruits and vegetables in my recipe are from my state, and some were even from my own garden. I substituted frying the cakes with baking as a healthier choice. The pickle sauce is like my mom's tartar sauce but healthier with yogurt. It tastes great now with all the healthy changes and I love it even more!" Gianna always serves this with a fresh green salad.

New Mexico

Baked Chicken Wrap with Nectarine Avocado Salsa

Emma Kenney, age 9 in 2012

"I decided to make this recipe because nectarine salsa is my favorite! I could eat it on anything," says Emma. "I chose a wrap because they are fun to take in my lunchbox." Emma likes to have these with corn-and-black bean salad, blueberries and strawberries, and milk.

Makes 4 servings

INGREDIENTS

1 pound chicken breast tenders, preferably organic

2 tablespoons olive oil

2 teaspoons ground cumin

Salt and pepper

2 nectarines, diced

1 avocado, pitted, peeled, and diced

1 bunch scallions, white and light green parts only, thinly sliced

1/4 cup fresh cilantro, chopped

Juice of 1/2 lime

4 whole-wheat tortillas

4 cups fresh baby spinach, preferably organic

PREPARATION

1. Preheat the oven to 375°F.
2. In a large ovenproof dish, drizzle the chicken with 1 tablespoon of the olive oil and sprinkle with the cumin. Season to taste with salt and pepper, and gently toss to coat the chicken in the oil and spices. Bake until the chicken is cooked through, 15 to 20 minutes. Let cool slightly.
3. In a medium bowl, combine the nectarines, avocado, scallions, and cilantro. Add the lime juice and the remaining 1 tablespoon olive oil, and gently toss to combine.
4. Place the wraps on individual plates and evenly distribute the chicken, salsa, and spinach. Roll each wrap around the filling from bottom to top, overlapping one end, burrito style. Slice the wraps diagonally, and enjoy!

Spinach Frittata

LOUIS TEICH, age 10 in 2013

"We started out with a basic Spanish tortilla (boiled potatoes and eggs) and added a lot of veggies to it," says Louis' father, Gabriele. "We like the spinach version, but any combination of vegetables will work. We usually serve it with salsa on the side. As a school lunch we put a wedge between two slices of bread and put some salsa for dipping in a separate container." For anyone allergic to nuts, Gabriele recommends substituting whole wheat flour for the almond flour.

Makes 6 servings

INGREDIENTS

6 ounces fresh spinach

1/2 bunch fresh flat-leaf parsley leaves

1/2 bunch fresh cilantro leaves

3 spring onions, ends trimmed

6 large eggs

3 tablespoons almond flour or whole wheat flour

Salt and freshly ground black pepper

2 tablespoons olive oil

2 small boiling potatoes, peeled, cut into cubes, and cooked

1/4 cup Parmesan

PREPARATION

1. In a food processor, chop the spinach, parsley, cilantro, and spring onions.

2. In a medium bowl, beat the eggs. Add the almond flour and season generously with salt and pepper. Add the spinach mixture and stir to combine.

3. In a large sauté pan over moderate heat, warm the olive oil. Pour the egg mixture into the pan then add the potato cubes, spreading them out evenly. Season with additional salt and pepper. Reduce the heat to low and cook, covered, until the underside is golden brown, about 10 minutes. Cut the frittata into quarters and flip each one over. Cover and cook until the frittata is firm and the potatoes are tender, about 10 minutes. During the last few minutes of cooking, sprinkle the frittata with Parmesan. Serve hot with salsa on the side or cold on sandwich bread.

250 calories; 13g protein; 20g carbohydrates; 13g fat (4g saturated fat); 264mg sodium

Max Johnson-Jimenez, age 11 in 2014

"We eat this meal often because it is a family favorite," says Max. "My parents made up the recipe before I was born, and we have continued to change the recipe over the years. Now I like to make it, too. We serve this with corn tortillas, brown rice, cucumber salad, and fruit."

Makes 6 servings • 429 calories • 23g fat • 27g carbohydrates • 19g protein

SOUTHWESTERN CASERA

INGREDIENTS

1 tablespoon vegetable oil
1¼ pounds ground turkey
4 large tomatoes, quartered
1 (14-ounce) can fire-roasted diced tomatoes
1 onion, peeled and coarsely chopped
1 jalapeño pepper, quartered and seeded
2 yellow bell peppers, quartered and seeded
1 scallion, trimmed and sliced
2 garlic cloves, peeled
1½ teaspoons salt
1 teaspoon Mexican oregano
1 teaspoon ground chipotle pepper or chili powder
½ cup fresh cilantro sprigs
1 lime, cut into wedges
Garnish: Corn tortillas, low-fat sour cream, brown rice, fruits and veggies

PREPARATION

In a large sauté pan, warm the oil over moderate heat. Add the turkey and cook for about 10 minutes or until cooked through. Drain any liquid from the pan.

Meanwhile, in a food processor or blender, place ¾ of the tomatoes, the canned tomatoes, ½ the onion, jalapeño, peppers, scallion, garlic, salt, oregano, and chili powder, and blend until ingredients are evenly mixed. Add the rest of the tomato and onion and all the cilantro. Pulse the food processor 5 or 6 times to reach a chunky consistency.

Add the salsa to the turkey and cook on moderate heat for about 5 minutes. Serve with lime wedges and garnishes.

New Mexican Style Layered Tostada with Cauliflower Tortilla

Makes 6 Servings • 508 calories • 20g fat • 51g carbohydrates • 35g protein

INGREDIENTS

For the Cauliflower Tortillas:

1 head cauliflower, cut up and stems removed
2 large eggs
1 teaspoon garlic salt
1 teaspoon peeled and minced onion
1 teaspoon pepper

For the Tostadas:

1 (15-ounce) can low-sodium black beans
1 cup instant brown rice
1 (10-ounce) can diced tomatoes
12 ounces lean ground turkey
2 tablespoons red chile powder
6 large eggs
Low-fat shredded Mexican-style cheese
1 avocado, chopped
1 tomato, sliced
¼ onion, peeled and sliced
¼ head of lettuce, shredded
1 cup plain Greek yogurt
Salsa

PREPARATION

1. **To make the Tortillas:** Preheat the oven to 375°F. In a blender or a food processor, pulse the cauliflower until you get a texture finer than rice. In a steamer set in a large stockpot filled with boiling water, cook the riced cauliflower for 5 minutes. Let cool. Place the steamed cauliflower in a dishtowel or paper towel and squeeze out as much excess water as you can. Transfer the cauliflower to a large bowl. Add the eggs, garlic salt, onion, and pepper (you can use any spices you like).
2. **Separate the mixture into 6 balls of equal size,** and spread/smash each ball out on a parchment-lined baking sheet to make 6 small circles, each about the size of corn tortillas. Bake for 8 to 10 minutes, then flip and cook for another 5 minutes. Set aside.
3. **To make the Tostadas:** In a medium sauté pan, heat the black beans over medium-high heat for 3 minutes. Mash the beans until they reach a refried bean consistency.
4. **In a medium saucepan,** bring 1 cup of water to a boil. Stir in the brown rice and return to a boil. Reduce the heat to a simmer, add ½ can diced tomatoes, and simmer for 5 minutes.
5. **In a large nonstick saucepan,** cook the turkey over medium-high heat, breaking up the meat with a wooden spoon, for about 8 minutes, or until no pink is left. Add the remaining ½ can diced tomatoes and the red chile powder. Mix thoroughly, then reduce the heat to low and simmer for 5 minutes.
6. **Meanwhile, in a large nonstick skillet,** fry the eggs over medium heat.
7. **To assemble:** Layer each tortilla with 2 tablespoons mashed black beans, ¼ cup rice, 2 tablespoons red chile–turkey sauce, a pinch of cheese, 1 egg, avocado, tomato, onion, lettuce, 1 tablespoon yogurt, and salsa!

Chef Hannah Torres,

age 10 in 2015

"A tostada is a very popular and versatile dish! Usually served on a corn tortilla, we substituted that for a gluten-free option: a cauliflower tortilla," says Hannah. "They are easy to make, and everyone can make their own! By replacing the corn tortilla with a cauliflower tortilla, we add more veggies to our plate. For some extra flavor, we included a red chile–turkey sauce for an authentic New Mexico taste."

Green Chili Cheese Roll and Lime Jicama Fries

Makes 6 servings • 425 calories • 22g fat • 33g carbohydrates • 26g protein

INGREDIENTS

For Green Chili Cheese Roll:

1 tablespoon olive oil
1 pound ground turkey
½ onion, peeled and chopped
1 tube canned thick crust pizza dough, whole-wheat if available
¼ teaspoon salt
½ teaspoon garlic powder
1 tablespoon red chili powder, or to taste
2 tomatoes, chopped
1 cup shredded low-fat sharp cheddar
½ cup Hatch green chili, or more to taste
¼ cup diced pickles

For Jicama Fries:

1 large jicama, peeled and thinly sliced
2 avocados, peeled, pitted, and cut into cubes
½ cup cilantro, stems removed, coarsely chopped
¼ cup olive oil
½ cup fresh lime juice
Salt and freshly ground black pepper to taste

PREPARATION

1. **For Green Chili Cheese Roll:** In a large nonstick skillet, warm the olive oil over medium heat. Add the ground turkey and onions and cook for 10 minutes, or until turkey is cooked through and onions are softened. Drain well, add remaining ingredients, and mix well. Cook for 2 minutes more.

2. **Preheat the oven to 425°F.** Roll out the pizza dough on a large nonstick baking sheet and stretch to make a rectangle. Spread the meat mixture on the dough. On the long side, carefully fold over the dough and roll it similar to a jelly roll. Pinch seam closed and gently put seam side down onto the sheet. Pinch ends closed. Bake for 15 to 20 minutes or until golden brown. Cut into six slices.

3. **To make the Jicama Fries:** In a large bowl, combine the jicama, avocado, and cilantro. In small bowl, whisk the olive oil, lime juice, salt, and pepper. Add to jicama mixture and stir gently. Serve with the Green Chili Cheese Roll.

CHEF

McLean Knight

age 10 in 2016

"McLean loves to make salsa, and this recipe combines his love of salsa making with the famous green chili cheeseburger New Mexico is known for," says McLean's mom, Kristin. "This recipe kept the feel of a green chili cheeseburger, but easier for lunch and healthier. Jicama is a great vegetable that is light and crisp but takes on other flavors, providing a healthy crunch to replace the greasy fries. The salsa is found in the form of a deconstructed guacamole. Our state question is 'red or green?' Every New Mexican knows that question refers to your green or red chili preference. This burger has both!"

New York

Fish-Fueled Pepper Rocket with Kale Chips and Quinoa

Samuel Wohabe, age 9 in 2012

"I came up with the recipe for Fish-Fueled Pepper Rockets when I was trying to find an interesting way to use a pretty orange bell pepper I saw in the grocery store," says Samuel. "I wanted to make fish that night too, so I decided it would be fun to stuff the pepper with the fish and mix the flavors. When it was done, it looked like a rocket ship. And I've always loved kale chips, and can eat the entire head of kale this way!"

Makes 3 servings

INGREDIENTS

1 tablespoon olive oil

1/2 pound halibut fillet

Salt and pepper

3 orange bell peppers, stemmed and seeds removed

1 cup shredded Manchego cheese

Kale chips (see below)

1 cup cooked quinoa

For Kale Chips:

1 bunch kale, stems removed and leaves torn into bite-size pieces

2 tablespoons olive oil

¼ teaspoon salt

PREPARATION

1. Preheat the oven to 350°F.
2. In a sauté pan over moderate heat, warm the olive oil. Add the halibut and sear, flipping once, until cooked through, about 4 minutes. Season to taste with salt and pepper. Cut the halibut into bite-size pieces.
3. Stuff each pepper with 1/3 of the cooked halibut and 1/3 of the shredded Manchego cheese. Place the peppers on a nonstick baking pan, open side up, and bake until soft, about 30 minutes. Serve with kale chips and quinoa.

For Kale Chips:

Preheat the oven to 400°F. On a large nonstick baking pan, drizzle the kale with olive oil, season with salt, and toss until evenly coated. Bake until crispy, about 15 minutes.

Super Rescue Soup

PETER MURPHY, age 9 in 2013

"We live on Long Island, and when Hurricane Sandy struck, we were without power for 15 days," reports Peter's mom, Jill. "The grocery stores had no produce, dairy, or meat, but it was harvest time at our local farmstand, so there was plenty of fresh produce available there. We filled a wagon with fresh produce, added some pantry staples, and came up with this soup, which we could cook on our gas stovetop. To round out the meal we would serve Peter's Banana Split Fruit Salad. Split a banana, top with berries and low-fat yogurt, and finish with ground flaxseed sprinkles."

Makes 6 servings

INGREDIENTS

1/2 cup dried cannellini beans or 1 (15-ounce) can, drained and rinsed

1/2 cup pearl barley

2 tablespoons olive oil

1 small onion, finely chopped

2 medium carrots, scrubbed and finely chopped

2 medium stalks celery, finely chopped

1 medium zucchini, quartered lengthwise and cut into 1/2-inch pieces

3/4 cup green beans, cut into 1/2-inch pieces

1 russet potato, peeled and cut into 1/2-inch cubes

1/2 cup tomato sauce or one medium tomato, chopped

1/2 teaspoon salt (or to taste)

PREPARATION

1. If using dried beans, soak them overnight or do a quick soak (boil for 2 minutes, then remove them from the heat and let soak for 1 hour).

2. In a medium saucepan over moderate heat, cover the presoaked beans with 2 inches of water and cook until tender, about 30 minutes. Add 1 1/4 cups water, bring to a boil, and add the barley. Lower the heat and simmer for 45 minutes. Set aside. (If using canned beans, wait to add them to the soup until step 4.)

3. In a large saucepan over moderate heat, warm the olive oil. Add the onion, carrots, and celery and sauté, stirring occasionally, until translucent, about 5 minutes. Add the zucchini and green beans and sauté until beginning to soften, about 3 minutes. Add the potato and sauté, stirring occasionally, for 3 minutes.

4. Add 6 cups of water and the tomato sauce, raise the heat, and bring the soup to a boil. Lower the heat and simmer for 20 minutes. Add the beans and barley and continue to simmer for 5 more minutes. Season with salt, and purée with an immersion blender, if desired.

187 calories; 5g protein; 31g carbohydrates; 5g fat (1g saturated fat); 440mg sodium (does not include banana split fruit salad)

MIKE'S CHICKEN & VEGETABLE DUMPLING CUPS

INGREDIENTS

2 tablespoons olive oil
2 tablespoons low-sodium soy sauce (or tamari)
Juice from 1 fresh tangerine
2 cups skinless, boneless chicken breasts, diced
¼ cup diced cilantro
1 carrot, peeled and diced
½ cup shredded cabbage
2 scallions, diced
2 minced garlic cloves
24 rice wrappers

PREPARATION

In a large bowl, mix 1 tablespoon of olive oil, the soy sauce, and the tangerine juice. Add the chicken, cilantro, carrot, cabbage, scallions, and garlic to this bowl. Set aside for 15 minutes to marinate.

In a large sauté pan over moderate heat, warm the remaining tablespoon of olive oil. Add the chicken and vegetable mixture to the pan and stir occasionally, cooking until the chicken is cooked through, about 10 minutes. Lower the heat to very low to keep warm.

Preheat oven to 350°F. Lightly spray a cupcake pan or muffin tin with olive oil or cooking spay. Dip rice paper wrapper in warm water. Place 2 of these wet wrappers in each cupcake cup and bake in the oven for 15 minutes. Let cool, remove the tin, then scoop chicken and vegetable mixture into the rice paper cup and serve.

Michael Lombardi, age 11 in 2014

"My grandparents take me out for Chinese dumplings for a good report card," says Mike. "We wanted to make a healthy version at home. Kids like finger foods, so I decided to make this fun. My aunt must eat gluten-free, so we used tamari instead of regular soy sauce. To complete a MyPlate-inspired meal, I would serve this with steamed broccoli and a glass of low-fat milk."

Makes 6 servings • 501 calories • 13g fat • 40g carbohydrates • 29g protein

CHEF MICHAEL

Chef Julia Rissberger,

age 11 in 2015

"I make Cheese Pennies that are a hit with everyone, but are very high in fat," says Julia. "I decided to make a modified version of the recipe, decreasing the amount of fat and including healthy whole grains without sacrificing the delicious taste of the New York extra-sharp cheddar cheese. I love the taste of sharp cheese with fruit, so I paired them with a salad featuring apples and blueberry dressing topped with homemade cinnamon almonds."

Spinach and Apple Salad with Blueberry Vinaigrette and Whole-Grain Cheese Pennies

Makes 6 Servings • 479 calories • 32g fat • 35g carbohydrates • 19g protein

---

INGREDIENTS

For the Cheese Pennies:

½ stick unsalted butter, softened
8 ounces grated New York extra-sharp low-fat cheddar cheese
⅓ cup all-purpose flour
⅓ cup whole-wheat flour
¼ cup oat bran
1 tablespoon sesame seeds
½ teaspoon salt
1 large egg white

For the Cinnamon Almonds:

2 tablespoons sugar
1 tablespoon water
½ teaspoon cinnamon
¾ cup almonds

For the Blueberry Vinaigrette:

½ cup fresh or frozen (defrosted) blueberries
¼ cup balsamic vinegar
¼ cup olive oil
1 tablespoon maple syrup
1 teaspoon water
Dash of pepper

For the Spinach Salad:

12 cups baby spinach
1 cucumber, peeled and sliced
1 apple, such as Gala or Honeycrisp, cored and thinly sliced

PREPARATION

1. **To make the Cheese Pennies:** Preheat the oven to 375°F. In a large bowl, combine the butter, cheese, all-purpose and whole-wheat flours, oat bran, sesame seeds, and salt. In a separate bowl, beat the egg white with an electric mixer until soft peaks appear. Fold the egg white into the cheese mixture. Roll into 24 small balls and place on an ungreased baking sheet. Flatten the balls with a fork. Bake for 15 minutes, or until lightly browned. Remove the pennies from the baking sheet, and let cool slightly.
2. **To make the Cinnamon Almonds:** In a nonstick sauté pan, bring the sugar, water, and cinnamon to a boil over medium heat. Add the almonds and stir continuously until the water evaporates and the sugar starts to harden on the almonds. Pour the nuts on a plate to cool.
3. **To make the Blueberry Vinaigrette:** In a medium bowl, smash the blueberries with a potato masher or fork. Add the remaining ingredients and mix well.
4. **To assemble,** divide the spinach, cucumber, and apple among 6 plates. Top each salad with 1 tablespoon lightly chopped cinnamon almonds and drizzle with blueberry vinaigrette. Serve with warm Cheese Pennies.

CHEF

Danielle Mazlish

age 10 in 2016

"In school, I did a report on Michelle Obama's *Let's Move!* program and now I try to eat based on the MyPlate picture," says Danielle. "I used chicken instead of beef for the meatballs, and I stuffed them with fresh mozzarella, because I love cheese! I put the meatballs on a stick, because I think it is fun to eat foods on a stick. I added carrots and yellow squash to make it colorful and taste even better. It looked like spaghetti, so I named it Veggie Spaghetti, and topped it with basil, which we grow. Everyone in my family loves it, even my brother, who is a picky eater. I hope you like it too!"

Chicken Cheeseball Kabobs on Veggie Spaghetti

Makes 6 servings • 351 calories • 16g fat • 27g carbohydrates • 27g protein

INGREDIENTS

For the Chicken Cheeseball Kabobs:

1 tablespoon olive oil
1 pound ground chicken
1 cup whole-wheat breadcrumbs
⅓ cup grated Parmesan cheese
¼ cup parsley, chopped
2 tablespoons Italian seasoning, dried
2 garlic cloves, peeled and minced
1 egg
½ teaspoon salt
⅛ teaspoon ground black pepper
¼ pound skim-milk mozzarella, cut into cubes
6 wooden skewers
1 ½ cups of marinara sauce for dipping (optional)

For the Veggie Spaghetti:

2 tablespoons olive oil
6 zucchini
3 yellow squash
2 garlic cloves, peeled and minced
1 ½ cups shredded carrots
2 tablespoons basil, finely chopped

PREPARATION

1. **To make the Chicken Cheeseball Kabobs:** Preheat oven to 375°F. Cover a large baking sheet with aluminum foil and grease with olive oil. In a large mixing bowl, combine chicken, breadcrumbs, cheese, parsley, seasoning, and garlic. In a small bowl, beat the egg with salt and pepper until well blended. Pour the egg into the chicken mixture and mix with a large spoon until blended. Using a soup spoon or tablespoon as a guide, scoop out the chicken mixture and form balls, about 1½ inches wide. Push two mozzarella cubes into the center of each ball and re-form the chicken over the cheese so they are covered and in a meatball shape. Bake for 15 minutes, or until golden on bottom, then turn over and cook 10 more minutes. When cooked, stick three chicken cheese balls per skewer to serve over the Veggie Spaghetti.
2. **To make the Veggie Spaghetti:** Using a spiral veggie slicer, mandolin or box grater, shred zucchini and yellow squash into thin strips so it looks like spaghetti. In a large nonstick skillet, warm oil on medium heat. Add zucchini, squash, garlic, and carrots, and cook until tender but not mushy, about 5 minutes.
3. **To Assemble:** Divide the Veggie Spaghetti onto 6 plates and sprinkle with chopped basil on top of each plate. Place the Chicken Cheeseball Kabobs on top. Serve marinara sauce on the side, for dipping.

North Carolina

Homerun Meatloaf Burger

Sydney Brown, age 11 in 2012

"My lunch is a healthy and fun take on a hamburger. I came up with this burger because I love meatloaf, and I thought I could show kids how delicious vegetables could be when you think of fun and creative ways to add them to your meal," says Sydney. She likes to serve this with Baked Zucchini Fries and fresh strawberry lemonade.

Makes 8 servings

INGREDIENTS

2 pounds lean ground beef

½ cup finely diced green bell pepper

½ cup finely diced zucchini

½ cup finely diced onion

½ cup unseasoned breadcrumbs

1 garlic clove, minced

¼ cup tomato sauce

1 egg

Salt and pepper

½ cup ketchup

½ cup barbecue sauce

Reduced-fat provolone cheese or any other type of melting cheese

8 whole-wheat or multigrain hamburger buns, toasted

For garnish:
Lettuce and tomato slices

For Baked Zucchini Fries:
1 large egg white

1/3 cup milk
½ cup Parmesan cheese

1/2 cup unseasoned breadcrumbs

Salt and pepper

2 large green or yellow zucchini, peeled, trimmed, and cut into (2-inch-long, ¼-inch-thick) strips

PREPARATION

1. Preheat the oven to 425°F.
2. In a large bowl, mix together the ground beef, green bell pepper, zucchini, onion, breadcrumbs, garlic, tomato sauce, egg, salt, and pepper. Make patties and place them on a baking sheet.
3. Bake for about 20 minutes, then flip them and cook for another 10 minutes.
4. While the burgers are cooking, make the zucchini fries: Combine the egg white and milk in a small bowl, and combine the Parmesan, breadcrumbs, salt, and pepper in another small bowl.
5. Dip the zucchini slices first in the milk mixture and then in the cheese mixture. Shake off any excess, then move to the baking sheet and place in the oven on another shelf while the burgers cook.
6. Mix together the ketchup and barbecue sauce, drizzle on the burgers, and bake for an additional 10 to 15 minutes.
7. Add a slice of cheese to each burger and bake until melted, about 1 minute.
8. Remove the burgers and lightly toasted fries from the oven and place the burgers on buns. Serve garnished with lettuce and tomato and Baked Zucchini Fries.

Spring Rolls

VIJAY DEY, age 12 in 2013

"This delicious recipe is inspired by my grandfather, who is a great person, and my role model," says Vijay. "He is very smart and strong. He is also a great chef, and he makes the best food I have ever eaten! Another reason I like this recipe is that it reflects my Chinese heritage. When I eat spring rolls, I think about the wonderful springtime, and I feel like the meal replenishes and refreshes me. Also, the wraps in this dish are not fried, and I think that it is not only healthier but tastes better that way."

Makes 6 to 8 servings

INGREDIENTS

1 pound boneless, skinless chicken breasts, cut into thin strips

1 tablespoon plus 1 teaspoon salt

1/2 teaspoon freshly ground black pepper

1 teaspoon reduced-sodium soy sauce

1 teaspoon cornstarch

2 tablespoons vegetable oil

2 teaspoons sesame oil

5 cups mung bean sprouts

2 cups chopped napa cabbage

1 cup grated carrots

5 fresh shiitake mushrooms, sliced

2 scallions, sliced

3 teaspoons minced fresh ginger

24 spring roll wrappers

PREPARATION

1. In a medium bowl, marinate the chicken with 1 teaspoon salt, pepper, soy sauce, and cornstarch.

2. In a wok or sauté pan over moderate heat, warm the vegetable and sesame oils. Add the bean sprouts, cabbage, carrots, mushrooms, scallions, and ginger and sauté, stirring occasionally, for 5 minutes. Add the marinated chicken and sauté, stirring occasionally, until cooked through, about 8 minutes.

3. Fill a pie plate with warm water. Immerse 1 spring roll wrapper in the water until pliable, about 15 seconds, then transfer to a cutting board. Place a heaping tablespoon of filling down the center of the wrapper. Fold the bottom of the wrapper over the filling then fold both sides into the center, and roll the wrapper up tightly to form a spring roll. Transfer the spring roll to a plate and keep covered with a damp paper towel. Repeat with the remaining spring roll wrappers and filling.

295 calories; 20g protein; 25g carbohydrates; 14g fat (2g saturated fat); 771mg sodium

YUMMY & HEALTHY KATI ROLL

INGREDIENTS

1 tablespoon vegetable oil
1 yellow onion, peeled and chopped
1 tablespoon finely chopped fresh ginger
1 minced garlic clove
½ cup chopped tomato
4 mushrooms, chopped
¼ teaspoon ground turmeric powder
¼ teaspoon ground garam masala
¼ teaspoon red chili powder (cayenne)
¼ teaspoon ground cumin
½ teaspoon ground coriander
1 pound boneless skinless chicken thighs, cut into small cubes
4 eggs
9 whole-wheat tortillas
½ red onion, peeled and chopped
3 carrots, peeled and chopped
½ cucumber, chopped
1 bunch cilantro, finely chopped
Juice from 2 limes
Salt to taste

PREPARATION

In a large sauté pan or wok, warm oil on moderate heat. Add the onion, ginger, and garlic and cook for 2 minutes. Add tomatoes and mushrooms and cook for 2 minutes. Add turmeric, garam masala, red chili powder, cumin, coriander, and chicken and cook, stirring often, until chicken is cooked, through about 15 minutes. Season with salt to taste and transfer to a bowl.

In a small bowl, whisk the eggs. Using a nonstick pan, cook the eggs over moderate heat. Place a tortilla on top of the egg while it's still cooking. Cook for 1 minute, then flip the eggs over. Cook 1 minute more, and slide the eggs onto a plate.

To make the roll: Diagonally on a tortilla, place a few tablespoons of the chicken mixture and eggs, as well as red onion, carrots, cucumber, and cilantro. Squeeze lime juice over the mixture and roll the tortilla up.

Rajen Dey, age 11 in 2014

"One summer, my family and I went to India. We went to a restaurant and ordered some rolls. When we got them, they were way too spicy. I drank almost a gallon of water! When we came back to the U.S., I was trying to make a roll that was healthy, delicious, and not spicy. When I was finished with experimenting, I cooked it for my family, and they all loved it. But, I wanted it to be even better. So, I added an egg to every roll, and I got the best roll ever made."

Makes 8 servings • 317 calories • 11g fat • 36g carbohydrates • 20g protein

Curried Chickpeas with Baked Tofu over Cilantro Rice

Makes 8 Servings • 464 calories • 10g fat • 76g carbohydrates • 18g protein

---

INGREDIENTS

1 (15-ounce) package extra-firm tofu
2 tablespoons whole-wheat flour
2 tablespoons nutritional yeast (optional)
1 garlic clove, peeled and minced
½ teaspoon salt
Nonstick cooking spray
4 cups vegetable broth
3 cups brown rice
¼ cup chopped fresh cilantro
1 teaspoon canola oil
1 large onion, peeled and diced
4 bell peppers, assorted colors, seeded and diced
2 garlic cloves, peeled and minced
2 teaspoons yellow curry powder
1 (14-ounce) can low-fat coconut milk
½ cup low-fat milk
1 can chickpeas, drained and rinsed well
½ teaspoon salt

PREPARATION

1. **Preheat the oven to 400°F.** Place the tofu on a paper towel-lined plate and press with another paper towel to squeeze excess water out of the tofu. Cut into bite-sized cubes.
2. **In a medium bowl,** combine the whole-wheat flour, nutritional yeast (optional), garlic, and salt. Add the cubed tofu and toss to coat the pieces in the flour mixture. Spray a baking sheet to prevent sticking and spread the tofu in a single layer. Bake for 30 minutes, gently stirring once during baking so all pieces are evenly browned.
3. **While the tofu is baking,** in a large stockpot, boil 2 cups of water, the vegetable broth, and rice over medium heat. Reduce the heat to a simmer, cover, and cook for 45 minutes, or until the rice is tender. Remove the rice from the heat and add the chopped cilantro.
4. **Meanwhile, in a large sauté pan,** heat the canola oil over medium heat. Add the onion and peppers and cook for about 8 minutes, or until softened. Add the garlic, curry powder, coconut milk, low-fat milk, chickpeas, and salt, reduce the heat to low, and simmer for 15 minutes.
5. **To assemble,** layer brown rice, curry sauce, and finally baked tofu on top.

Chef Alexander Tschegg,

age 8 in 2015

"My mom used to make white rice with curry for dinner, but I thought it would be good to make it more healthy, so I used brown rice instead and added chickpeas to the curry," says Alexander. "I like tofu, so I decided to add baked tofu to the top layer. We usually have a salad with most of our dinners, and I think that is healthy."

Korean Lentil Patties

Makes 6 servings • 276 calories • 7g fat • 39g carbohydrates • 15g protein

INGREDIENTS

For Korean Lentil Patties:

¾ brown lentils, rinsed and drained
2 cups vegetable broth
1 yellow onion, peeled and chopped
1 teaspoon minced garlic
2 tablespoons Korean hot pepper paste or red chili paste
¼ cup dried cranberries
¼ cup chopped walnuts
Juice from ½ fresh lemon
1 teaspoon kosher salt
½ teaspoon freshly ground black pepper
1 cup rolled oats
1 egg
½ cup panko breadcrumbs
Olive oil

For Greek Dill Yogurt:

1 cup low-fat Greek yogurt
1 tablespoon dill

PREPARATION

1. **To make the Korean Lentil Patties:** In a large stockpot, combine lentils with the broth and bring to a boil over medium-high heat. Cover, reduce heat to low, and simmer until tender, about 30 minutes. Once tender, drain the lentils to remove any extra liquid and let cool for 10 minutes. In a large mixing bowl, combine the lentils with the remaining ingredients except the breadcrumbs. Form into 6 balls with your hands. Place breadcrumbs on a plate and roll the balls in the breadcrumbs, flatten into patties, and refrigerate for at least 30 minutes. Meanwhile, preheat the oven to 400°F. Place the patties on a large baking sheet and drizzle olive oil over the top of the patties. Bake for 25 minutes or until golden brown. Serve with Greek Dill Yogurt.
2. **To make Greek Dill Yogurt:** In a small bowl, whisk together the yogurt and dill and serve with the patties.

CHEF

Mena Choi

age 10 in 2016

"I created this dish because I like to cook with my mom in the kitchen," says Mena. "I wanted to make a healthy meal that highlights my Korean background and also learn more about nutrition when I cook. I made this recipe for my dad and he loved the taste. I am very lucky to live in North Carolina because I can choose so many wonderful vegetables to cook with, including sweet potatoes, which are so tasty!" Mena serves this with roasted sweet potatoes.

North Dakota

Turkey Vegetable Soup

Logan Rosene, age 8 in 2012

Logan's mom says, "Ever since my children have been babies, we as a family have stayed away from the fast foods and frozen foods section of the grocery store. I lost my father at a young age due to health issues from being obese, and I make it a priority to teach my children the importance of healthy eating and longevity of life." Logan likes to round out this meal with whole-wheat bread, milk, and raspberries.

Makes 8 servings

INGREDIENTS

1 pound ground turkey

32 ounces low-sodium chicken broth

2 cups thinly sliced carrots

6 celery ribs, trimmed and cut into ¼-inch-thick slices

2 cups thinly sliced cabbage

2 (15-ounce) cans kidney beans, drained and rinsed

1 (28-ounce) can crushed tomatoes

Salt and pepper

PREPARATION

1. In a large sauté pan over moderate heat, cook the turkey until browned and cooked through, about 8 minutes.
2. While the turkey is cooking, in a large stockpot, combine the chicken broth with the carrots, celery, cabbage, beans, and tomatoes. Add the cooked turkey and simmer, over moderate heat until the vegetables are soft, about 30 minutes. Season to taste with salt and pepper

Asian Fajitas

CHARLI MCQUILLAN, age 8 in 2013

"Charli fell in love with a sweet and sour meatball recipe," said mom Heidi Lynn. "But it was lacking in vegetables and the meatballs were frozen, and not something I wanted to serve my kids. This challenge was the perfect thing for us, as it pushed me to find a better option. In doing so, I realized how much fun we have cooking together and how quickly you can make a meal with a helper! We would add low-fat yogurt, strawberries, and a couple of tablespoons of her grandma's homemade granola as a side to this dish."

Makes 6 servings

INGREDIENTS

2 tablespoons packed brown sugar

1/2 teaspoon paprika

1/2 teaspoon garlic powder

1/2 teaspoon freshly ground black pepper

Crushed red pepper to taste

3 medium boneless, skinless chicken breasts, cut into thin strips

1 teaspoon sesame oil

1 green bell pepper, seeded and sliced

1 orange bell pepper, seeded and sliced

5 scallions, chopped

1 cup canned pineapple, cut into bite-size pieces, plus 2 tablespoons pineapple juice reserved from the can

6 whole wheat tortillas

Garnish: 1/4 head red cabbage, thinly sliced; 1/2 cup toasted sliced almonds

PREPARATION

1. In a medium bowl, combine the brown sugar, paprika, garlic powder, black pepper, and crushed red pepper. Add the chicken and rub it all over with the spice mixture. Transfer the chicken to a large resealable plastic bag and refrigerate for at least 20 minutes and up to several hours.

2. In a large sauté pan or wok over moderately high heat, warm the oil. Add the chicken and cook, stirring occasionally, until completely cooked through, about 7 minutes. Transfer the chicken to a plate and set aside. Do not wash the pan. Add the bell peppers, scallions, and pineapple juice to the pan and cook for about 5 minutes. Add the pineapple pieces and cooked chicken and cook, stirring occasionally, for about 3 minutes.

3. Warm the tortillas in the microwave for 30 seconds. Divide the chicken and vegetable mixture among the tortillas, top each with some red cabbage and almonds, and serve.

303 calories; 14g protein; 42g carbohydrates; 8g fat (1g saturated fat); 345mg sodium

Tegan Lancaster, age 11 in 2014

"Tegan loves grilled food and she's a vegetarian, so grilling gets creative at our house," says Tegan's mom, Kathryn. "She also loves breakfast, so she decided that she would like to share our grilled veggies egg-white omelet recipe. With the omelet, she likes something sweet so we added a side of fruit and Greek yogurt with our toasted honey/cinnamon tortilla chips."

Makes 1 serving • 421 calories • 20g fat • 37g carbohydrates• 18g protein

CHEF TEGAN

GRILLED VEGGIE BRUNCH

INGREDIENTS

♥ For the Omelet:
4 asparagus, chopped
1 portobello mushroom
2 teaspoons olive oil
2 egg whites
Pinch sea salt and pepper
1 tablespoon chopped Roma or plum tomato
1 tablespoon feta cheese

♥ For the Fruit & Yogurt:
1 whole-wheat tortilla
½ tablespoon honey
1 teaspoon cinnamon
¼ cup sliced banana, raspberries and blackberries
3 ounces Greek yogurt, preferably lemon

PREPARATION

Preheat the grill. Place the asparagus and portobello mushroom on a grill pan and drizzle with olive oil; sprinkle with sea salt and pepper. Grill for 10 minutes, turning occasionally, and set aside.

In a nonstick pan over moderate heat, cook the egg whites, letting the eggs set for 1 minute. Add the asparagus, mushrooms, tomato, and feta cheese, turn the heat off, and cover for 2 minutes.

To make Fruit & Yogurt dessert: Preheat the oven to 350°F. Place tortilla on a cookie sheet, spread honey and cinnamon, and bake for 7 minutes then slice. In a bowl, mix the lemon-flavored Greek yogurt with fruit and serve with tortilla chips.

Chef Carter Cassola,

age 11 in 2015

"This is one of my favorite dishes because there is so much color, and it's also a very healthy dish," says Carter. "My mom is a licensed registered dietitian and always encourages healthy colorful plates. Also, in this dish you can easily get three servings of fruits and vegetables. These are the reasons and my inspiration for creating this flavorful, delicious dish."

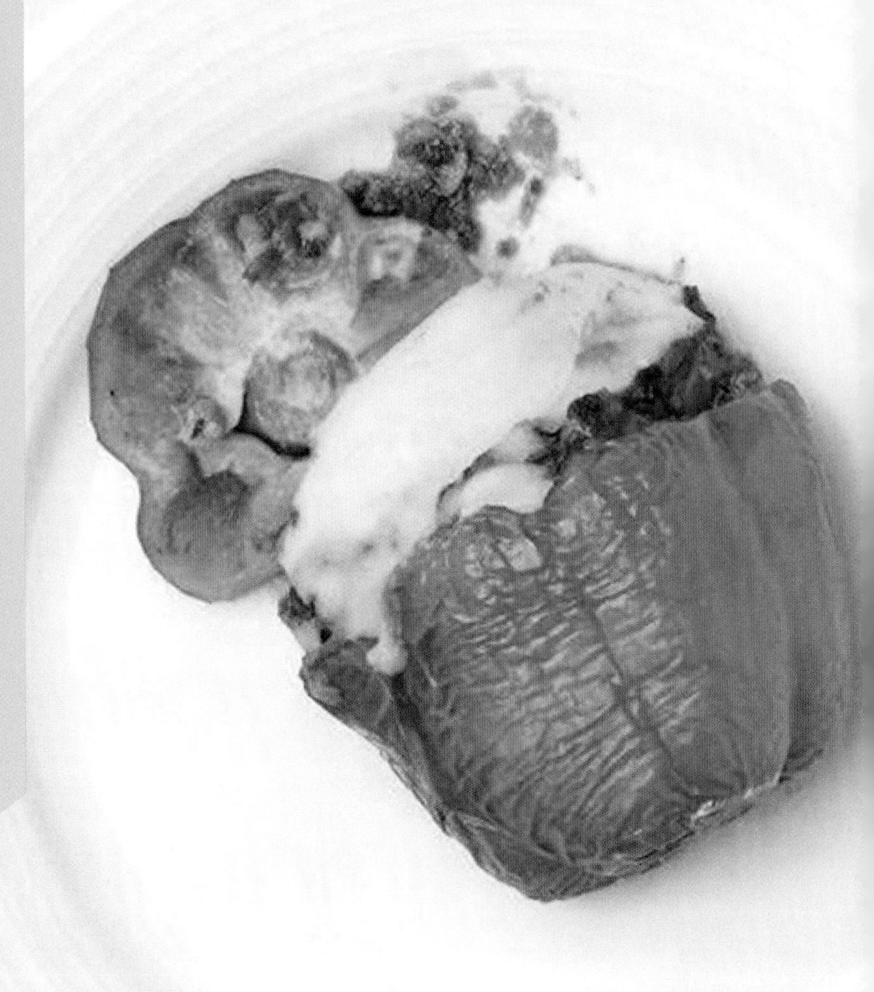

Stuffed Peppers Delite

Makes 8 Servings • 234 calories • 7g fat • 26g carbohydrates • 19g protein

INGREDIENTS

1 tablespoon canola oil
1 pound ground turkey
¾ cup diced celery
¾ cup diced mushrooms
¾ cup diced yellow bell pepper
½ cup peeled and diced yellow onion
¼ cup chopped kale
8 ounces tomato sauce
8 ounces green chilies
1 cup whole-grain rice
8 assorted bell peppers, tops and seeds removed
Low-fat mozzarella cheese to taste
1 can pineapple rings (or you can use fresh pineapple)

PREPARATION

1. **In a large stockpot,** heat the canola oil over medium heat. Add the turkey and cook, breaking up the meat with a wooden spoon, for about 10 minutes, or until cooked through. Add the celery, mushrooms, yellow bell pepper, onion, and kale and cook for about 7 minutes, or until the vegetables are softened. Add the tomato sauce and chilies and cook for 10 minutes.
2. **Meanwhile, in a medium saucepan,** combine the rice with 1 ½ cups water and bring to a boil over medium-high heat. Reduce the heat to low, cover, and simmer for 20 to 30 minutes, or until the rice is tender. Add to the turkey-veggie mix and stir to combine.
3. **Preheat the oven to 350°F.** Place the bell peppers in a 13- x 9-inch baking dish. Scoop about ½ cup of the turkey-veggie mixture into each pepper. Bake, uncovered, for 30 minutes. Remove the peppers from the oven and sprinkle lightly with cheese. Bake an additional 10 minutes. Serve with grilled pineapple slices and enjoy!

CHEF

Stella Halverson

age 8 in 2016

"We are potato farmers—Stella is a part of the fifth generation of our family that will farm potatoes," says Stella's dad, Eric. "So a potato had to be a big part of the recipe. We made chili to put in the potato to show one example of how a potato can be healthy. We selected bison meat because it is lower in fat and cholesterol than beef. We used dried beans because North Dakota is the largest producer of dried beans in the world. Stella loves to cook—we cook together every chance we get."

Red Potato Boat with 3 Bean Bison Chili

Makes 6 servings • 557 calories • 11g fat • 86g carbohydrates • 32g protein

INGREDIENTS

For Red Potato Boats:
6 red potatoes
Olive oil

For 3 Bean Bison Chili:
1 pound ground bison
3 14-ounce cans diced tomatoes
1 8-ounce can tomato sauce
1 green bell pepper, seeded and chopped
1 medium onion, peeled and chopped
1 cup chopped celery
2 tablespoons minced garlic
¾ teaspoon salt
½ teaspoon cayenne pepper
3 tablespoons chili pepper
1 15-ounce can pinto beans, rinsed and drained
1 15-ounce can black beans, rinsed and drained
1 15-ounce can red kidney beans, rinsed and drained

Garnishes:
½ cup shredded low-fat cheese
¼ cup chopped green onions
1 avocado, peeled, pitted, and cubed

PREPARATION

1. **To make the Red Potato Boats:** Preheat the oven to 350°F. On a large baking sheet, bake the potatoes for 1 hour, or until soft all the way through. Let cool. Using a spoon, scoop out the center of the potato to create the boat. Drizzle the inside with oil and set aside.
2. **To make the 3 Bean Bison Chili:** Meanwhile, in a large stockpot, brown the bison meat over medium heat and cook for 10 minutes, or until cooked through. Drain. Add the remaining ingredients, mix to combine, reduce heat to low and simmer for 1 hour.
3. **To Assemble:** Spoon chili into the scooped-out potato, sprinkle with cheese, green onions, and avocado.

Northern Mariana Islands

Pitaya Healthy Salad

Esther Huh, age 11 in 2012

Esther's mom, Dae Young, is a big fan of the high-fiber pitaya fruit (dragonfruit), and happily, so is Esther. They combined it with chicken and cabbage to make a healthy, vibrant salad. They like to layer the salad ingredients when they serve it and if you do this, serve the dressing on the side.

Makes 1 serving

INGREDIENTS

1 cup diced cooked chicken breast

½ pitaya (dragonfruit) or 2 kiwi, peeled and diced

2 slices pineapple, peeled, cored, and diced

½ head cabbage, cored, cut into ¼-inch-thick slices, and chopped

1/3 cup plain reduced-fat yogurt

1 tablespoon low-sodium soy sauce

2 teaspoons white vinegar

1 teaspoon sugar

Pinch cayenne or minced hot red chile to taste

2 teaspoons black sesame seeds

PREPARATION

In a large bowl, combine the chicken, pitaya, pineapple, and cabbage. In a small bowl, whisk together the yogurt, soy sauce, vinegar, sugar, and cayenne. Add the yogurt sauce to the fruit and cabbage, and toss to coat. Sprinkle with sesame seeds and serve.

Kangkong Pomegranate Salad

GENZO GONZALES, age 11 in 2013

"I wanted to feature locally grown produce that is abundant most everywhere in my island's villages, but more importantly is healthy and affordable," writes Genzo. "Our parents always remind us to eat the seasonal fruits and vegetables around us because they are locally grown naturally and are healthy and free from preservatives and chemicals. I would serve along with it a fresh and tropical coconut-avocado shake. I also enjoy fresh papaya salad." To make it heartier, add turkey breast, as well as chunks of avocado.

Makes 2 servings

INGREDIENTS

1/2 cup pomegranate seeds or dried cranberries

1/2 cup freshly and roughly grated young coconut, or shredded unsweetened coconut

1 large guava, cut into bite-size pieces

1/2 cup cherry tomatoes, cut in half

2 cups freshly cut young sprouting kangkong leaves, or spinach

Juice of 1 tangerine

1 teaspoon olive oil

1 teaspoon honey

Salt and freshly ground black pepper

PREPARATION

1. In a large bowl, stir together the pomegranate seeds or dried cranberries, coconut, guava, tomatoes, and kangkong leaves or spinach.

2. In a small bowl, whisk together the tangerine juice, oil, honey, salt, and pepper.

3. Pour the dressing over the salad and toss to coat. Serve and enjoy.

209 calories; 3g protein; 31g carbohydrates; 10g fat (6g saturated fat); 120mg sodium

Chef Claire Park,

age 9 in 2015

"My parents grew up in Korea. My father said many Koreans believe eating five colored foods a day is the best way to maintain our general health," says Claire. "I like colored food also. The best purple food is purple potatoes, especially the ones grown on Rota, one of the Northern Mariana Islands. They are really pretty and yummy. I think I am pretty healthy because of colored foods."

Rota Sweet Potato Salad with Grilled Chicken Breast

Makes 2 Servings • 518 calories • 19g fat • 68g carbohydrates • 24g protein

---

INGREDIENTS

2 purple or regular sweet potatoes, peeled and halved lengthwise
¼ cup nuts, crushed
¼ cup dried cranberries
¼ cup cooked corn
¼ cup plain yogurt
2 tablespoons mustard
1 tablespoon honey
1 large skinless, boneless chicken breast
Pinch salt and pepper
1 teaspoon dried basil
1 tablespoon lime juice
1 tablespoon olive oil
1 tablespoon honey
2 teaspoons low-sodium soy sauce

PREPARATION

1. **In a steamer set** in a large pot of boiling water, steam the sweet potatoes for about 20 minutes, or until tender.
2. **In a large bowl,** mash the potatoes. Add the nuts, cranberries, corn, yogurt, mustard, and honey.
3. **Preheat the grill to medium-high.** Sprinkle the chicken with salt, pepper, and basil and grill, turning once, about 5 minutes per side, or until cooked through. Cut the chicken in half.
4. **Meanwhile, in a small bowl,** whisk together the lime juice, olive oil, honey, and soy sauce.
5. **Divide** the sweet potato salad and grilled chicken breast between 2 plates. Drizzle the chicken with the lime-soy sauce and serve.

CHEF

Fanai Staffler

age 9 in 2016

"This recipe was inspired by my mom's workouts and the diverse cultures that live in our community," says Fanai. "The coleslaw is like our community—full of different flavors from all of the different cultures that live here."

Chicken Kebab Lettuce Wraps

Makes 4 servings • 422 calories • 12g fat • 60g carbohydrates • 19g protein

INGREDIENTS

For the Chicken Kebabs:

2 ½ cups water
1 cup brown rice
½ pound ground chicken
½ teaspoon cumin
½ teaspoon garlic powder
½ teaspoon salt
1 tablespoon fresh lemon juice
3 tablespoons chopped parsley
1 egg
¼ cup breadcrumbs

For the Coleslaw:

¼ cup bell pepper, seeded and thinly sliced
¼ cup finely chopped celery
½ green apple, peeled and thinly sliced
¼ cup sliced grapes
½ cup peas
¼ onion, peeled and thinly sliced
¼ cup carrot, peeled and thinly sliced
¼ cup raisins
¼ cup low-fat plain yogurt
¼ cup low-fat mayonnaise
Salt and freshly ground black pepper

To Assemble:

Nonstick spray
8 romaine lettuce leaves

PREPARATION

1. **To make the Chicken Kebabs:** In a large stockpot, boil water with the rice over medium-high heat, cover, reduce heat to low, and simmer for 45 minutes, or until tender and water has been absorbed. Preheat the oven to 350°F. In a large bowl, combine all the kebab ingredients, and using your hands, form into 4 patties and place on a large non-stick baking sheet. Bake for 40 minutes, or until golden brown.
2. **To make the Coleslaw:** In a large mixing bowl, combine all of the ingredients and mix well.
3. **To Assemble:** Place patty on top of lettuce leaves and top with coleslaw.

Ohio

Shredded Veggie Wrap

Logan Kendall, age 11 in 2012

"I came up with this idea one Memorial Day. My grandma made a Veggie Pizza, and when I heard about this contest, I made up my own wrap," says Logan. "I would serve grapes or carrots with this."

Makes 3 servings

INGREDIENTS

8 ounces low-fat cream cheese

½ teaspoon fresh flat-leaf parsley, minced

½ cup light mayonnaise

½ cup diced onions

¼ cup diced green bell pepper

¼ cup diced celery

1/8 teaspoon each salt and pepper

3 multigrain wraps

1 (12-ounce) bag broccoli slaw (broccoli, carrots, and red cabbage)

12 slices of turkey pepperoni or turkey breast

PREPARATION

1. In a small bowl, thoroughly mix together the cream cheese, parsley, mayonnaise, onions, green bell pepper, celery, salt, and pepper. Divide among the wraps, spreading evenly and not getting too close to the edge. Take ¼ cup of broccoli slaw and place on top of cream cheese spread. Top with 4 slices of turkey pepperoni.
2. Roll the wraps up tight, wrap each in plastic wrap, and refrigerate for at least 1 hour or serve at room temperature.

Kickin' Colorful Bell Peppers Stuffed with Quinoa

ANISHA PATEL, age 11 in 2013

"I came up with this recipe by watching my mom cook a lot of healthy vegetarian dishes that had a little kick to them with some spice," says Anisha. "I love eating lots of different types of fresh vegetables and fruits. For vegetarians my dish can be served with a garden salad and any nice fresh fruit. And for non-vegetarians I would serve it with grilled chicken or any other protein and fruit on the side."

Makes 4 to 6 servings

INGREDIENTS

For the pesto:

1 cup roughly chopped fresh cilantro leaves

1/4 cup olive oil

1/4 cup pine nuts

2 cloves garlic, peeled and mashed

2 tablespoons freshly squeezed lime juice

2 tablespoons freshly grated Parmesan

1/2 teaspoon crushed red pepper (add more if you want it spicier)

Salt and freshly ground black pepper

For the filling:

1 cup cooked quinoa

1 (16-ounce) can chickpeas, drained and thoroughly rinsed

1/3 cup diced tomatoes

1/4 cup diced red onion

1/4 cup diced green bell pepper

1/4 cup diced zucchini

1/2 cup freshly grated Parmesan

3 tablespoons panko or plain bread crumbs

Olive oil

For the peppers:

1 green bell pepper, stem and seeds removed

1 red bell pepper, stem and seeds removed

1 orange bell pepper, stem and seeds removed

PREPARATION

Make the pesto:

1. In a blender or food processor, combine the cilantro, olive oil, pine nuts, garlic, lime juice, Parmesan, and crushed red pepper and blend until smooth. Season to taste with salt and pepper. If the pesto is too thick, add a couple more drops of olive oil.

Make the filling:

1. In a large bowl, combine the quinoa, chickpeas, tomatoes, red onion, green bell pepper, and zucchini. Add the pesto, season with salt and pepper, and stir to combine.

2. In a small bowl, stir together the Parmesan, bread crumbs, and a little olive oil to lightly moisten the mixture.

Make the peppers:

1. Preheat the oven to 375°F.

2. Arrange the peppers in a large baking dish and stuff each one with an equal amount of the quinoa-vegetable mixture. Top each pepper with an equal amount of the Parmesan–bread crumb mixture. Pour about 1/4 inch of water into the bottom of the baking dish, cover it with foil, and bake until the peppers are tender, about 20 minutes. Remove the foil and place the peppers under the broiler, broiling just until the Parmesan–bread crumb mixture is light golden brown.

371 calories; 11g protein; 19g carbohydrates; 27g fat (7g saturated fat); 332mg sodium

Abigail Cornwell, age 9 in 2014

"I came up with my recipe because I love Italian food, and wanted to share my recipe with everyone!" says Abigail. "I love fresh ingredients, especially in the summertime, going to the farmers' market with my mom to shop. I have included my 'sunshine' in the recipe, and it is a tangerine with fresh strawberries. I also included a lean protein, whole grain pasta, spinach as my vegetable."

Makes 8 servings • 468 calories • 17g fat • 39g carbohydrates • 24g protein

SUNRISE TUSCAN CHICKEN

INGREDIENTS

♥ For Chicken:
2 tablespoons olive oil
1 pound skinless, boneless chicken breasts
Handful fresh basil leaves
Juice of 1 lemon
♥ For Pasta & Sauce:
1 pound whole-wheat penne pasta
3 tablespoons olive oil
2 minced garlic cloves
2½ cups low-sodium chicken broth
1 pint cherry tomatoes, halved
1 lemon, thinly sliced
3 cups fresh spinach, stems removed
½ teaspoon salt
½ teaspoon pepper
⅓ cup grated Parmesan cheese
♥ For Sunrise:
3 tangelos, halved
6 large strawberries, sliced

PREPARATION

Place chicken in a large plastic resealable bag. Add basil, lemon juice, and olive oil. Place in the refrigerator for 20 minutes to marinate.

In a large sauté pan, warm the olive oil over moderate heat. Add the chicken and cook, stirring often, for 10 minutes, or until fully cooked. Set aside, let cool, and then slice.

In the meantime, bring a large pot of water to a boil, and cook pasta until al dente, about 8 minutes. Drain and set aside.

In a large sauté pan on medium-low heat, warm the remaining tablespoon of olive oil. Add the garlic and cook for 2 minutes. Add the chicken broth, cherry tomatoes, lemon, spinach, and salt and pepper and cook for 5 minutes or until the broth is reduced by half. Add the pasta and stir. Serve pasta with sliced chicken and a sprinkle of Parmesan cheese. Place the tangelo on the plate, face up, and add strawberry slices around to create the sun!

Chef Sydney Mazik,

age 12 in 2015

"My mom and I created this recipe five years ago while having to live in Florida (my surgeon is there) for five months due to my surgery," says Sydney. "We were always trying new recipes and cooking a lot because I was in a wheelchair then. We have always eaten spaghetti squash in our house and I had asked my doctors, nurses, and therapists if they had ever tried it, but most of them had not even heard of it. We decided to come up with a dish for them to try and they loved it! It was so popular that I made it at least once a week as well as every surgery since. My nickname is now S.S. Sydney." (S.S. stands for spaghetti squash.)

S.S. Asparagus Pie

Makes 6 to 8 Servings • 151 calories 8g fat • 10g carbohydrates • 11g protein

---

INGREDIENTS

1 spaghetti squash, halved and seeds removed
2 teaspoons olive oil
½ cup peeled and diced yellow onion
1 bunch asparagus, ends removed, cut into 1-inch pieces
3 garlic cloves, peeled and minced
5 large eggs
1 cup low-fat or skim milk
1 cup shredded low-fat cheese
Salt and pepper to taste

PREPARATION

1. **Preheat the oven to 400°F** and grease a 9-inch cake or pie pan. Place the squash, cut side up, on a large baking sheet, and bake for about 50 minutes, or until tender. Set aside to cool slightly.
2. **In a large sauté pan,** heat the olive oil over medium heat. Add the onion and sauté for 3 minutes. Add the asparagus and garlic and sauté for about 5 minutes, or until the asparagus is soft and bright green. Remove from the heat and set aside to cool.
3. **In a large bowl**, whisk together the eggs, milk, cheese, salt, and pepper, then add the cooled onion-asparagus mixture and stir to combine.
4. **Using a fork,** scrape the strands from the spaghetti squash and transfer to the bottom and sides of the greased cake pan, creating an even crust. Press paper towels onto the crust to remove any excess moisture (or you can wring the squash out ahead of time). Pour the egg mixture onto the "crust" and bake for 40 minutes, or until the pie is firm and not wiggly. Enjoy!

CHEF

Wyatt Rosengarten

age 9 in 2016

"Wyatt loves pizza, but his grandmother is gluten free and can't join us for build-your-own-pizza night," says Wyatt's mom, Tiffany. "He found a recipe for a cauliflower crust, but decided it needed to taste more like a seasoned flatbread crust. The flavor of the pizza was amazing since he added his own blend of spices into the crust. Serving it with a salad and fruit smoothie is our favorite way to have lunch."

Chicken Sausage Cauliflower Crust Pizza

Makes 4 servings • 398 calories • 22g fat • 20g carbohydrates • 32g protein

INGREDIENTS

For the Crust:

1 cauliflower, stemmed and roughly chopped
1 tablespoon olive oil, plus more for drizzling
1 tablespoon minced onion
2 garlic cloves, peeled and minced
1 teaspoon dried oregano
2 tablespoons Parmesan cheese
¼ cup shredded low-fat mozzarella cheese
2 egg whites

For the Sauce:

1 15-ounce can tomato sauce
2 garlic cloves, peeled and minced
2 tablespoons minced fresh onion
1 teaspoon dried parsley
1 ½ teaspoon dried oregano
1 tablespoon grated Parmesan cheese
½ teaspoon dried basil

For the Sausage:

1 pound ground chicken
½ teaspoon black pepper
½ teaspoon dried parsley
½ teaspoon Italian seasoning
½ teaspoon garlic powder
½ teaspoon fennel seed
½ teaspoon paprika
½ teaspoon onion powder
1 teaspoon sea salt
1 tablespoon olive oil

Toppings:

½ cup shredded low-fat mozzarella cheese
Optional Toppings:
green pepper slices, mushrooms,
olives, onions, tomatoes, spinach

PREPARATION

1. **To make the Crust: Preheat the oven to 375°F.** In a food processor, add the cauliflower in sections and pulse 10 times until it has a rice-like consistency. Place into a dry dishcloth, squeeze and wring out any water into the sink. Pour out on a parchment-lined baking sheet and drizzle with olive oil. Bake for 25 minutes, or until dry and lightly golden. Remove and cool. In a large mixing bowl, add cauliflower and remaining crust ingredients. Mix together until dough forms, then press mixture into two 8-inch circles on the parchment-lined baking sheet. Drizzle with olive oil if desired. Turn oven up to 450°F and bake for 20 minutes.

2. **To make the Sauce:** In a large stockpot, combine all ingredients, stir, and cook over medium heat for 20 minutes.

3. **To make the Sausage:** In a large mixing bowl, combine all of the ingredients except the olive oil. In a large nonstick skillet, warm the olive oil over medium heat. Add the chicken mixture and cook, stirring, for 10 minutes, or until cooked through and starting to brown.

4. **To Assemble:** To each crust, add 3 tablespoons sauce, any toppings, sausage, and ¼ cup mozzarella cheese. Return to oven and bake 8 minutes, or until cheese is melted and toppings warm. Cut into 4 slices and enjoy.

Oklahoma

Power Pesto Pasta

Harrison Booker, age 9 in 2012

"I like garlic so much I decided to make pesto, and now I like to eat Power Pesto Pasta," says Harrison. "After Thanksgiving I plant my garlic in our garden. I like to plant as much garlic as I can. In the spring I grow basil in our backyard in pots. In the summer we have basil that is ready to be picked and garlic ready to pull out of the ground. The spinach puts Power in the Pesto!"

Makes 4 servings

INGREDIENTS

8 ounces whole-wheat pasta, such as rotelle

3 cups loosely packed fresh basil

1 1/4 cups fresh baby spinach leaves

2 tablespoons walnuts or pine nuts

1 garlic clove, peeled

¼ cup plus 1 tablespoon extra-virgin olive oil

3 tablespoons freshly grated Parmigiano-Reggiano cheese

Pinch of salt

1/4 teaspoon black pepper

1 cup sliced yellow squash

½ cup halved cherry tomatoes

1 cup halved green beans

PREPARATION

1. In a large pot of boiling salted water, cook the pasta until al dente, about 6 minutes.
2. While the past is cooking, in a food processor or blender, blend the basil, spinach, walnuts or pine nuts, garlic, 1/4 cup of olive oil, Parmigiano-Reggiano, salt, and pepper. If it's too thick, add a few more teaspoons of olive oil.
3. In a large saucepan over moderate heat, warm the remaining 1 tablespoon olive oil, then cook the squash, cherry tomatoes, and green beans until soft and slightly brown, about 4 minutes. Add the cooked pasta and the pesto, and stir to combine.
4. Divide the pasta, veggies, and pesto among four bowls and serve.

Taco de Camarón

OGDEN JOHNSON, age 10 in 2013

"One of my favorite foods is shrimp and we eat a lot of tacos," says Ogden. "We like to eat it with corn tortillas because they are gluten-free. My other favorite food is broccoli and I like that I can heat it up all by myself. Pico de gallo is what my dad always makes with tacos and I love the fresh cilantro from our garden. He leaves the jalapeños out of mine. Cheese and sour cream are both good on tacos, too."

Makes 6 servings

INGREDIENTS

For the pico de gallo:

6 medium plum tomatoes, diced

1/2 medium red onion, minced

3 tablespoons chopped fresh cilantro leaves

1/2 jalapeño, seeded and minced (optional)

Juice of 1/2 lime

1 clove garlic, minced

1 pinch garlic powder

1 pinch ground cumin

Salt and freshly ground black pepper

For the shrimp tacos:

2 tablespoons olive oil

2 pounds shrimp, peeled and deveined

1/4 cup water

1 1/2 teaspoons chili powder

1 1/4 teaspoons paprika

1 1/4 teaspoons ground cumin

1 teaspoon onion powder

1 teaspoon salt

1/2 teaspoon garlic powder

1/2 head of fresh broccoli

12 corn tortillas

PREPARATION

Make the pico de gallo:

1. In a medium bowl, stir together the tomatoes, red onion, cilantro, jalapeño, lime juice, fresh garlic, garlic powder, cumin, salt, and pepper. Cover and chill in the refrigerator for at least 3 hours before serving.

Make the shrimp tacos:

1. In a medium sauté pan over moderate heat, warm the oil. Add the shrimp, water, chili powder, paprika, cumin, onion powder, salt, and garlic powder and sauté, stirring occasionally, until the shrimp is no longer pink, about 5 minutes.

2. In a microwave-safe dish, steam the broccoli in the microwave until tender, about 3 minutes.

3. Warm the corn tortillas in the microwave.

4. Divide the shrimp mixture among the tortillas and serve with broccoli and pico de gallo.

238 calories; 33g protein; 18g carbohyrates; 3g fat (.5g saturated fat); 790mg sodium

Ranger Lemaster, age 8 in 2014

"My kids love any snacks with dip," says Ranger's mom, Ashley. "We came up with this recipe as a healthy alternative to some of the chip-and-dip options out there. It is just as good with baked tortilla chips or whole-grain pita wedges as it is with celery sticks. We would include a side of fresh fruit, as this recipe lacks nothing else. The spices give it the extra kick, and the sunflower seeds give it a salty crunch and a boost of lean protein."

Makes 8-10 appetizer servings • 314 calories • 8g fat • 41g carbohydrates • 18g protein

CHEF RANGER

SMOKY SOUTHWESTERN VEGETABLE DIP

INGREDIENTS

4 whole-grain pitas
Baked corn tortilla chips
Grape seed oil or olive oil, for drizzling
Himalayan pink salt or any sea salt or coarse salt to taste
1 (16-ounce) container of low-fat cottage cheese, drained
1 (15-ounce) can black beans, rinsed and drained
1 (15-ounce) can sweet whole kernel corn, rinsed and drained
½ cup peeled and seeded cucumber, chopped
½ red bell pepper, seeded and chopped
Juice of 1 lime
1 teaspoon chili powder
½ teaspoon smoked paprika
½ teaspoon ground cumin
1 small avocado, cubed
¼ cup roasted salted sunflower seeds
Celery Sticks

PREPARATION

To make the crisps: Preheat the oven to 375°F. Cut pita wedges and corn tortillas into bite-size wedges and lightly sprinkle with oil and salt. Bake in oven for 10 minutes, turning over after 5 minutes. Let cool.

In a large bowl, mix cottage cheese, black beans, corn, cucumber, and red pepper. Add the lime and spices, stir and refrigerate for about 15 minutes. Add avocado and sunflower seeds just before serving.

M‘eggs’ican Quesadillas with Pineapple Dipping Sauce

Makes 8 Servings • 591 calories • 29g fat • 53g carbohydrates • 33g protein

INGREDIENTS

1 cup plain Greek yogurt
¾ cup crushed pineapple, drained
2 tablespoons olive oil, plus more as needed
½ cup diced red bell pepper
1 cup chopped fresh spinach
¾ cup diced tomato
½ cup canned black beans, rinsed and drained
8 large eggs
½ avocado diced
16 whole-wheat flour tortillas
1 (16-ounce) package shredded low-fat hot pepper jack cheese

PREPARATION

1. **In a medium bowl,** combine the Greek yogurt and crushed pineapple and set aside.
2. **In a large sauté pan,** heat 1 tablespoon of the olive oil over medium heat. Add the red bell pepper and sauté for about 2 minutes. Add the spinach and stir for 1 minute. Add the tomato, beans, and eggs and cook, stirring, until the eggs are scrambled. Turn off the heat, add the avocado, and stir to combine.
3. **In another sauté pan,** heat the remaining 1 tablespoon olive oil over medium heat. Place 1 tortilla in the skillet, spread some egg mixture on the tortilla until it's covered, sprinkle the cheese on top of the egg mixture and place another tortilla on top. Cook until the tortilla is a little crispy, then carefully flip it over. Once the other side is a little crispy, place the quesadilla on a cutting board and let it sit for a minute. Using a pizza cutter, slice it into sixths. Repeat with the remaining ingredients to make more quesadillas, adding more oil as necessary.
4. **Serve the quesadillas with** the Greek yogurt-pineapple sauce and a side of fruit for a well-balanced meal!

Chef Riley Higgins,

age 9 in 2015

"I tried different recipes out and let my family be my taste testers and decide which one would be best," says Riley. "My mom and dad like our family to eat healthy most of the time, but I don't always like some of the vegetables, so I hid them in the quesadilla so everyone is happy! This dish uses all of the food groups in one dish, but we added some mini fruit kabobs for extra vitamins. I hope you enjoy it!"

Okie Pride Brown Rice with Chicken and Vegetables

Makes 6 servings • 499 calories • 8g fat • 68g carbohydrates • 37g protein

INGREDIENTS

4 cups water
2 cups brown rice
1 tablespoon canola oil
¼ cup chopped onion
1 ½ pounds boneless skinless chicken breast, cut into small pieces
3 garlic cloves, peeled and minced
1 teaspoon grated fresh ginger
¼ teaspoon turmeric
½ teaspoon salt
¼ teaspoon freshly ground black pepper
½ teaspoon cayenne pepper
1 teaspoon paprika
2 cups frozen mixed veggies
1 cup black-eyed peas, rinsed and drained
½ cup diced tomatoes
3 cups fresh spinach
1 cup garbanzo beans, rinsed and drained
½ cup diced red or green bell pepper
1 bunch fresh cilantro
½ cup chopped pecans (optional)

PREPARATION

1. **In a large stockpot,** combine water with the rice and bring to a boil over medium-high heat. Reduce the heat to low, cover, and simmer for 45 minutes or until the rice is tender. Set aside.
2. **Meanwhile,** in a large nonstick skillet, warm the oil over medium heat. Add the onion and chicken and cook for about 7 minutes, or until chicken is cooked through and onions are softened. Add the garlic, ginger, turmeric, salt, pepper, cayenne pepper, and paprika, and continue cooking for about 10 minutes. Add the mixed vegetables, black-eyed peas, tomatoes, spinach, garbanzo beans, and pepper and cook for an additional 5 minutes. Add the cooked brown rice and mix thoroughly. Sprinkle on pecans and cilantro as a garnish (optional).

CHEF

Maya Jacob

age 10 in 2016

"I'm a first generation-born American and proud to be born and raised in the great state of Oklahoma," says Maya. "I wanted to create a recipe that represents my Pakistani heritage and my lovely state's homegrown products. My inspirations to cook healthy are my precious 14-year-old twin brothers who have cerebral palsy and also a severe seizure disorder. We found out that certain foods or even too many carbs or sugar can trigger seizures. I thought, wow, if we can help reduce their seizures just by what they eat, then I will definitely help prepare recipes for them. I had no idea that food played that big a part in our health. Ever since we decided to start eating healthy we noticed a huge decrease in their seizures and a bonus is I can focus much better at school."

Oregon

Veggie Pizza

Robert Robinson, age 9 in 2012

Robbie's mom Cassie learned how to make a dessert fruit pizza and began making a vegetable version for her family, including her son Robert. "My children have their own favorite toppings, and we change these based on the season, what is available locally and at our farmer's market. Any of the herbs or vegetables you can grow in your own garden make this more fun to make," she says. The family uses an already-baked thin-crust pizza and puts their just-picked veggies on the pizza. This version is a more traditional way of making pizza, but the Robinsons' version is great for summer evenings, as you don't turn the oven on.

Makes 6 servings

INGREDIENTS

1 (12-inch) thin store-bought pizza crust

1 tablespoon olive oil

2 cups finely chopped broccoli florets

6 scallions, white and light green parts only, chopped

2 cups local mushrooms, trimmed and sliced

3 small green zucchini, trimmed and chopped

3 small yellow squash, trimmed and chopped

12 grape tomatoes, halved

1/2 cup reduced-fat cream cheese

2 tablespoons 1 percent milk or rice milk

1/2 cup pitted, sliced black olives

½ cup minced fresh basil

½ cup minced chives

1/2 cup shredded Parmesan

PREPARATION

1. Preheat the oven to 425°F. Lightly oil a large baking sheet or get out a pizza stone.
2. Cook the pizza crust on the pan or stone until lightly brown on top, about 10 minutes.
3. While the crust is baking, in a large sauté pan over moderate heat, warm the olive oil. Add the broccoli, scallions, mushrooms, zucchini, squash, and tomatoes, and cook until just tender, about 5 minutes.
4. Remove the pizza crust from the oven and let cool for 5 minutes, leaving the oven on. In a small bowl, whisk together the cream cheese and milk. Spread on the pizza crust, leaving a ½-inch border, and top with the vegetables, olives, basil, chives, and Parmesan. Bake until the cheese is bubbling and lightly brown, about 10 minutes. Serve hot or cold.

Salmon Fried Rice

AUDREY RUSSELL, age 10 in 2013

"We eat a lot of salmon in Oregon because it is a super healthy and delicious local fish," says Audrey. "Fried rice makes a great lunch because it combines protein, grains, and veggies all in one meal. I can even take it in my lunch box! My favorite thing to make with it is Caprese salad. My mom lets me cut cherry tomatoes in half and mix them with fresh mozzarella, basil, and olive oil to serve with the fried rice. We don't have dessert at lunch, but Greek yogurt, honey, and berries would be good."

Makes 4 servings

INGREDIENTS

2 tablespoons oil

1 tablespoon minced ginger or garlic

2 medium carrots, diced

1 cup chopped fresh vegetables such as red bell pepper, broccoli, asparagus, or snow peas

2 cups flaked cooked salmon

3 cups cooked and chilled brown rice

2 tablespoons gluten-free soy sauce or tamari

Chopped fresh cilantro leaves for garnish (optional)

PREPARATION

1. In a large nonstick sauté pan over moderately high heat, warm the oil. Add the ginger or garlic and sauté, stirring occasionally, until sizzling. Add the carrots and the vegetables of your choice and sauté, stirring occasionally, until they start to soften, about 3 minutes. Add the salmon and cook until heated through, about 2 minutes. Add the rice and soy sauce and continue to cook until the rice is hot. Top with cilantro, if using, and serve.

552 calories; 34g protein; 41g carbohydrates; 23g fat (5g saturated fat); 750mg sodium

HEALTHY STUFFED RAINBOW PEPPERS

INGREDIENTS

♥ For the Stuffed Bell Peppers:

2 tablespoons coconut oil

½ yellow onion, peeled and chopped

4 minced garlic cloves

1 pound ground turkey

½ cup fresh basil leaves, chopped

4 medium bell peppers, tops removed and seeded

Parmesan cheese to sprinkle on top

Salt and pepper to taste

♥ For the Israeli Couscous:

1 box of Israeli couscous

1 (16-ounce) container low-sodium chicken broth

1½ cups cannellini beans, rinsed and drained

4 grape tomatoes, halved

1½ cups spinach, chopped

¼ cup Parmesan cheese

PREPARATION

To make the Stuffed Bell Peppers: Preheat your oven to 350°F. In a large sauté pan, warm the oil over moderate heat. Add the onion and garlic and cook until onions are soft, about 3 minutes. Add the turkey and cook, stirring often, for 10 minutes, until the turkey is cooked. Add in the basil. Stuff the peppers and sprinkle cheese on top. Season with salt and pepper. Place the peppers in a 9-by-9-inch baking pan and bake for 20 minutes.

To make the Israeli Couscous: In a large saucepan, cook the couscous with the broth according to the directions. Add the beans and tomatoes and let sit, covered, for 5 minutes. Meantime, put the spinach in a large bowl. Pour the couscous on top of the spinach and stir it in gently. Add in the cheese and stir once more. Serve with the stuffed peppers.

Grace Wetzler, age 12 in 2014

"My lunch is a variety of color, flavor, and fun. Looking down at the plate it is like a rainbow," says Grace. "I am a strong believer that a meal should look good and taste good. It should please your eyes and your stomach. This was an easy lunch I whipped up in no time." Grace likes to finish the meal with Greek yogurt with fresh fruit and a drizzle of honey.

Makes 8 servings • 392 calories • 10g fat • 40g carbohydrates • 27g protein

Phoebe's Phish Tacos with Kale Chips

Makes 4 to 8 servings • 759 calories • 40g fat • 36g carbohydrates • 78g protein

INGREDIENTS

For the Tacos:

1 pound asparagus, tough ends removed
1 tablespoon naval orange juice
¼ cup olive oil
1 pound or 4 fillets salmon
½ teaspoon garlic powder
¼ teaspoon salt
8 corn tortillas
2 avocados, halved and pitted
Juice from ½ lime
¼ teaspoon salt
¼ cup chopped fresh cilantro
4 ounces shredded low-fat mozzarella cheese
Blueberries, optional

For the Kale Chips:

½ pound curly kale, stalks discarded and leaves torn into bite-sized pieces
1 tablespoon olive oil
Sea salt to taste

PREPARATION

1. **Preheat the oven to 400°F** and line a baking sheet with parchment paper. Spread the asparagus on the baking sheet, drizzle with the orange juice and 1 tablespoon olive oil, and toss to coat. Roast for 8 to 10 minutes and set aside.
2. **To make the Kale Chips:** Once the asparagus is done, reduce the oven temperature to 250°F. In a large bowl, combine the kale with 2 tablespoons olive oil and salt and toss to evenly coat. Arrange in single layer on a baking sheet and bake for about 25 minutes, or until crisp.
3. **To make the Salmon:** Sprinkle the salmon fillets with garlic powder and salt. In a large sauté pan, heat the remaining 1 tablespoon olive oil over medium heat. Add the salmon and cook, flipping once, about 5 minutes per side, or until the fish flakes when touched by a fork. Cut each fillet in half.
4. **Warm** the tortillas in the microwave.
5. **In a medium bowl,** mash the avocadoes with a fork. Add the lime juice and salt and continue to mash until you get the desired texture. Stir in the cilantro.
6. **To assemble,** place 2 small pieces of salmon, and 2 pieces of asparagus inside each warm tortilla. Sprinkle with cheese then top with homemade guacamole. Arrange on a plate with kale chips and blueberries. Enjoy!

Chef Phoebe Garrett,

age 11 in 2015

"My inspiration for this is also my favorite story. I was at a barbecue while on vacation and set my eyes on my first suckling pig," says Phoebe. "The sight convinced me to become a vegetarian. After studying with my parents about vegetarianism and how much protein my body needs, I decided that I would eat fish and chicken, but not mammals. Making this choice has forced us to find creative protein options. Fish is both high in protein and the good types of fats we need."

All Kale Caesar!

Makes 4 servings • 462 calories • 34g fat • 21g carbohydrates • 20g protein

INGREDIENTS

4 slices whole-wheat bread, cut into ½-inch cubes
¼ cup olive oil, plus 3 tablespoons
½ teaspoon salt, truffle flavor or regular
Freshly ground black pepper
8 ounces salmon fillets
1 head kale (about 5 cups), stems removed, cut into bite-sized pieces
1 tablespoon Worcestershire sauce
Juice of ½ fresh lemon
2 tablespoons grated Parmesan cheese
¼ cup chopped black olives
1 egg

PREPARATION

1. **Preheat the oven to 275°F.** In a large bowl, combine bread cubes with 2 tablespoons of olive oil, salt, and pepper. Bake for 15 minutes or until golden and dry.
2. **Meanwhile,** season the salmon with salt and pepper. In a nonstick skillet, warm 1 tablespoon of olive oil over medium heat, add the salmon skin-side down and cook for 5 minutes, turn over and cook 2 minutes more, or until salmon is firm. Remove skin.
3. **In a large salad bowl,** add the kale. Place the whole uncracked egg into a cup with hot water and let sit for 5 minutes. In a small bowl, whisk together remaining ¼ cup olive oil, Worcestershire sauce, lemon juice, salt, and pepper. Crack the egg into the dressing and whisk until combined. Add the dressing to the kale and massage in so that the kale is well coated. Flake the salmon and add to the kale along with Parmesan, olives, and croutons. Toss well to combine.

CHEF

Hannah Conte

age 12 in 2016

"This recipe is for hungry kids who like salad and want to make it a meal," says Hannah. "In this recipe, I've added protein (salmon) and a heartier base (kale) to turn one of my favorite dishes into a satisfying meal. Every year my grandma serves Caesar salad as a starter on Christmas Eve. I request Caesar salads for my special meals and as I've grown, I make the salad myself. I was inspired to create All Kale Caesar so that my favorite salad wasn't just a side dish—it's a satisfying meal. I hope you enjoy this salad as much as I do!"

Pennsylvania

Falafel Wrap with Apple, Carrot & Cranberry Slaw

Evan Clark, age 9 in 2012

Evan's mom, Jami, reports that they have always enjoyed cooking together. "I knew he liked hummus, so I introduced this version of falafel that was not deep-fried," she says. "I offered to make this in pita, but he said he preferred it in a tortilla, which he then assembled with his favorite toppings! We made a healthy, sweet salad to serve on the side as a complement."

Makes 2 servings

INGREDIENTS

1 (15-ounce) can garbanzo beans (chickpeas), drained and rinsed

1 small red onion, finely chopped

3 garlic cloves, minced

1/4 cup chopped fresh cilantro

¼ cup plus 2 tablespoons sesame tahini

3 tablespoons lemon juice

2 tablespoons plus 1 teaspoon olive oil

1 1/2 teaspoon ground cumin

1 teaspoon ground coriander

1/4 teaspoon cayenne pepper

1 teaspoon baking powder

2 tablespoons flour, if necessary

Kosher salt

1/4 cup plain nonfat yogurt

2 large multigrain tortillas

1 tomato, thinly sliced

½ cup arugula or fresh baby spinach

1 medium carrot, peeled and shredded

Fresh cilantro (optional)

PREPARATION

1. In a medium bowl, mash the beans with a fork. Add the onion, 2 garlic cloves, cilantro, 2 tablespoons tahini, 1 tablespoon lemon juice, 1 teaspoon olive oil, cumin, coriander, cayenne powder, and baking powder. If the mix is too wet or dry, adjust with flour or water, 1 teaspoon at a time. Season to taste with salt.

2. In a large skillet over moderate heat, warm the remaining 2 tablespoons olive oil. Form the bean mixture into four patties and cook, flipping, until lightly browned on both sides, about 6 minutes total. Cut each patty in half.

3. While the patties are cooking, in a small bowl, combine the yogurt, the remaining ¼ cup tahini, and the remaining 2 tablespoons lemon juice.

4. Place the wraps on individual plates and top with the patties, tomatoes, arugula, carrot, cilantro, and some yogurt-tahini sauce. Roll up the wrap, and slice in half for easier eating.

Lentil-Spinach Soup and Mint Chutney

GANESH SELVAKUMAR, age 9 in 2013

"When I was younger, I would love to play with lentils until I realized from my mom that they are very nutritious," says Ganesh. "I love green vegetables and decided to make a new recipe with vegetables and lentils. Last summer my mom and I planted a few mint plants in our garden. I loved to eat the fresh leaves. I don't want to waste those precious leaves and came up with a mint recipe with lentils. I would serve this with 2 cups of rice, a glass of 2% milk, and a bowl of berries with ½ cup yogurt."

Makes 6 servings

INGREDIENTS

For the mint chutney:

1/2 cup soaked dried split chickpeas

1 teaspoon olive oil

2 cups packed fresh mint leaves

1 cup chopped onion

2 fresh green chiles, seeded and thinly sliced

1 clove garlic, minced

1 teaspoon tamarind paste

1/2 teaspoon salt

1/2 cup water

For the lentil soup:

2 cups cooked red lentils

2 cups chopped spinach

1/4 cup chopped onions

1/2 teaspoon salt

6 cups water

1 teaspoon olive oil

2 fresh green chiles, seeded and thinly sliced

1/4 teaspoon mustard seed

1/4 teaspoon crushed red pepper

Pinch of turmeric

Pinch of cumin seeds

PREPARATION

Make the mint chutney:

1. In a medium bowl, soak the split chickpeas in 4 cups of water for 30 minutes. Drain the chickpeas and set aside.

2. While the chickpeas are soaking, in a small sauté pan over low heat, warm the oil. Add the mint, onion, green chiles, and garlic and sauté, stirring occasionally, for 3 minutes. Remove the pan from the heat and let the mixture cool. Transfer to a blender, add the tamarind paste and salt along with the soaked chickpeas and ½ cup water and blend to make a paste.

Make the lentil soup:

1. In a large saucepan over moderate heat, combine the red lentils, spinach, onion, and salt and cook for 10 minutes. Add the 6 cups of water, reduce heat to low, and simmer for 20 minutes.

2. While the soup is simmering, in a small sauté pan over low heat, warm the oil. Add the green chiles, mustard seed, crushed red pepper, turmeric, and cumin seeds and toast, stirring, until the mustard seeds pop, about 2 minutes. Stir the spice mixture into the soup, divide the soup among bowls, and top with the mint chutney.

352 calories; 23g protein; 58g carbohydrates; 4g fat (.5g saturated fat); 452mg sodium

SEAFOOD TACOS WITH LIME COLESLAW & PEACHY SALSA

INGREDIENTS

♥ For the Fish:
5 fresh tilapia fillets
15 medium (20 count) shrimp, shelled and deveined
1 tablespoon olive oil
⅛ teaspoon garlic powder
¼ teaspoon ground cumin
3 tablespoons low-fat mayonnaise
1 teaspoon fresh lime juice
2 cups shredded cabbage and carrots
5 whole-grain tortilla shells
♥ For the Peach Nectarine Salsa:
½ cup diced fresh peaches
¼ cup diced fresh nectarines
½ medium red sweet pepper, seeded and finely chopped
2 tablespoons thinly sliced scallions
½ jalapeño chile pepper, seeded and finely chopped
1¼ teaspoons olive oil
¼ teaspoon fresh lime zest
1¼ teaspoons fresh lime juice
1¼ teaspoons vinegar
¼ teaspoon salt
⅛ teaspoon black pepper

PREPARATION

Preheat the oven to 450°F. Rinse fish and shrimp and pat dry with paper towels. Place fish and shrimp in a greased shallow baking dish. In a small bowl, combine olive oil, garlic powder, and cumin and brush mixture over both sides of fish. Bake for about 6 minutes, turn over, and bake for another 5 minutes or until the fish flakes easily with a fork. With fork, break fillets into smaller pieces and chop shrimp.

In a small bowl, combine mayonnaise and lime juice. Add cabbage/carrot mix and toss to coat.

In a small bowl, combine all salsa ingredients and mix together.

To assemble tacos, warm tortillas, wrapped in damp paper towels, in microwave for 45 seconds, and top each with a fifth of the fish, shrimp, some of the coleslaw and salsa, and grilled asparagus.

Hannah Foley, age 10 in 2014

"I love to cook, and hope to one day be a chef with my own show on the Food Network called *H to the F to the Hannah Foley Chef*," says Hannah. "Our family really loves seafood, and we try to eat healthy. My recipe includes whole grains with a whole-wheat tortilla; lean protein with tilapia fillets and shrimp; veggies in the coleslaw, salsa, and side of grilled asparagus; and fruit with the peaches and nectarines in the salsa."

Makes 5 servings • 351 calories • 15g fat • 18g carbohydrates • 39g protein

CHEF HANNAH

Chef Sydney Tyner,

age 11 in 2015

"I'm just a normal kid, so when my stepmom got breast cancer I was scared. When I found out we were going to change our eating habits to be healthier I was mad," says Sydney. "But once we started eating healthy, I realized it wasn't a bad thing at all. I love tacos and I came up with this new version so I could still eat healthy and have my favorite food. In the summer we use vegetables out of our own garden. It tastes even better then."

Chicken Taco Tower

Makes 6 Servings • 316 calories • 19g fat • 24g carbohydrates • 17g protein

---

INGREDIENTS

For the Chicken Taco Meat:

2 tablespoons olive oil
⅓ cup peeled and diced onion
⅓ cup diced green bell pepper
1 garlic clove, peeled and minced
1 pound ground chicken
1 tablespoon chili powder
½ teaspoon ground cumin
½ cup fat-free refried beans
1 tablespoon chopped fresh cilantro
¼ teaspoon lime juice
Pinch of salt
6 (6-inch) corn tortillas
Shredded low-fat cheddar cheese, for serving
Shredded romaine lettuce, for serving

For the Corn and Avocado Salsa:

1 ear of corn, shucked
1 avocado, peeled and diced
½ diced tomato
1 tablespoon peeled and minced onion
1 tablespoon chopped fresh cilantro
¾ tablespoon lime juice
Salt to taste

PREPARATION

1. **To make the Chicken Taco Meat:** Preheat the oven to 350°F. In a large nonstick skillet, heat 1 tablespoon of the olive oil over medium heat. Add the onion and bell pepper and sauté for about 3 minutes. Add the garlic and cook for 2 minutes, then add the chicken and cook, breaking the meat up with a wooden spoon, for about 10 minutes, or until the chicken is cooked through. Add the chili powder and cumin and cook for 1 minute. Add ¾ cup water and bring to a boil. Reduce the heat to low and simmer until the water is almost gone. Stir in the refried beans and cook for about 3 minutes, or until the beans are incorporated. Add the cilantro, lime juice, and salt.

2. **Lightly grease** both sides of the tortillas with the remaining 1 tablespoon olive oil and place on a large baking sheet. Bake for 15 minutes, or until crisp.

3. **To make the Corn and Avocado Salsa:** In a medium bowl, combine all the salsa ingredients.

4. **To assemble the Taco Tower:** Divide the turkey-refried bean mixture among the baked tortillas. Top with cheddar cheese and romaine lettuce. Finish with a heaping tablespoon of the corn and avocado salsa.

CHEF

Ava Terosky

age 9 in 2016

"My little sister Caitlin was born with a serious heart problem and got a pacemaker at one day old," says Ava. "My mom, dad, and the doctors were worried, especially because she was a very picky eater, even as a baby! So, my dad and I work hard to create healthy, animal-shaped meals that Caitlin will eat—she loves animals! When my mom told me about this contest, my first thought was making a healthy meal that Caitlin would love, which meant a breakfast-at-lunch theme in the shape of Bo and Sunny Obama. A lot of my ingredients are from Pennsylvania, including the eggs, mushrooms, and fruit. It's shaped like Portuguese Water Dogs because what kid doesn't like breakfast for lunch in the shape of adorable dogs?"

Sunny's Omelette and Bo's Patriotic Parfait

Makes 2 servings • 578 calories • 28g fat • 50g carbohydrates • 35g protein

INGREDIENTS

For the Omelettes:

2 teaspoons olive oil
4 ounces white mushrooms, sliced
4 ounces baby spinach
Sprig fresh thyme,
or pinch dried thyme
Salt and freshly ground black pepper
4 large eggs
2 teaspoons unsalted butter
Ketchup (optional)

For the Patriotic Parfait *(not pictured)*:

1 cup nonfat plain Greek yogurt
1 teaspoon honey or maple syrup
⅔ cup favorite low-sugar granola
6 strawberries, hulled and sliced
1 medium apple,
peeled, cored and sliced
½ cup blueberries

PREPARATION

1. **To make the Omelette Filling:** In a large nonstick skillet, warm the olive oil over medium heat, add the mushrooms and thyme to the pan, and cook for 3 minutes. Add the spinach, salt, and pepper to taste, and cook for 2 minutes, or until the spinach is wilted but still bright green. Transfer to a plate.

2. **To make the Omelettes:** Break 2 eggs into a bowl, add salt and pepper to taste, and whisk with a fork. In the same pan you cooked the veggies in, melt 1 teaspoon of butter over medium heat. Add the eggs to the pan and as they cook, continuously lift and swirl the pan so that the liquid portion of the eggs goes all the way around the edge of the pan to form a circle. Continue cooking about 30 seconds more, then flip using a spatula. You can either add ½ the veggie filling now and fold the eggs over, or do as we do, and cook 30 seconds on the second side, slide the omelettes from pan onto a plate, and top with the filling. Make the second omelettes with the remaining teaspoon butter and two eggs. Cut omelettes into four dog shapes using a large cookie cutter or use any type of cookie cutter. Top each with half of the filling if you didn't do the traditional fill-and-fold method.

3. **To make Patriotic Parfaits:** In two flat bowls, divide the honey and yogurt, and stir to combine. Fill a cookie cutter—we used a dog shape—with granola. Surround with strawberries, apple, and blueberries.

Puerto Rico

Sushi for Kids

Ariana Lugo, age 9 in 2012

Ariana's mom, Tania, says, "Sushi for Kids is a recipe that I have been trying with my kids, and they love it. It's easy to make, healthy, and fun to prepare with the kids," she says. "They usually prepare it and serve a papaya shake on the side."

Makes 1 serving

INGREDIENTS

2 slices oven-roasted ham

4 ounces low-fat cream cheese

1 cup cooked white rice

1/2 avocado, pitted, peeled, and thinly sliced

1 small tomato

PREPARATION

On a plate, evenly spread the cream cheese on the ham slices. Divide the rice between the slices and press it into the cream cheese. Place the avocados and tomatoes in the center of each slice of ham. Roll the ham tightly around the filling, and cut each roll into 4 pieces.

Yummy Eggplant Lasagna Rolls

ALIANA ARZOLA-PIÑERO, age 9 in 2013

"I practice rhythmic gymnastics, and my coaches always talk about the importance of good nutrition. They advise us to eat a balanced diet, including veggies," says Aliana. "My mom loves eggplants. I do not like eggplants that much; they have millions of seeds! However, I do love pasta, so we came up with this recipe: eggplant lasagna rolls. We combined the eggplant with other veggies. We spread the eggplant filling over the lasagna pasta and rolled them up. As a pasta lover, I had to cover the rolls with a bit of tomato sauce and cheese. Yummy! For dessert, we chose fresh clementine oranges."

Makes 6 servings

INGREDIENTS

6 whole-grain lasagna sheets

1/4 cup olive oil

1 small onion, diced

2 cloves garlic, finely chopped

1/4 cup water

2 small eggplants, peeled and diced

2 small carrots, diced

1 red bell pepper, seeded and diced

18 black olives, pitted and finely chopped

1 tablespoon finely chopped fresh cilantro leaves

1/4 teaspoon salt

1 cup shredded low-fat mozzarella cheese

3/4 cup tomato sauce

PREPARATION

1. Preheat the oven to 350°F.

2. In a large pot of boiling water, cook the lasagna until tender, about 7 minutes. Drain the lasagna and let it cool on a flat surface.

3. While the lasagna is boiling, in a large sauté pan over moderate heat, warm the olive oil. Add the onion, garlic, water, eggplants, carrots, bell pepper, olives, cilantro, and salt and cook, stirring occasionally, until the veggies are tender, about 8 minutes.

4. On a work surface, spread about 2 tablespoons of the eggplant filling over each lasagna noodle. Using about half of the total amount, divide the cheese among the lasagna noodles. Starting with the edge closest to you, roll each lasagna noodle tightly then secure with a toothpick. Place the lasagna rolls in a large baking dish and cover each one with some tomato sauce and the reserved cheese. Bake until the cheese is golden, 15 to 20 minutes.

373 calories; 15g protein; 45g carbohydrates; 16g fat (4g saturated fat); 619mg sodium

SALMON & SALAD ISLAND DELUXE

INGREDIENTS

1 tablespoon olive oil
2 4-ounce salmon fillets
½ teaspoon low-sodium salt
½ teaspoon white ground pepper
½ teaspoon parsley, optional
1 head of lettuce, shredded
¼ cup diced tomatoes
¼ cup shredded carrots
¼ cup corn
¼ cup tortilla strips
¼ cup shredded low-fat mozzarella and cheddar mix
2 teaspoons lemon-and-herb vinaigrette or healthy dressing of your choice

PREPARATION

In a large sauté pan, warm the oil over moderate heat. Season the salmon with salt, pepper, and parsley and cook for 5 minutes, then flip over and cook for 4 more, or until golden and firm.

In a large salad bowl, add the lettuce, tomatoes, carrots, corn, tortilla strips and cheese. Drizzle with the dressing and toss well. When the salmon is ready, put each fillet on a plate with half the salad and serve.

Karla Gonzalez, age 10 in 2014

"At science class, we did an awesome project. We had to keep record for a week of all the food we ate at breakfast, lunch, and dinner, and also the snacks," says Karla. "That made me more aware of the importance of eating healthy. Since I am a fan of salmon with white rice, I am making a variation and replacing the rice with salad. The salmon is so easy to prepare that I do it myself. For the salad, I help my mom in the preparation to make sure there are no secret ingredients."

Makes 2 servings • 425 calories • 26g fat • 18g carbohydrates • 31g protein

CHEF KARLA

Chef Felix Gonzalez,

age 11 in 2015

"One day I was very hungry after my soccer practice so I was inspired to create a nutritious chicken meal that was easy to prepare," says Felix. "I decided to make this dish as a wrap because I was thinking about the fun times when my dad wrapped me up as a burrito with a blanket when I was a small child. This recipe is versatile because I can change the chicken for fish, or just make it a salad not using the tortilla. This plate goes perfectly with a nonfat Greek yogurt with berries."

Wrap It Up

Makes 2 Servings • 427 calories • 17g fat • 44g carbohydrates • 27g protein

INGREDIENTS

For the Chicken:

4 ounces skinless, boneless chicken breast, thinly sliced
Pinch salt and pepper
Pinch garlic powder
Pinch dried cilantro or parsley
1 teaspoon olive oil
¼ cup peeled and minced onions
¼ cup minced red and green bell peppers
2 high-fiber tortillas

For the Salad:

1 cup romaine lettuce
¼ cup minced tomatoes
¼ cup corn
1 tablespoon sliced almonds
1 tablespoon sweetened dried cranberries
1 tablespoon low-fat feta cheese or low-fat mozzarella-cheddar cheese blend
1 teaspoon of cranberry-almond vinaigrette

PREPARATION

1. **To make the Chicken:** Place the chicken in a large bowl, and season with salt, pepper, garlic powder, and cilantro. In a large sauté pan, heat the olive oil over medium heat. Add the onions and red and green bell peppers and sauté for about 5 minutes. Add the chicken and sauté for 10 minutes, or until light brown and cooked through.
2. **To make the Salad:** In a medium bowl, mix the lettuce, tomatoes, corn, almonds, cranberries, cheese, and vinaigrette. Warm the tortillas in the microwave or heat them in a pan. Put half of the salad mix and chicken in each tortilla. "Wrap it up" and enjoy. For a "berry" happy ending, serve a small cup of yogurt with berries!

CHEF

Victor Junniel Rivera

age 10 in 2016

"Being raised by my mother, a health teacher, and my father, a disabled veteran, it is not new to me to have a healthy lifestyle," says Victor. "On a Saturday after a basketball game, the most convenient thing to have is a healthy lunch and I would think of making a pizza in a pan. My recipe includes ingredients we picked from our backyard like oregano and spinach. With my parents I learned to make a healthy pizza with a twist, one in which anyone can add the ingredients of their choice. I like the mix of flavors and the idea of me cooking it. I would like to motivate others to learn or keep up healthy food habits."

Oat! My Tropical Pizza

Makes 2 servings • 275 calories • 6g fat • 37g carbohydrates • 20g protein

INGREDIENTS

For the Pizza Crust:

4 egg whites
1 whole egg
1 cup rolled oats
Pinch sea salt
½ teaspoon garlic powder
½ teaspoon dried parsley
1 teaspoon fresh oregano or ½ teaspoon dried
Coconut oil, or any nonstick cooking spray

For the Topping:

½ tomato, chopped or crushed
1 tablespoon chopped onion
1 teaspoon garlic powder
½ teaspoon dried parsley
Pinch sea salt
¼ cup nonfat plain Greek yogurt
½ cup fresh spinach, chopped
¼ cup fresh pineapple, diced

PREPARATION

1. **To make the Crust:** In a blender, mix together the egg whites, whole egg, oats, sea salt, garlic, and parsley for 20 seconds, or until blended. After blending, add the oregano and mix with a whisk. In a large nonstick skillet, grease the pan with coconut oil or any cooking spray and pour the mix in. Cook over medium heat for 6 minutes, flip over, and cook for another 6 minutes, or until it is golden and cooked through.

2. **To make the Topping:** Meanwhile, in a separate nonstick skillet, cook the tomato over medium heat for 1 minute. Add the onion, garlic, parsley, and sea salt, and cook for 5 minutes. Spread the sauce on the pizza crust still in the pan, reduce the heat to low, and add the yogurt, spinach, and pineapple. Let it warm up for 2 minutes, plate, and cut.

Rhode Island

Broccoli and Cheese Egg-White Omelet

Caroline Cowart, age 12 in 2012

Caroline's mom, Jennifer, says, "We came up with this lunch recipe because Caroline prefers egg whites instead of regular eggs, and she likes broccoli quite a bit." They like to serve this with wheat toast and mixed fruit.

Makes 1 serving

INGREDIENTS

3 large egg whites

¼ cup shredded mozzarella cheese

¾ cup cooked chopped broccoli

PREPARATION

Warm a nonstick sauté pan over low heat. Add the egg whites and let them set for a minute. Add the broccoli to one side of the egg whites, leaving the other side of the omelet empty. Sprinkle the mozzarella cheese over the broccoli, cover the pan, and cook until the cheese is melted and the eggs are cooked, about 4 minutes. (You can also cook the omelet under the broiler for 3 minutes.) Fold the empty half of the omelet over the broccoli-cheese side and serve.

Italian Garden Salsa with Crunchy Chicken Tenders

SAMANTHA MASTRATI, age 12 in 2013

"This lunch is brimming with the flavors of an Italian vegetable garden and is very nutritious. We love Italian food and the salsa is something we can make with vegetables from our garden," says Samantha. "It's very tasty with chicken combined with the crunchy coating." Her lunch also includes a 1/2 cup of strawberries, 1 ounce of whole-grain flatbread crackers, and an 8-ounce glass of fat-free milk.

Makes 4 to 6 servings

INGREDIENTS

For the Italian garden salsa:

2 cups diced ripe plum tomatoes

1/2 cup diced green bell pepper

1/2 cup diced Vidalia onion

1/4 cup diced celery

1 tablespoon minced garlic

1/8 teaspoon dried rosemary

1/8 teaspoon dried thyme

1/2 cup chopped fresh basil leaves

1/4 cup chopped fresh parsley leaves

For the chicken tenders:

3/4 cup plain panko bread crumbs

1 1/2 teaspoons dried basil

1 teaspoon garlic powder

1 teaspoon dried parsley

2 tablespoons freshly grated Parmesan

2 large egg whites

2 tablespoons fat-free milk

1 pound skinless chicken tenders (about 8 to 10 pieces)

1 tablespoon olive oil

PREPARATION

Make the Italian garden salsa:

1. In a small saucepan over low heat, combine the tomatoes, peppers, onion, celery, garlic, rosemary, and thyme and cook, stirring occasionally, for 5 minutes. Add the basil and parsley and continue to cook, stirring occasionally, for 1 minute.

Make the chicken tenders:

1. Preheat the oven to 400°F. Spray a dark baking sheet with cooking spray.

2. In a small bowl, stir together the bread crumbs, 1 teaspoon basil, garlic powder, parsley, and Parmesan.

3. In a second small bowl, beat the egg whites, milk, and remaining ½ teaspoon basil.

4. Working with 1 piece at a time, dip the chicken tenders into the egg mixture, making sure to coat both sides. Dip one side of the chicken tender into the bread crumb mixture, then flip it over to coat the other side. Dip the chicken tender back in the egg mixture and then back in the bread crumb mixture so it has two coats of each. Place the coated chicken tenders on the prepared baking sheet and repeat with the remaining chicken, egg mixture, and bread crumb mixture. Drizzle olive oil over the chicken and bake for 10 minutes. Flip the chicken tenders over, drizzle with more olive oil, and bake until golden brown, about 10 minutes. Serve with salsa.

301 calories; 15g protein; 28g carbohydrates; 14g fat (3g saturated fat); 556mg sodium

MEDITERRANEAN KEBAB WRAP WITH CILANTRO TABBOULEH

INGREDIENTS

♥ For the Kebabs:

1 pound ground turkey
1 bunch parsley, chopped
½ bunch cilantro, chopped
1 medium sweet onion, peeled and finely chopped
1 teaspoon black pepper
2 teaspoons allspice
½ teaspoon cinnamon
¼ teaspoon ground nutmeg
¼ teaspoon cloves
1½ teaspoons salt
1 minced garlic clove
Olive oil
Garnish: whole-wheat pita, lettuce, tomato, hummus

♥ For the Cilantro Tabbouleh:

½ cup coarse bulgur
2 bunches cilantro
5 medium scallions, sliced
4 tomatoes, seeded and diced
Juice of 4 fresh lemons
¼ cup and 1 tablespoon extra-virgin olive oil
1 teaspoon dried mint
2 tablespoons pine nuts
Salt and black pepper to taste

♥ For the Refreshing Cucumber Salad:

16 ounces low-fat plain Greek yogurt
1 large cucumber, peeled and seeded
1 tablespoon dried mint
4 minced garlic cloves
Juice of 3 fresh lemons
Salt to taste

PREPARATION

To make the Mediterranean Kebab Wraps: In a large bowl, mix ground turkey, parsley, cilantro, and onion. In separate bowl, mix the spices and garlic. Add to the turkey and mix well.

Form the kebabs by hand. Each should be about 4 inches long and about 1½ to 2 inches wide. Place on lightly greased tray. Lightly brush the kebabs with olive oil. Place in preheated broiler on low (or grill) and cook for 15 minutes, flip them over, and cook an additional 15 minutes. Place in pita-wrap with lettuce, tomatoes, and hummus.

To make the Cilantro Tabbouleh: In a large pot bring 1½ cups water and pinch of salt to boil over moderate heat. Add the bulgur, stir, remove from heat, and let cool. Add cilantro, scallions, tomatoes, lemon juice, ¼ cup olive oil, and mint to bulgur and stir.

In a small sauté pan over moderate heat, warm the remaining tablespoon of olive oil. Add the pine nuts and toast until lightly brown, about 2 minutes. Let cool, then toss into salad. Season with salt and pepper.

To make Refreshing Cucumber Salad: In a large bowl, add all of the ingredients and mix thoroughly. Chill before serving.

Kinnan Hammond-Dowie, age 12 in 2014

"I've always enjoyed learning to cook with my grandmother, who is of Middle Eastern heritage," notes Kinnan. "I like to experiment with our family recipes and try to make them healthier and still delicious. I decided to make the kebabs out of ground turkey rather than the traditional lamb. Since ground turkey can sometimes be bland, I tried adding some healthy herbs to boost the flavor. I serve this meal with a Refreshing Cucumber Salad. Yummy!"

Makes 6 servings • 318 calories • 20g fat • 21g carbohydrates • 19g protein

CHEF KINNAN

Mexican–Jewish Barley Pozole

Makes 8 servings • 423 calories • 18g fat • 50g carbohydrates • 20g protein

---

INGREDIENTS

For the Pozole:

1 tablespoon olive oil
½ medium onion, peeled and finely chopped
2 carrots, peeled and diced
1 stalk celery, diced
1 small zucchini, diced
2 skinless, boneless chicken breasts, diced
1 quart chicken broth
½ cup pearled barley
1 (15.5-ounce) can hominy, drained
1 teaspoon dried oregano
Salt and pepper to taste

For Garnish:

1 cup shredded romaine lettuce
2 large radishes, sliced very thinly
1 lime, cut into 4 wedges
1 avocado, cut into cubes
¼ onion, peeled and finely chopped
Hot sauce or ground dried chile peppers

PREPARATION

1. **In a large stockpot,** heat the olive oil over medium heat. Add the onion, carrots, celery, and zucchini and sauté for about 10 minutes, or until the vegetables are soft. Add the chicken and sauté for about 10 minutes, or until light brown and cooked through. Add the chicken broth, barley, hominy, and oregano, season to taste with salt and pepper, and simmer for about 30 minutes, or until the barley is soft. If the soup is too thick or there isn't enough liquid, add 1 more cup of water or chicken broth.

2. **To serve, ladle soup into bowls.** Place the garnishes on small serving plates in the middle of the table. Squeeze the juice from one lime wedge into each soup bowl. Each person can sprinkle whatever garnishes they choose onto their soup as desired.

Chef Clara Aizenman,

age 11 in 2015

"I created this soup because it represents my heritage, which is Jewish, Mexican, and Eastern European," says Clara. "I first made this recipe when my grandmother came to visit from Mexico. She was convinced the ingredients wouldn't go well together, but the result was delicious. This soup combines vegetable barley soup, common to Jewish cooking, with Mexican pozole. I also really love soup."

Peace in the Middle East Soup and Salad

Makes 4 servings • 451 calories • 18g fat • 57g carbohydrates • 22g protein

INGREDIENTS

For the Soup:

2 tablespoons olive oil
2 large carrots, peeled and thinly sliced
1 large celery stalk, thinly sliced
1 onion, peeled and chopped
½ cup dry lentils
¾ teaspoon cumin
¼ teaspoon coriander powder
½ teaspoon paprika
¼ teaspoon salt
¼ teaspoon freshly ground black pepper
8 cups low-sodium chicken broth (or vegetable broth)
4 large kale leaves, stemmed and chopped

For the Salad:

⅓ Vidalia onion, peeled and finely chopped
1 large cucumber, peeled and cut into ½-inch cubes or slices
1 pint grape tomatoes, sliced in half
10 fresh mint leaves, finely chopped
Juice from ½ fresh lemon
2 tablespoons olive oil
¼ teaspoon salt
¼ teaspoon freshly ground black pepper
¼ teaspoon sugar
2 large whole-wheat pita breads, cut in half and lightly warmed

Optional:

Nonfat plain Greek yogurt, as topping

PREPARATION

1. **To make the Soup:** In a large stockpot, warm the olive oil over medium heat and add the carrots, celery, and onions. Cook for 7 minutes, or until the vegetables are softened and golden brown. Add in the remaining ingredients except for the kale, cover, reduce heat to low, and simmer for 25 minutes. Add the kale and continue to simmer for another 20 minutes, or until lentils are soft. Remove 3 cups of the soup and puree in a blender. Return pureed soup to the main pot and heat through.
2. **To make the Salad:** In a large salad bowl, combine all of the ingredients. Carefully open the pocket in the pita bread half and add a quarter of the salad inside. Add some yogurt in the soup or salad for extra flavor and serve pita and soup together.

CHEF

Pablo Aizenman

age 10 in 2016

"I think war causes too much suffering in the world. One problem I see is that people often focus on their differences, rather than things they have in common," says Pablo. "In the Middle East there have been wars going on for a long time because people often fail to get past their differences. I wanted to create a dish that takes parts of different cultures in the Middle East and shows how they can come together to make a delicious and healthy lunch. The lentil soup brings in many Middle Eastern flavors and is joined by a crunchy Israeli salad stuffed into a pita. My dish highlights things that different regions in the Middle East have in common, and shows that, in the end, everyone is more alike than different."

South Carolina

Fun with Lunch

Lauren Kuperman, age 12 in 2012

"My daughter Lauren loves Asian cuisine," says her mom, Faye. "This can be challenging to pack for a lunch. I have come up with this satisfying 'Asian-style' lunch for her. I usually cook the noodles the night before. They are very easy to cook: It only takes 2 minutes in boiling water."

Makes 1 serving

INGREDIENTS

1 cup vermicelli noodles

1 cup cooked chopped chicken breast

1 tablespoon chopped red bell pepper

1 tablespoon chopped celery

2 tablespoons chopped peanuts

1 teaspoon chopped onion

Pinch freshly ground black pepper

1/8 teaspoon lime zest

1 teaspoon minced fresh lemon basil

1/4 cup rice-wine vinegar

PREPARATION

1. In a large pot of boiling salted water, cook the vermicelli noodles for 2 minutes. Drain, rinse in cold water, and return the noodles to the pot.
2. Add the chicken, bell pepper, celery, peanuts, onion, pepper, lime zest, lemon basil, and rice-wine vinegar, and stir to combine. Cook over moderate heat, stirring occasionally, for two minutes. (This can be prepared the evening before.) Serve hot or cold.

Bring It On Brussels Sprout Wrap!

CORBIN JACKSON, age 9 in 2013

"I have been on a Brussels sprout kick lately so that is the first thing I thought of. And I knew that Brussels sprouts were healthy, so I picked that," says Corbin about his recipe. He recommends combining 2/3 cup of kefir with 1/3 cup pomegranate juice for a delicious drink to accompany the wrap.

Makes 10 servings

INGREDIENTS

2 tablespoons chili powder

1 tablespoon ground cumin

1/2 tablespoon paprika

1/2 teaspoon garlic powder

1/2 teaspoon onion powder

1/2 teaspoon dried oregano

1 teaspoon salt

1 teaspoon freshly ground black pepper

2 tablespoons coconut oil

10 ounces Brussels sprouts, trimmed and finely chopped

1 (15-ounce) can organic pinto beans, rinsed and drained

2 small avocados, pitted

Juice from 2 limes

2 tablespoons chia seeds

10 whole wheat tortillas

PREPARATION

1. In a medium bowl, stir together the chili powder, cumin, paprika, garlic powder, onion powder, oregano, salt, and pepper.

2. In a large sauté pan over moderate heat, warm the coconut oil. Add the Brussels sprouts and the seasoning mixture and cook until the Brussels sprouts soften and wilt slightly, about 5 minutes. Add the beans, lower the heat to low, and cook, stirring often, until the beans are heated through, about 3 minutes.

3. In a small bowl, use a fork to mash the avocados and lime juice into a creamy paste. Add the chia seeds and stir to combine.

4. Spread a thin layer of the avocado mixture on each tortilla then top with the Brussels sprout-bean mixture. Roll up the tortillas, tucking the sides in as you roll.

289 calories; 7g protein; 35g carbohydrates; 13g fat (3g saturated fat); 455mg sodium

Julia Pascoe, age 8 in 2014

"About every two weeks, we go buy a rotisserie chicken from wherever it's on sale. On that night we eat chicken breast with two veggies and a fruit," says Julia. "The next afternoon is my favorite, because we make Carolina Chicken Chili, which is a recipe I helped my mom make up. It's healthy and doesn't cost much—we make one rotisserie chicken go really far this way, and we're all eating healthy two or three nights and lunch."

Makes 8-10 servings • 404 calories • 16g fat • 36g carbohydrates • 24g protein

CHEF JULIA

CAROLINA CHICKEN CHILI

INGREDIENTS

¼ cup olive oil
2 yellow onions, peeled and chopped
1 minced garlic clove
4 (15.2-ounce) cans white kidney beans, rinsed and drained
10 ounces rotisserie chicken, shredded (or cooked chicken, shredded)
2 (32-ounce) boxes of low-sodium chicken broth
1 (15-ounce) can corn, rinsed and drained
1 (4.5-ounce) can chopped green chiles, or less if you don't like spicy flavors
2 tablespoons ground cumin
2 tablespoons red chili powder
1 teaspoon smoked paprika
1 teaspoon salt
1 teaspoon pepper
Garnish: whole-wheat chips, low-fat Monterey Jack cheese shredded, chopped avocado, chopped tom to, chopped fresh cilantro

PREPARATION

In a large stock or pasta pot, warm the oil over moderate heat. Add the onions and sauté until soft, stirring often, about 10 minutes. Add the garlic and cook about 2 minutes more.

Add three cans of the beans, chicken, broth, corn, chiles, cumin, chili power, paprika, salt, and pepper. Raise heat to medium high and stir. While the chili is cooking, mash up the remaining can of beans in a bowl with a fork. Add to the chili and stir. Reduce heat to low and cook for 10 minutes. Serve with the garnishes.

Chef Summer LaPress,

age 9 in 2015

"My mom and I first made this recipe after visiting the beach in Charleston, South Carolina," says Summer. "Every restaurant had the most delicious fresh fish. Before we left, we bought some grouper at a fish shack that had been caught that morning, and we took it home in a cooler. We also ate rice native to South Carolina, and we were able to find it in stores back home in Greenville. So we came up with this recipe to remind us of our trips to the beach!"

Pan-Roasted Grouper with Carolina Gold Rice Salad

Makes 8 Servings • 561 calories • 23g fat • 46g carbohydrates • 33g protein

---

INGREDIENTS

For the Rice Salad:

2 cups Carolina Gold rice or wild rice
10 ounces baby spinach, stems trimmed and leaves roughly chopped
½ red onion, peeled and diced
1 pint multicolor cherry tomatoes, halved
3 cups red grapes, halved

For the Vinaigrette:

½ cup ruby red grapefruit juice
¼ cup balsamic vinegar
1 teaspoon yellow miso paste
2 teaspoons salt
1 teaspoon pepper
¾ cup extra-virgin olive oil

For the Grouper:

4 (4-ounce) grouper fillets or another firm fish
Salt and pepper to taste
2 tablespoons canola oil
1 tablespoon unsalted butter (optional)

PREPARATION

1. **In a large stockpot,** bring 12 cups of water to a boil over medium heat. Add the rice, bring back to a boil, then reduce the heat to low and simmer, uncovered, for 30 minutes, or until the rice is tender. Drain the rice in a colander and keep warm.
2. **Meanwhile, make the Vinaigrette:** In a small bowl, whisk together the grapefruit juice, balsamic vinegar, miso paste, salt, and pepper. Add the oil in a thin stream, whisking until emulsified. Reserve ¼ cup of the vinaigrette.
3. **Pat the fish fillets dry** with a paper towel and place in a plate or in a shallow dish. Sprinkle both sides of the fish with salt and pepper, and then brush both sides with the reserved vinaigrette. Marinate as you make the salad.
4. **When the rice is done,** fluff with a fork and transfer to a very large bowl. Add the spinach, red onion, tomatoes, grapes and remaining vinaigrette, and toss.
5. **To cook the fish:** Heat a heavy 10-inch nonstick or cast-iron skillet over high heat. When the pan is hot, add the canola oil. Place the fillets in the pan (skin side down if you're using fish with skin), laying them down away from your body. Reduce the heat to medium and let sizzle 2 to 3 minutes, or until the fish is golden. Carefully flip the fillets and add butter to pan, if using. Continue cooking until golden all over and cooked through, 1 minute more, depending on the thickness of your fish. Serve ½ a fillet with rice salad.

CHEF

Kiana White

age 12 in 2016

"Every fall, shrimp season opens in South Carolina," says Kiana. "My grandpa and I always go out and watch the shrimpers head into the ocean on their huge shrimp boats. We always buy shrimp fresh from the ocean and go home to think of creative new ways to cook them. This recipe is a combination of spicy flavors my grandpa likes, complimented by the sweet flavors I like."

Carolina Shrimp Tacos with Pineapple Salsa

Makes 4 servings • 383 calories • 13g fat • 53g carbohydrates • 14g protein

INGREDIENTS

For the Salsa:

½ chopped seedless jalapeño
¼ cup chopped sweet Vidalia onions
¼ cup chopped yellow bell pepper
½ cup finely chopped red cabbage
2 fresh limes, juiced
1 garlic clove, peeled and minced
½ avocado, peeled, pitted, and diced
½ cup chopped pineapple
¼ cup chopped fresh cilantro

For the Shrimp Tacos and Quinoa:

1 tablespoon plus 1 teaspoon olive oil
1 garlic clove, peeled and minced
½ teaspoon ground cumin
½ teaspoon chili powder
¼ teaspoon kosher salt
¼ teaspoon cayenne pepper (optional)
20 medium shrimp, peeled and deveined
4 whole-wheat tortillas
1 cup quinoa rinsed
½ cup spinach, chopped

PREPARATION

1. **To make the Salsa:** In a medium bowl, combine all the salsa ingredients. Cover and chill.
2. **In a medium bowl,** whisk together the tablespoon olive oil, garlic, cumin, chili, salt, and cayenne pepper (if using). Add in shrimp and toss to coat completely. Cover and refrigerate for 15 minutes to marinate.
3. **Meanwhile, in a medium pot,** bring 2 cups of water and the quinoa to a boil over medium heat; reduce heat to low and cook for about 20 minutes, or until tender. Remove from heat and mix in spinach. Set aside.
4. **In a large nonstick skillet,** warm the remaining teaspoon of oil over medium high heat. Add the shrimp and cook until pink and cooked through, about 5 minutes. Turn off heat and cover to keep warm.
5. **To Assemble:** Warm the tortillas in the microwave. Arrange ¼ cup of the quinoa-fish mixture down the middle of each tortilla. Add ¼ of cooked shrimp and top with salsa. Tightly wrap the tortillas and cut in half to serve. Repeat with remaining ingredients. Serve with additional salsa, if desired.

South Dakota

Miss Kitty's Egg Salad Sensation

Eva Farley, age 8 in 2012

Eva's family loves egg salad, but they know it needed "a healthy makeover. Enter Greek yogurt," says Eva. They use yogurt instead of mayo and sour cream. Their egg-cellent sandwich is on whole-wheat bread, and they pair it with fruit kabobs, layering grapes, strawberries, and bananas.

Makes 4 servings

INGREDIENTS

8 large eggs

1 cup Greek yogurt

1 teaspoon brown mustard

½ teaspoon dried dill

¼ teaspoon sea salt

¼ teaspoon freshly ground black pepper

4 whole-wheat buns

PREPARATION

1. Fill a saucepot with water and add the eggs. Cook over high heat until the water boils. Remove the pot from the heat and let the eggs sit in the water for 10 minutes. Drain the eggs and place them in a bowl of cool water. In the cool water, peel the shells off the eggs.
2. In a large bowl, combine the eggs, yogurt, mustard, dill, salt, and pepper. Gently mash and stir until well combined. Place ½ cup egg salad on the bottom of each whole-wheat bun, top with the other half of the bun, and serve.

Hidden Veggie Lasagna

OWEN KERKVLIET, age 9 in 2013

"I do not like eating vegetables when they are plain on my plate at home," admits Owen. "My mom hides vegetables in the food she makes sometimes, and she doesn't tell me they are in there until I am done eating. My mom and I came up with the recipe together. I love lasagna, and we hid the vegetables in the lasagna. I would serve it with grapes, my favorite fruit."

Makes 12 servings

INGREDIENTS

1 (16-ounce) box whole-grain lasagna noodles

3 tablespoons olive oil

1 cup shredded carrots

1 medium head broccoli, chopped

1 medium red bell pepper, seeded and chopped

1 medium yellow onion, chopped

3 cups tomato sauce

32 ounces part-skim ricotta cheese

9 ounces chopped fresh spinach or thawed frozen spinach

1 1/2 cups part-skim shredded mozzarella cheese

PREPARATION

1. Preheat the oven to 350°F.

2. In a large pot of boiling water, cook the lasagna noodles, according to package directions, until al dente. Drain the noodles and set them aside.

3. While the noodles are boiling, in a large saucepan over moderate heat, warm the olive oil. Add the carrots, broccoli, bell pepper, and onion and cook until tender, about 5 minutes. Add the tomato sauce to vegetables, and continue to cook, stirring occasionally, for 3 minutes.

4. In a large bowl, stir together the ricotta and spinach.

5. In a 9- by 13-inch baking dish, spread 1/3 of the vegetable-tomato sauce on the bottom. Arrange lasagna noodles lengthwise over the sauce. Spread the ricotta cheese mixture evenly over the noodles. Add more vegetable-tomato sauce, another layer of lasagna noodles, and another layer of the ricotta cheese mixture. Continue to layer the lasagna with the remaining sauce, noodles, and ricotta mixture. Top the lasagna with the mozzarella cheese, cover the baking dish with aluminum foil, and bake until the top is browned and the lasagna is heated through, about 45 minutes.

349 calories; 21g protein; 41g carbohydrates; 13g fat (6g saturated fat); 505mg sodium

Sabrina Swee, age 12 in 2014

"A year ago we traveled to Maui for a family vacation and enjoyed many Hawaiian dishes, which inspired us to create this wrap," says Sabrina. "We wanted to incorporate many ingredients that we can grow locally and/or purchase locally at our small town grocery store. This recipe is very versatile, as you can use a kale leaf or other lettuce for the wrap."

Makes 5 servings • 404 calories • 17f fat • 39g carbohydrates • 23g protein

HAWAIIAN KALE WRAPS

INGREDIENTS

♥ For the Wrap:

1 pound lean ground beef
1 cup water
½ cup uncooked quinoa
½ cup thinly sliced red bell pepper
¾ cup shredded carrot
¾ cup canned pineapple, drained and chopped
2 cups coleslaw mix or broccoli slaw mix
⅓ cup chopped scallions
10 kale leaves

♥ For the Sauce:

½ cup pineapple juice
⅓ cup low-sodium soy sauce
2 minced garlic cloves
½ teaspoon dried ginger
⅛ teaspoon cayenne
½ teaspoon sesame oil
1 tablespoon lime juice
1 tablespoon honey
1 tablespoon cornstarch

PREPARATION

In a large sauté pan over moderate heat, cook the ground beef until browned and cooked through, about 10 minutes. Drain any excess fat.

Meanwhile, in a small stockpot, add 1 cup water and the quinoa and bring to a boil. Reduce heat to low, cover, and simmer for 15 minutes until quinoa is cooked. While quinoa is cooking, combine the sauce ingredients in a medium bowl, mix together, and set aside.

When quinoa is done, increase heat to medium-high and add the sauce, red bell pepper, carrots, pineapple, and coleslaw mix. Mix thoroughly and cook for 3 minutes then add the scallions. Place about ¼ or ½ cup (depending on the size of your kale leaf) of the cooked mixture in the middle of a washed kale leaf, wrap, and eat.

Storm of Deliciousness BBQ Chicken Soup

Makes 8 Servings • 461 calories • 12g fat • 42g carbohydrates • 48g protein

---

INGREDIENTS

For the BBQ Sauce:

1 tablespoon olive oil
½ yellow onion, peeled and diced
2 cups tomato sauce
5 tablespoons tomato purée
2 garlic cloves, peeled and minced
5 tablespoons honey
3 tablespoons balsamic vinegar
2 tablespoons Worcestershire sauce

For the Soup:

1 pound skinless, boneless chicken breasts
1 (10.8-ounce) bag frozen corn
1 (15-ounce) can black beans, drained and rinsed
1 red bell pepper, chopped
1 yellow bell pepper, chopped
1 cup fresh mushrooms, chopped
¼ red onion, peeled and chopped
2 cups BBQ sauce (see recipe for our homemade BBQ sauce)
3 cups low-sodium chicken broth
1 tablespoon chili powder
½ teaspoon salt
½ teaspoon pepper
Reduced-fat sour cream, for serving
Reduced-fat shredded cheddar cheese, for serving

Equipment:

Slow cooker

PREPARATION

1. **To make the BBQ Sauce:** In a sauté pan, heat the olive oil over medium heat. Add the onion and sauté for about 5 minutes, or until translucent. Add the remaining ingredients, stir, and sauté for about 10 minutes.
2. **To make the Chicken Soup:** Place uncooked chicken breasts in a large slow cooker. Add corn, black beans, red and yellow bell peppers, mushrooms, and red onion.
3. **In a separate bowl,** mix 2 cups BBQ sauce, chicken broth, chili powder, salt, and pepper. Pour the BBQ sauce mixture into the slow cooker, covering the chicken and vegetables completely. Cook, covered, on high heat for 6 hours. About 30 minutes before serving, remove the chicken breasts, and shred the chicken. Place the shredded chicken back into the slow cooker and stir. Keep the lid off for the last 30 minutes of cooking time. Serve topped with sour cream or cheddar cheese.

Chef Griffin Storm,

age 8 in 2015

"I love BBQ sauce and I also love homemade soups, especially my grandma's chicken noodle and vegetable," says Griffin. "When I was thinking about my recipe I thought, why not make a BBQ vegetable soup? I love red and yellow peppers, so I knew I wanted to add them to the recipe. My mom loves slow cooker recipes for our busy family of six. My parents and I worked on the recipe together to come up with what I like to call a Storm of Deliciousness." This recipe uses a slow cooker. If you don't have one, slowly simmer the soup ingredients in a pot for 1 hour or more.

Catch of the Day Fish Tacos

Makes 4 servings • 499 calories • 8g fat • 68g carbohydrates • 37g protein

INGREDIENTS

For the Fish:

1 pound walleye fillets
(or any flaky white fish, like cod or haddock)
¼ cup nonfat plain Greek yogurt
2 cups panko breadcrumbs
¼ cup milk
2 eggs
Salt and freshly ground black pepper

For the Salsa:

½ cup peach-pineapple salsa,
or any flavor salsa
¼ cup nonfat plain Greek yogurt

For the Tacos:

3 cups finely shredded green cabbage
¼ cup shredded carrots
½ cup chopped fresh pineapple
6-inch whole-wheat flour tortillas
Juice of 1 fresh lime

PREPARATION

1. **To make the Fish:** Preheat oven to 400°F. Line a large rimmed baking pan with parchment paper or grease with nonstick cooking spray or oil. In a shallow dish combine the eggs, milk and Greek yogurt. Whisk until combined. Place breadcrumbs on another dish. Season the fish with salt and pepper, to taste. Lightly dunk the walleye into the egg mixture, draining any excess, and then place in the breadcrumbs, rolling and pressing to help the breadcrumbs adhere. Place the breaded fish onto the prepared baking pan. Bake for 12 minutes; turn on broiler, place under the broiler for 1 minute, then flip over and brown on the other side. (Or, leave in the oven for 5 more minutes.) Cut into small, bite-sized pieces.
2. **To make the Salsa:** In a small bowl, combine salsa and Greek yogurt and blend until smooth.
3. **To make the Tacos:** In a large bowl, toss together cabbage, carrots, and pineapple. On a plate, heat one tortilla in the microwave for 10 seconds or until warm and pliable. Top with ¼ of the cabbage and carrot mixture and fish. Drizzle 2 teaspoons salsa on top, then top with a squirt of lime juice. Repeat with remaining tortillas, veggies, fish, and salsa.

CHEF
Josh Weissenberger
age 11 in 2016

"Every summer, I go fishing on the Missouri River with my dad and two grandpas," says Josh. "We spend the week catching and eating lots of fresh walleye, the state fish of South Dakota. When you catch a lot of fish, you have to eat a lot of fish, so we come up with new ways to cook walleye. Since tacos are another favorite food, I thought it'd be fun to make fish tacos. Fish is really healthy; my mom says it's got lots of protein and is low in fat. Lots of people batter and fry fish, but baking it is great. What's even better is that I can make it since my mom doesn't want me to get splattered by hot oil. Cooking is fun! I like to eat these tacos with fruit and milk."

Tennessee

Tuna Schooners

Logan Guleff, age 9 in 2012

"I came up with my recipe by thinking what could I do to my favorite tuna salad to make it healthier and tasty," says Logan. "I decided to try quinoa, a whole grain that I had never had before. I added it to my favorite canned tuna and all my favorite veggies, and WOW, was it good! If you don't like my veggie choices, have fun experimenting with your own." Logan always adds fruit to the side of his plate.

Makes 4 servings

INGREDIENTS

1 cup cooked quinoa, at room temperature

½ cup minced onion

½ cup diced red and orange bell peppers

½ cup diced cucumber

½ cup diced celery

1 (6-ounce) can white tuna, drained

¼ cup low-fat mayonnaise

Salt and pepper

4 long sweet peppers, cut in half lengthwise and seeds removed

2 lettuce leaves, cut in triangles

PREPARATION

In a large bowl, combine the quinoa, onion, bell peppers, cucumber, celery, tuna, and mayonnaise. Season to taste with salt and pepper, and stir well to combine. Divide the salad among the sweet pepper halves, insert the lettuce like a boat's sail, and serve.

Makenna's Bodacious Banana Muffins

MAKENNA HURD, age 9 in 2013

"My mommy and I bake lots of muffins to raise awareness for Down syndrome. I walk in 'Walk for Success' each year with my family and almost always win a medal," says Makenna. "I would have my muffins alongside a yogurt parfait with strawberries and blueberries, and a nice green salad with only dark greens like kale and spinach and some cherry tomatoes and cucumbers." Her dad Mark reports that Makenna wants to open her own bake shop when she's older, and that she sells muffins to schools and businesses in the community to raise money for research and programs for Down syndrome.

Makes 12 servings

INGREDIENTS

3 ripe bananas, mashed

2 large eggs

3/4 cup packed brown sugar

3/4 cup unsweetened applesauce

1/4 cup vegetable oil, plus more for pans

1 teaspoon pure vanilla extract

2 cups whole wheat flour

1 teaspoon baking soda

1 tablespoon ground cinnamon, plus more for pans

PREPARATION

1. Preheat the oven to 350°F. Grease a 12-cup muffin pan with the vegetable oil and sprinkle a little cinnamon in the bottom of each cup.

2. In a large bowl, beat together the bananas, eggs, brown sugar, applesauce, oil, and vanilla.

3. In a medium bowl, whisk together the flour, baking soda, and cinnamon. Add the flour mixture to the banana mixture and stir until incorporated. Spoon the batter into the prepared muffin tray and bake until the tops of the muffins spring back when pressed lightly, about 30 minutes. Let cool and enjoy!

201 calories; 4g protein; 35g carbohydrates; 6g fat (1g saturated fat); 123mg sodium

TENNESSEE TABBOULEH

INGREDIENTS

♥ For the Couscous:

1 teaspoon olive oil

¼ teaspoon salt

1 cup whole-wheat couscous

♥ For the Tabbouleh:

Juice of 3 lemons

2 tablespoons olive oil

½ teaspoon salt

2 cups cherry tomatoes, halved

3 small or 1 large cucumber, chopped

2 scallions, sliced thin

1 bunch parsley, stems removed and chopped

1 large dark green leafy lettuce

2 boneless skinless chicken breasts, cooked and sliced into strips

¼ cup low-fat feta cheese

PREPARATION

In a medium pot, bring 1 cup water, olive oil and salt to a boil on moderate heat. Remove from the heat, stir in the couscous, cover, and let it sit for 5 minutes. Fluff with a fork and pour into a large serving bowl to cool.

In a medium bowl, whisk together the lemon juice, olive oil, and salt and set it aside. Add the cherry tomatoes, cucumber, scallions, and parsley to the couscous. Drizzle the dressing on top and toss. Lay a large lettuce leaf or two smaller ones on each plate. Divide the tabbouleh, top with chicken and feta.

Lily Sahihi, age 9 in 2014

"I live in a three-generation home, and I love watching my grandma and mom cook," says Lily. "I've learned so much from them about using fresh ingredients. We grow our own herbs and some fruits and veggies too. I call this dish Tennessee Tabbouleh because it's a Mediterranean recipe. I added my own twist by using whole-wheat couscous instead of cracked wheat because it's easier to find in the grocery store and has lots of good-for-you protein and fiber."

Makes 4 servings • 445 calories • 14g fat • 41g carbohydrates • 34g protein

Chef Evie Braude,

age 9 in 2015

"My inspiration for this recipe was a soup my mom makes. My sister and I adore this soup," says Evie. "So, I decided to make a version of the soup as a salad that would be easier to take to school in a lunchbox. I was also inspired by the local farmer's market here in Knoxville, TN. The farmer's market has food trucks, pastries, vegetables, meat, and more! I love the salad by itself, but it would also be tasty with my dad's grilled salmon."

Farro with a Tennessee Twist

Makes 6 to 8 Servings • 611 calories • 19g fat • 83g carbohydrates • 31g protein

---

INGREDIENTS

For the Salad:

1 ½ cups farro
2 tablespoons olive oil
2 garlic cloves, peeled and roughly chopped
1 small bunch dinosaur kale or your favorite variety of kale, stems removed and leaves sliced into strips
3 stalks celery, chopped
5 green onions (scallions), white and light green parts only, chopped
1 pint grape tomatoes, halved
2 (15-ounce) cans white beans, drained and rinsed
¾ ounce fresh mint, chopped
Salt and pepper to taste
5 ounces shaved or shredded Parmesan cheese

For the Buttermilk Dressing:

1 cup buttermilk
Juice of 1 lemon
6 tablespoons olive oil
2 tablespoons honey
Salt and pepper to taste

PREPARATION

1. **To make the Salad:** In a medium saucepan, bring 4 cups of water to a boil. Add the farro, reduce the heat to low, cover, and cook until tender, 20 to 30 minutes. Set aside to cool.
2. **In a large sauté pan,** heat the olive oil over medium heat. Add the garlic and cook for 1 minute. Add the kale and cook for about 5 minutes, or until wilted. Add the celery, green onions, tomatoes, white beans, and mint and cook for about 10 minutes. Season to taste with salt and pepper. Set aside to cool.
3. **To make the Buttermilk Dressing:** In a small bowl, whisk together all of the ingredients.
4. **Drizzle the dressing** over the salad and mix well. Top with Parmesan cheese.

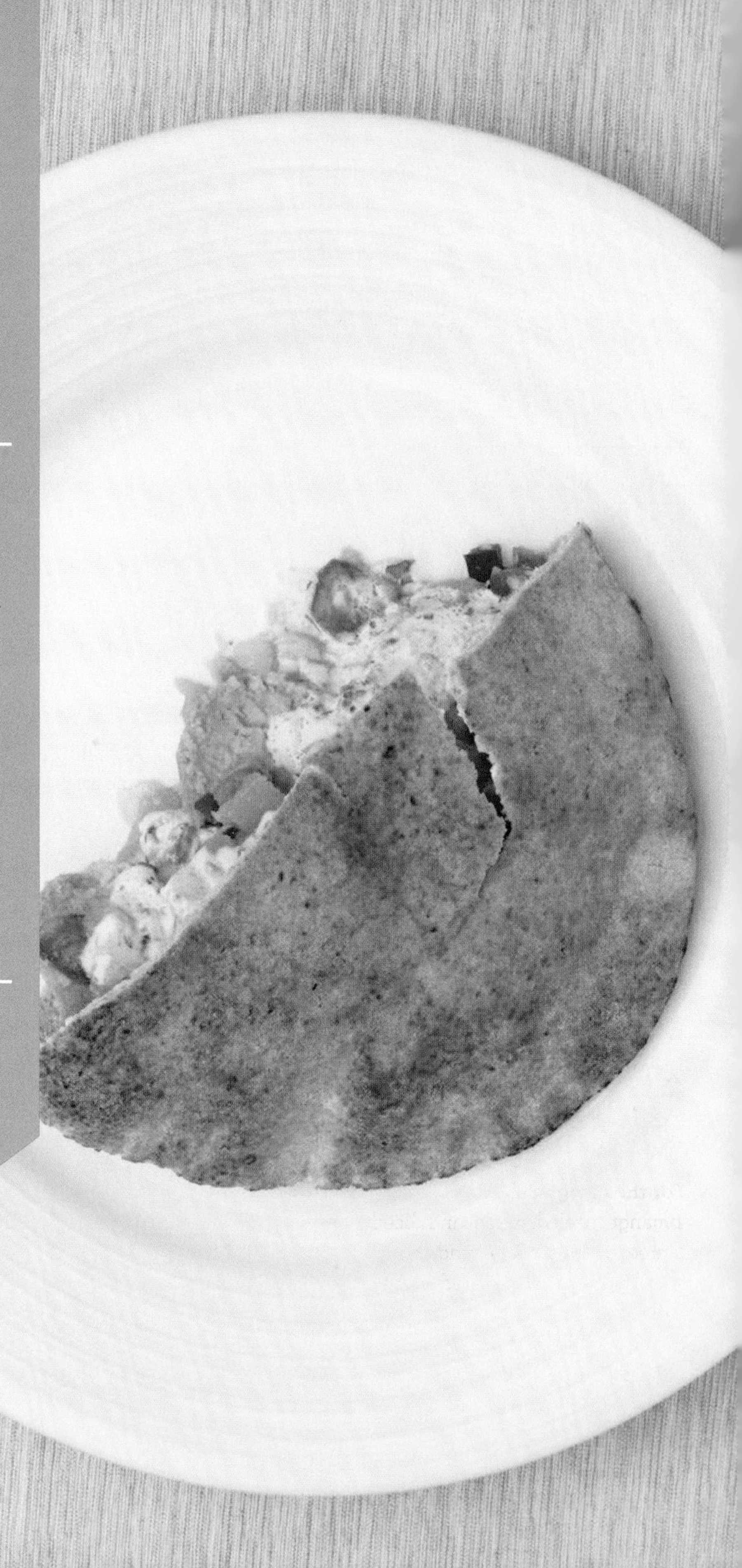

CHEF

Leya Alani

age 9 in 2016

"Leya was inspired to make this dish by her uncle," says Leya's mom, Deena. "As a family of Middle Eastern descent, Leya and her uncle love to create traditional dishes with a twist. Falafel and mango salsa are a favorite in the Middle East, so this was an attempt to make a healthier version. Falafels are usually deep fried, whereas in this recipe they are baked and are just as delicious. The salsa includes tomatoes, which is Tennessee's state fruit. Tennessee is now home to a large Middle Eastern immigrant population, so there are many falafel places opening their doors in the state."

Awesome Baked Falafel with Mango Salsa

Makes 6 servings • 494 calories • 14g fat • 75g carbohydrates • 21g protein

INGREDIENTS

For the Falafel:

2 15-ounce can chickpeas, rinsed and drained
1 ½ teaspoon cumin
¼ teaspoon coriander powder
¼ cup chopped chives
¼ cup minced onion
2 garlic cloves, peeled and minced
¼ cup chopped cilantro
¼ cup chopped parsley
¼ teaspoon salt
2 tablespoons all-purpose flour
1 teaspoon baking powder
2 cups water
2 tablespoons olive oil, plus more for coating
½ cup breadcrumbs
2 cups instant oats
Toasted sesame seeds

For the Yogurt Sauce:

1 cup nonfat plain Greek yogurt
2 tablespoons fresh lemon juice
2 garlic cloves, peeled and minced
Salt

For the Mango Salsa:

1 mango, peeled, pitted, and diced
2 green onions, peeled and chopped
2 red bell peppers, seeded and diced
2 diced tomatoes
3 tablespoons fresh lime juice
2 tablespoons fresh lemon juice
6 whole-wheat pita breads, halved
Salt

PREPARATION

1. **To make the Falafel:** Preheat the oven to 425°F. In a blender, combine all ingredients except breadcrumbs, oats, and sesame seeds. Puree mixture until well blended. Transfer to a large mixing bowl. Add breadcrumbs and oats to mixture and mix by hand. Let stand for 10 minutes, then shape into balls and place on a greased or nonstick baking sheet. Brush balls with olive oil and sprinkle sesame seeds on top. Bake for 20 minutes, then flip falafel balls over and bake for an additional 20 minutes.
2. **To make the Yogurt Sauce:** In a medium bowl, combine all ingredients and toss well.
3. **To make the Mango Salsa:** In a medium bowl, combine all ingredients and toss well.
4. **To Assemble:** Spread the yogurt sauce on the inside of the halved pita bread, place 2 to 3 falafels inside the bread and top with salsa. You can have 1 or 2 halves, depending on how hungry you are. Enjoy!

Texas

Secret Service Super Salad

Michael Lakind, age 9 in 2012

"I came up with this idea because I love to eat fresh, healthy, and light food. I came up with the name for the salad because I am very interested in the important job of the Secret Service." Michael likes to have this with a tasty carrot soup he calls Bunny Bisque.

Makes 4 servings

INGREDIENTS

4 slices whole-grain bread, cut into cubes

2 tablespoons unsalted butter, melted

Kosher salt and freshly ground black pepper

1 teaspoon parsley

3/4 cup extra-virgin olive oil

1/4 cup white-wine vinegar

1 (8-ounce) package fresh baby spinach

2 skinless boneless chicken breasts, grilled or cooked and cut into thin slices

1 pint strawberries, stemmed and sliced

PREPARATION

1. Preheat the oven to 300°F.
2. On a baking sheet, drizzle the bread cubes with butter, stirring so each piece gets a little butter. Season to taste with salt and pepper, and sprinkle with parsley. Bake until the bread is crisp, about 20 minutes.
3. While the bread is baking, in a small bowl, whisk together the olive oil and vinegar. Season to taste with salt and pepper.
4. In a large bowl, combine the spinach, chicken, strawberries, and croutons. Drizzle with the dressing, and serve

Slam Dunk Veggie Burger

DEVANSHI UDESHI, age 12 in 2013

"When I went grocery shopping with my mom, I came across quinoa in the grains aisle, so we decided to try it," says Devanshi. "I guess it tastes really good, so my mom and I created a burger recipe, which includes quinoa, a good source of protein. My healthy and delicious recipe can be served with a side dish of Super Scrumptious Strawberry Salad," which has spinach, strawberries, and red onion.

Makes 6 servings

INGREDIENTS

1 cup quinoa, rinsed

2 cups of water

1/2 teaspoon kosher salt

1 cup chopped fresh cilantro leaves

1/2 cup whole wheat bread crumbs, unseasoned

1 medium white onion, finely chopped

1 large egg

1/3 cup chopped carrot

1/3 cup chopped green beans

1/3 cup sweet corn

1/4 cup feta cheese

1 clove garlic, minced

1 tablespoon extra-virgin olive oil

1 teaspoon ground cumin

1/4 teaspoon freshly ground black pepper

6 whole wheat hamburger buns

For garnish:

Avocado, lettuce, and tomato

PREPARATION

1. Preheat the oven to 400°F.

2. In a medium saucepan combine the quinoa, 2 cups of water, and 1/4 teaspoon salt. Bring to a boil then reduce the heat to low and simmer until the quinoa is tender, about 15 minutes. Transfer to a large bowl. Add the cilantro, bread crumbs, onion, egg, carrot, green beans, corn, feta, garlic, oil, cumin, pepper, and the remaining 1/4 teaspoon salt and stir to thoroughly combine. Let the mixture sit for 5 minutes so the bread crumbs can absorb some moisture.

3. Divide the mixture into 6 even parts and shape each one into a 1-inch-thick patty. Arrange the patties on a baking sheet and bake for 20 minutes. Flip the patties over and continue baking until light brown, about 5 minutes. Serve the patties on the buns, garnished with avocado, lettuce, and tomato.

346 calories; 12g protein; 57g carbohydrates; 9g fat (2g saturated fat); 552mg sodium

Ariel Derby, age 8 in 2014

"We chose to make falafel because of our heritage. It is a Mediterranean/Middle Eastern staple," noted Ariel. "This version is baked and not fried, making it lower in fat. I choose to top it with low-fat Greek yogurt, but you could choose any dairy-free yogurt that you want. I serve it with a Tomato Cucumber Salad on the side, which is very refreshing in the summer."

Makes 4 servings • 325 calories • 14g fat • 42g carbohydrates • 12g protein

BAKED FALAFEL & TOMATO CUCUMBER SALAD

INGREDIENTS

♥ For the Falafel:
1 cup dried chickpeas, soaked overnight
2 tablespoons olive oil
⅓ cup chopped red onion
½ cup chopped fresh parsley
½ cup chopped cilantro
¼ teaspoon ground cumin
¼ teaspoon ground turmeric
¼ teaspoon ground coriander
Splash of lemon juice
Dash of cayenne, if desired
Garnishes: Lettuce leaves, plain low-fat Greek yogurt

♥ For the Tomato Cucumber Salad:
3 large tomatoes, chopped
2 cucumbers, peeled and chopped
¼ cup cilantro, chopped
1 tablespoon olive oil
1 tablespoon lemon juice

PREPARATION

To make the Falafel: Preheat the oven to 425°F. Blend all ingredients in a blender until the texture is like a very fine meal. Transfer to a large bowl. Form 2-inch balls, like meatballs, and place onto a greased cookie sheet. Bake for 15 minutes, turn them over, and bake 10 more minutes, or until lightly browned. Serve wrapped in a lettuce leaf with Greek yogurt and the salad.

To make the Tomato Cucumber Salad: In a medium bowl, combine the tomatoes, cucumbers, and cilantro. Drizzle with olive oil and lemon juice and toss.

Chef Jianna Garcia,

age 10 in 2015

"I was inspired to make this as I love eating healthy, and I especially love any salad, more than chips and soda," says Jianna. "Greek food is also one of my very favorites. I love how the flavors of the couscous, parsley, feta, and fresh veggies combine with my Lemon-Honey Vinaigrette. By adding delicious Chicken Skewers and Texas Tzatziki, I turned this already scrumptious salad into a super fresh, healthy, and very tasty meal."

Couscous Salad with Chicken, Artichoke, and Lemon Skewers and Tangy Texas Tzatziki

Makes 4 to 6 Servings • 655 calories • 34g fat • 58g carbohydrates • 31g protein

---

INGREDIENTS

For the Chicken Skewers:
12 chicken tenderloins, halved
Salt and pepper to taste
⅔ cup lemon juice
¼ cup olive oil
12 canned artichoke hearts, halved
24 grape tomatoes

For the Salad:
2 cups cooked couscous, cooled
1 cup chopped fresh parsley
1 cup peeled, seeded, and diced cucumber
1 cup rinsed and drained canned garbanzo beans
½ cup grape tomatoes, halved
⅓ cup crumbled feta cheese
¼ cup peeled and minced onions

For the Vinaigrette:
⅓ cup olive oil
¼ cup lemon juice
¼ cup white wine vinegar
1 tablespoon honey
Salt and pepper to taste

For the Tzatziki:
1 peeled, seeded cucumber, finely grated
1 cup Greek yogurt
1 garlic clove, peeled and minced
1 teaspoon lemon juice
2 tablespoons chopped fresh dill
2 tablespoon chopped fresh mint
2 teaspoon olive oil
Salt and pepper to taste

Equipment: 12 wooden skewers

PREPARATION

1. **To make the Chicken Skewers:** Make sure to soak the wooden skewers in water for about 10 minutes before using. Season the chicken tenderloins with salt and pepper and put in a gallon-sized plastic bag with a seal. Add the lemon juice, olive oil, salt, and pepper. Seal the bag and let the chicken marinate in the refrigerator for 30 minutes.
2. **Preheat the oven to 350°F.** Slide 1 wooden skewer though 1 piece of chicken twice, add 1 artichoke heart and 1 grape tomato then repeat with another piece of chicken, 1 artichoke heart, and 1 tomato. Lay the completed skewer on a foil-lined baking sheet. Repeat the process until all the skewers are filled. Bake for 20 minutes, or until the chicken reaches 165°F.
3. **To make the Salad:** Mix all ingredients in a large bowl and chill.
4. **To make the Vinaigrette:** Place all the ingredients in a Mason jar with a lid and shake for 30 seconds. Drizzle over the salad and toss to combine.
5. **To make the Tzatziki:** Squeeze all the water out of the cucumber and place it in a bowl. Add the remaining ingredients and whisk to combine. Season to taste with salt and pepper as needed. Chill.
6. **Serve Chicken Skewers** atop a mound of the Parsley Couscous Salad with a side of the Tangy Texas Tzatziki.

CHEF

Priya Patel

age 10 in 2016

"I was first inspired to make this recipe by my mom. She always tells us to add vegetables to everything we make and to experiment," says Priya. "I love Tex-Mex food and also lasagna so we thought this was a good way to combine both. My mom also tells us to be flexible so we use canned or frozen vegetables if we're out of fresh. You can substitute any veggies and fruits you like. The possibilities are endless. My mom says not having or liking one ingredient is not an excuse to not try a recipe or to buy fast food!"

Tex-Mex Veg-Head Lasagna

Makes 4 servings • 342 calories • 8g fat • 56g carbohydrates • 16g protein

INGREDIENTS

For the Lasagna Filling:

1 tablespoon olive oil
¼ red onion, peeled and chopped
2 garlic cloves, peeled and minced
1 15-ounce can black beans, rinsed and drained
2 tomatoes, seeded and chopped
½ jalapeno, seeded and chopped
Juice of ½ fresh lime
1 teaspoon cumin
1 teaspoon chili powder
1 teaspoon paprika
½ teaspoon salt
½ teaspoon Mexican oregano or regular oregano
1 teaspoon freshly ground black pepper
½ cup vegetable stock or broth

For the Tortilla Lasagna:

1 8-ounce can tomato sauce
6 corn tortillas
2 corn cobs, kernels removed or 1 cup frozen corn
½ cup low-fat cheddar or jack cheese
1 cup fresh spinach
1 large red or green bell pepper, seeded and chopped
Cilantro, for garnish

PREPARATION

1. **To make the Lasagna Filling:** Preheat oven to 400°F. In a large nonstick skillet, warm the oil over medium heat, and cook onions for 2 minutes, then add garlic and cook for 1 minute more. Add remaining ingredients and bring to a slow boil, about 4 minutes. Turn off heat and mash beans with back of wooden spoon or masher.
2. **To make Tortilla Lasagna:** In a round or square oven-safe dish, put 2 tablespoons tomato sauce, followed by a tortilla, 3 tablespoons black bean filling, 1 tablespoon cheese, 5 spinach leaves, ⅕ of the corn, and bell pepper. Repeat with remaining tortillas and ingredients. (You will have a little tomato sauce, cheese, corn, and bell pepper remaining.) On the 6th and last tortilla, top with remaining 3 tablespoons tomato sauce and bake, uncovered, for 20 minutes. Add the remaining cheese on top and bake for another 10 minutes. Remove from oven and let sit for 10 minutes. Slice into wedges and garnish with any remaining peppers, corn, and cilantro.

U.S. Virgin Islands

Vegetarian Lasagna

Gabriel Reed, age 11 in 2012

"We grew fresh greens at Gabriel's school," reports his mom, Vanessa. "We chose kale, tomatoes, and basil from the garden, and made lasagna. We served samples to 84 fourth-graders, and they loved it!" Gabriel often has this with fresh slices of mango and milk.

Makes 8 servings

INGREDIENTS

3 pounds ripe tomatoes, chopped
1 (24-ounce) jar marinara sauce
1 cup shredded fresh basil
Salt and freshly ground black pepper
9 whole-wheat lasagna noodles (about half a 1-pound box)
4 bunches kale (about 3 pounds total)
1 (15-ounce) container part-skim ricotta cheese
1 pound part-skim mozzarella cheese, shredded
¼ cup finely grated imported Parmesan cheese
1 large egg

PREPARATION

1. Preheat the oven to 325°F.
2. In a large saucepan over moderate heat, combine the tomatoes, marinara sauce, and basil, and bring to a simmer. Cover the pot, then transfer it to the oven to cook gently, stirring once or twice, until the tomatoes are tender, 2 to 2 ½ hours.
3. Carefully remove the pot from the oven. Transfer the tomato sauce to a food mill set over a large saucepan, and force the sauce through the mill to remove the skins. Discard the skins. (If you don't have a food mill, skip this step.) Season to taste with salt and pepper, and let cool. (You will have about 4 cups of sauce.)
4. In a large pot of boiling salted water, cook the lasagna until al dente, about 10 minutes. Drain and rinse.
5. While the lasagna is boiling, fill a second large pot halfway up with water and bring to a boil. Add half the kale and cook, stirring occasionally, until wilted, 3 to 4 minutes. Using a slotted spoon, remove the kale from the water, place it in a colander, and rinse with cold water until cool. Repeat with the remaining kale. Using a clean towel, squeeze excess moisture from the cooked kale then coarsely chop it.
6. Preheat the oven to 400°F.
7. In medium bowl, stir together the ricotta , 3/4 cup mozzarella, the Parmesan, and the egg. Season lightly with salt and pepper.
8. Lightly oil a 13-by-9-inch baking dish. Add 1 cup of the tomato sauce to the bottom, tilting to coat. Arrange 3 cooked lasagna noodles in the bottom of the pan, then top with 1 cup tomato sauce. Top with about a third of the kale then dot with about a third of the cheese mixture. Repeat with 2 more layers. Cover the lasagna tightly with foil and bake 45 minutes. Remove the foil, sprinkle the lasagna with the remaining mozzarella, and continue baking until the cheese is melted and the lasagna is bubbling, 10 to 15 minutes. Let stand for 20 minutes before serving.

Zucchini Pancakes & Passion Fruit Banana Smoothie

SAKARI CLENDINEN, age 8 in 2013

"On the weekend, we make pancakes from scratch in shapes that go along with family celebrations. These have a healthy twist and are delicious," says Sakari. "At first we were going to use sour cream, but I don't like that. So we made a cream cheese and yogurt mixture that I love. Bananas and passion fruit grow in our yard, and we make really tasty smoothies with them to go along with the pancakes."

Makes 4 servings

INGREDIENTS

For the zucchini pancakes:

2 medium zucchinis, trimmed and grated

Salt

1/2 cup fat-free plain Greek-style yogurt

3 ounces cream cheese

1 large egg plus 2 large egg whites

1 clove garlic, minced

1/3 cup whole wheat pastry flour

1/4 cup Parmesan

Freshly ground black pepper

2 tablespoons oil

For the passion fruit banana smoothies:

8 passion fruits, seeded and flesh removed

4 bananas

2 cups fat-free plain Greek-style yogurt

2 tablespoons honey

8 ice cubes

PREPARATION

Make the zucchini pancakes:

1. In a colander, combine the grated zucchini with a pinch of salt and let it sit for 15 minutes to drain any excess liquid. Wrap the zucchini in paper towels and wring out any excess liquid.

2. In a small bowl, stir together the yogurt and cream cheese.

3. In a large bowl, beat the egg, egg whites, and garlic. Fold in the flour and Parmesan, and season with pepper. Add the zucchini and stir just until combined.

4. In a large sauté pan over moderate heat, warm the oil. Spoon 1 heaping tablespoon of batter into the pan and cook until golden brown, 2 to 3 minutes per side. Continue with the rest of the batter, covering the finished pancakes to keep them warm. Serve the pancakes topped with a dollop of the yogurt and cream cheese mixture.

Make the passion fruit banana smoothies:

1. In a blender, combine the passion fruits, bananas, yogurt, honey, and ice cubes, and blend until smooth.

409 calories; 18g protein; 64g carbohydrates; 12g fat (7g saturated fat); 324mg sodium

Ahlissa Pierce, age 9 in 2014

"My mom always said that it was important to eat different-colored vegetables, but it wasn't until I saw a beautiful rainbow last week that I felt encouraged to add colorful vegetables to my mother's traditional chicken soup," says Ahlissa. "Adding these vegetables to soups is an easy way to try new vegetables. My soup has 13 different vegetables in it. I challenge the nation to eat as many different-colored vegetables as they can!"

Makes 10 servings • 300 calories • 11g fat • 32g carbohydrates • 19g protein

CHEF AHLISSA

AHLISSA'S RAINBOW CARIBBEAN SOUP

INGREDIENTS

♥ For the Soup:
2 tablespoons vegetable oil
1½ yellow onions, peeled and minced
4 skinless boneless chicken breasts, chopped
6 minced garlic cloves
2 tablespoons chopped parsley
3 bell peppers—red, orange, and yellow—seeded and chopped
3 carrots, peeled and chopped
2 red potatoes, chopped
1½ cups chopped purple cabbage
1½ cups cubed pumpkin or sweet potato
1 zucchini, chopped
3 okras, sliced
1½ cups chopped baby spinach
Sea salt and black pepper to taste

♥ For the Wheat Dumplings:
1 cup whole-wheat flour
1 tablespoon olive oil
1 teaspoon sea salt

PREPARATION

Make the Soup: In a large stockpot, warm the oil over moderate heat. Add the onions and cook until soft, about 5 minutes. Add the chicken, garlic, parsley, peppers, and 1 cup of water and cook for 5 minutes. Add the remaining ingredients and 11 cups of water. Bring to a boil, then reduce the heat to low and simmer for 30 minutes.

Meanwhile, make the Wheat Dumplings: In a large bowl, combine the whole-wheat flour, sea salt, and olive oil. Drizzle ¼ cup water in slowly and knead for 2 minutes. Shape into small balls and flatten. Add to soup during its last 10 minutes of cooking and then serve.

Hurricane Salmon and Lentil Patties

Makes 4 Servings • 700 calories • 21g fat • 58g carbohydrates • 72g protein

---

INGREDIENTS

8 ounces lentils
Pinch dried thyme
Pinch dried oregano
Pinch salt
Pinch pepper
2 cans salmon, any bones removed
2 large eggs
1 onion, peeled and diced
2 tablespoons olive oil
4 whole-wheat buns
Sprouts, optional
1 mango, sliced

PREPARATION

1. **Place the lentils in a bowl,** cover with cold water, and let sit for 1 hour. Fill a large stockpot with water, add the lentils, and bring to a boil over medium-high heat. Cook for 20 minutes, or until tender. Drain the lentils and place in a large bowl. Add the thyme, oregano, salt, and pepper and toss to combine.
2. **Add the salmon,** egg, and onion to the bowl with the cooked lentils. Shape into 4 patties.
3. **In a large sauté pan,** heat the olive oil over medium-high heat. Cook the patties, flipping once, for 5 minutes per side, or until cooked through and light brown. Place on buns, and serve with sprouts and mango on the side.

Chef Jalani Phillips Jr.,

age 10 in 2015

"Living on an island can be a task at times, especially during hurricane season. Power is knocked out, grocery stores closed or damaged, and fresh food items are often limited," says Jalani. "My recipe can be prepared under these circumstances. The salmon doesn't have to be refrigerated, nor are many supplies needed. If the power is out, I can prepare my meal using our gas stove with mom's help."

Healthy Chicken

Makes 4 servings • 335 calories • 13g fat • 20g carbohydrates • 33g protein

---

INGREDIENTS

Juice of 1 fresh lime
2 boneless, skinless chicken breasts
1 teaspoon Cajun seasoning
2 green apples, peeled and minced
2 celery stalks, thinly sliced
½ Jerusalem artichoke, peeled and thinly sliced
2 tablespoons dried cranberries
2 tablespoons minced walnuts
½ cup minced red onion
⅓ cup mayonnaise
⅓ cup Dijon mustard
Freshly ground black pepper
4 lettuce leaves

PREPARATION

1. **Preheat the oven to 350°F.** In a medium bowl, combine the lime juice with the chicken and marinate in the refrigerator for 30 minutes. On a large nonstick baking sheet, bake the chicken for 15 minutes on each side. Remove from the oven and cut into ½-inch cubes.

2. **In a large salad bowl,** combine the chicken with the remaining ingredients and stir thoroughly to combine. Refrigerate before serving on top of the lettuce leaves. Enjoy!

CHEF
Orin Hayes
age 12 in 2016

"I can eat chicken for breakfast, lunch, and supper, all by itself," says Orin. "On St. Thomas you can meet chickens everywhere. We have about two dozen of them now around my house. Also, my grandma grows some fruit and vegetables. We kids are helping her to take care of it. My responsibility is to water them early in the morning and right before dusk. The lettuce and lime I used in my recipe is locally grown."

Utah

Lentil Veggie Soup

Lahav Ardi, age 9 in 2012

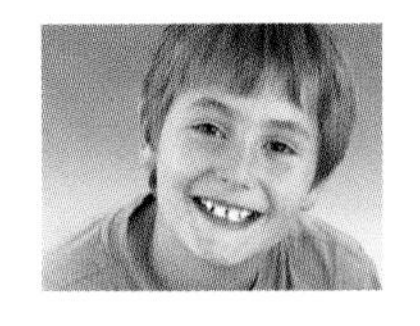

"I first made this soup when Mom was sick and I was 6½ years old," says Lahav. "I told Mom to 'lay down and rest, I'll make lunch.' I convinced her I could do it. I made this soup, and she felt better that night." Sometimes she adds cut-up skinless, boneless chicken breast slices. Lahav always has this with multigrain bread with gouda and mozzarella melted on top, followed by mixed berries and kiwi.

Makes 8 servings

INGREDIENTS

6 cups vegetable broth, plus more if needed

1 cup assorted lentils (red and green)

1/3 cup barley

½ onion, peeled and finely chopped

¼ cup finely chopped celery

4 small red potatoes, cut into ½-inch cubes

6 carrots or 12 baby carrots, peeled and thinly sliced

1 cup fresh or frozen peas

1 cup fresh or frozen corn

1 cup sliced white mushrooms

1/2 teaspoon parsley

1/2 teaspoon oregano

½ teaspoon basil

½ teaspoon cilantro

½ teaspoon sage

Salt and pepper

PREPARATION

In a large stock or soup pot over moderate heat, combine the vegetable broth, lentils, barley, onion, celery, potatoes, carrots, peas, corn, mushrooms, parsley, oregano, basil, cilantro, and sage. Bring to a boil, then lower the heat and gently simmer, stirring occasionally, until the lentils and potatoes are fully cooked, about 45 minutes. Serve hot.

Lucky Lettuce Cups

CECILY ASPLUND, age 10 in 2013

"Me and my mom love to be in the kitchen! I was in Mandarin immersion at my school for three years, and when we had Chinese dumplings, I became interested in Chinese food," recalls Cecily. "Mom and I experimented with these delicious Chinese-style lettuce cups. I love how the crunchy lettuce, peanuts, and veggies go with the tender rice. I like to have it with a side of grilled pineapple, Greek honey yogurt, and a good old glass of water!"

Makes 4 servings

INGREDIENTS

2 tablespoons safflower oil

3/4 pound boneless, skinless chicken breasts, cut into 1-inch cubes

4 scallions, thinly sliced, plus 2 scallions sliced diagonally, for garnish

1 (2-inch) piece fresh ginger, peeled and grated

2 large cloves garlic, minced

1 cup zucchini, cut into 1-inch cubes

1 cup red bell pepper, cut into 1-inch dice

1 cup yellow bell pepper, cut into 1-inch dice

1 cup lightly salted roasted peanuts

1 cup cooked short-grain brown rice

1 tablespoon brown sugar

1 tablespoon soy sauce

1 1/2 teaspoons rice wine vinegar

1/2 teaspoon salt

1/4 teaspoon hot chile sauce (optional)

1 head butter lettuce, washed and separated

PREPARATION

1. In a large sauté pan over moderate heat, warm 1 tablespoon oil. Add the chicken and sauté, stirring occasionally, until cooked through and brown, 5 to 7 minutes. Transfer to a plate and set aside. Do not wash the pan.

2. In the same pan over moderate heat, warm the remaining 1 tablespoon oil. Add the 4 thinly sliced scallions, along with the ginger and garlic and sauté, stirring occasionally, for 1 minute. Add the zucchini, red and yellow bell peppers, peanuts, and rice, and cook, stirring occasionally, for 3 minutes. Add the brown sugar and cook, stirring occasionally, for 3 minutes. Add the cooked chicken, along with the soy sauce, vinegar, salt, and hot chile sauce, if using.

3. Mound the rice and vegetable mixture in the middle of a large serving plate and garnish with diagonally sliced scallions. Surround the rice with lettuce cups. To serve, spoon the rice and vegetable mixture into lettuce cups and eat with your fingers, taco-style.

400 calories; 28g protein; 19g carbohydrates; 25 fat (3g saturated fat); 649mg sodium

Andrew Chardack, age 9 in 2014

"This recipe has its origins from Grandma's Polish heritage," says Andrew. "It's a delicious mix of cucumbers, sour cream, lemon juice, and salt. Our recipe eliminates the high-fat sausage and adds protein-rich toasted quinoa and melted Muenster cheese. We added a fresh vegetable mix including the traditional beets, but also added red onion, asparagus, corn, and peas."

Makes 4 servings • 308 calories • 14g fat • 38g carbohydrates • 10g protein

CHEF ANDREW

NEW POLISH POTATOES

INGREDIENTS

♥ For the Cucumber Salad:
½ cucumber, peeled and chopped
½ cup Greek kefir sour cream (or low-fat sour cream)
Juice of 1 lemon
½ teaspoon salt
♥ For the Vegetable Medley:
1 tablespoon olive oil
1 red onion, peeled and diced
6 asparagus stalks, cut in ¼-inch pieces
½ cup fresh or frozen corn
½ cup fresh or frozen peas
1 beet--peeled, cooked, and cubed
Salt and pepper to taste
♥ For the Potato Mixture:
2 medium red-skin potatoes, cooked and cubed
½ cup cooked quinoa
2 slices Muenster cheese

PREPARATION

Make the Cucumber Salad: In a medium bowl, mix the cucumber, sour cream, lemon juice, and salt together. Set aside.

Make the Vegetable Medley: In a large sauté pan, warm the oil over moderate heat. Add the onion and cook until soft, about 4 minutes. Add the asparagus, corn, and peas and cook for 2 minutes. Add the beet, season with salt and pepper to taste, and set aside.

Make the Potato Mixture: In a large microwavable bowl, combine the potatoes and quinoa and top with the cheese. Microwave for 45 seconds on high, until hot and bubbly. Add ½ cup of the cucumber salad, using more to taste, and the vegetables, gently stir, and serve.

Chef Indiana Coyle,

age 8 in 2015

"Sushi is my favorite food. I like making sushi with my mom. She cuts up all the food and then I can pick what goes inside," says Indiana. "We roll it up together and I eat it. When it was time to pick which sushi I thought was best, I couldn't choose! So we used the food in all of them for the recipe. We used brown rice because it is healthy and it tastes great. I think it would be healthy for kids to eat sushi."

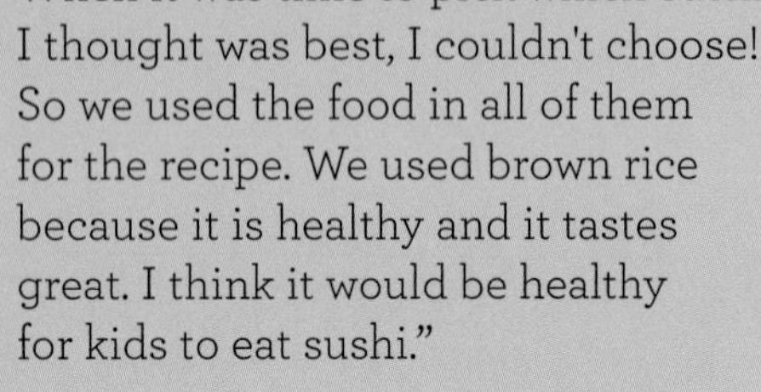

Mix It Up Sushi

Makes 8 sushi rolls • 311 calories • 10g fat • 49g carbohydrates • 11g protein

INGREDIENTS

2 cups brown rice
1 teaspoon kosher salt
¼ cup seasoned rice wine vinegar
8 to 10 roasted seaweed papers
1 cucumber, peeled, seeded, and cut into long matchsticks
1 avocado, peeled, seeded, and cut into thin slices
1 large broccoli stem, outer layer peeled and stem cut into small matchsticks
¼ small pineapple, peeled, cored, and cut into matchsticks
½ small mango, peeled and cut into matchsticks
4 ounces softened low-fat cream cheese, cut into large matchsticks
8 ounces cooked shrimp, crab, or even imitation crab
1 small bundle watercress, washed

Equipment:
Bamboo sushi mat, covered in plastic

PREPARATION

1. **In a large stockpot,** bring 3 quarts of water to a boil. Add the rice and salt and boil, uncovered, for 35 minutes. Remove from the heat and drain the rice in a strainer set in the sink. Return the rice to the pot, place a kitchen towel over the pot opening, and cover with a lid. Let sit for 10 minutes to allow the remaining water and heat to steam the rice and cook it the rest of the way through.
2. **Turn the warm rice out into a non-metal bowl.** Drizzle the rice wine vinegar over the rice while gently stirring and folding the rice with a wide spoon. Continue stirring until the rice is no longer warm, about 10 minutes.
3. **On your plastic-covered bamboo sushi mat,** place one seaweed wrapper with the shiny surface facing down. Wet your hands and gently spread a thin, even layer of rice over the seaweed wrapper. Re-wet your hands as needed. Spread the rice to the edges of the mat.
4. **On the nearest L of the wrapper,** place a few matchsticks or slices of veggies and fruit horizontally across the rice. Make sure the ingredients reach both edges of the seaweed paper. Add a little cream cheese and shrimp or crab. Top with a few leaves of watercress.
5. **Lift the bamboo mat with your thumbs,** while gently keeping the filling in place with your fingers. Fold the wrapper over the filling and continue rolling in a jelly roll style. When the edge of bamboo mat has almost been rolled under the sushi, pull out that edge and continue rolling.
6. **Unroll the bamboo mat** and allow the sushi roll to sit for a few minutes before cutting. Repeat with the remaining ingredients to make more sushi rolls. Cut each roll into 8 equal pieces with a wet knife.

CHEF

Daniela Bergantz

age 10 in 2016

"I saw a cool way to put designs into pasta and thought I could try to make red stripes for the American Flag," says Daniela. "My favorite parts of making this were when I made the nest in the flour to hold the ingredients. I loved mixing the beet dough and seeing the red color pop out! I also really liked to turn the pasta crank. My dad grinds all of our flour. We grow a lot of vegetables used to make the garden sauce for the ravioli."

American Flag Ravioli in Creamy Garden Sauce

Makes 6 servings or 30 Ravioli • 494 calories • 18g fat • 61g carbohydrates • 26g protein

INGREDIENTS

For the Whole-Wheat Dough:
1 cup whole-wheat flour
1 cup 9-grain flour
(or you can substitute all-purpose or semolina)
2 eggs, beaten
2 teaspoons olive oil
¼ teaspoon salt
1 egg, beaten, for sealing

For the Red Flag-Stripe Dough:
½ beet, peeled, halved, and quartered
½ cup whole-wheat flour
½ cup 9-grain flour
(or you can substitute all-purpose or semolina)
1 egg, beaten
1 teaspoon olive oil
⅛ teaspoon salt
Water if needed, to form dough

For the Sauce:
1 tablespoon olive oil
2 garlic cloves, peeled and minced
8 tomatoes, seeded and chopped
1 squash, peeled and chopped
1 zucchini, peeled and chopped
Sprig of fresh oregano or ¼ teaspoon dried
2 sprigs of thyme or ½ teaspoon dried
Sprig of rosemary or ¼ teaspoon dried
1 tablespoon agave
⅓ cup heavy cream

For the Filling:
1 tablespoon olive oil
½ onion, peeled and diced
1 garlic clove, peeled and minced
2 cups shrimp, peeled,
tails removed, finely chopped
1 tablespoon dried parsley
¼ cup ricotta cheese
Salt

PREPARATION

1. **To make the Whole-Wheat Dough:** In a large mixing bowl, combine the two flours. Form a hole or nest in the flour and add eggs, oil, and salt; stir to mix. Add a bit of flour or water, if needed, to form a dough. Separate the dough into two equal pieces and feed into the pasta maker to form a long, thin sheet of pasta dough. Or, flatten the dough with a rolling pin into a sheet, ¼-inch thick or less.
2. **To make the Red Flag-Stripe Dough:** In a medium saucepan filled with cold water, boil beets over medium-high heat, about 5 minutes, or until soft. In a blender, combine the beets with ¼ cup of the beet water, and blend into a puree. In a large mixing bowl, combine the flours. Form a hole or nest in the flour and add beet puree, eggs, oil, salt; stir to mix. Add a bit of flour or water, if needed, to form a dough. Separate the dough into two equal pieces and feed into the pasta maker to form long, thin pasta strands, like spaghetti noodles. Or, flatten the dough with a rolling pin into a sheet, ¼-inch thick or less and use a knife to make skinny long strips. Lay the red dough strips on top of the sheets of whole-wheat dough, ½-inch apart in a stripe pattern, and press into pasta. Lay it flat.
3. **To make the Sauce:** Toss all the sauce ingredients into a crockpot on low heat for 10 hours or more. Or, in a large stockpot, warm olive oil over medium heat, cook the garlic for 2 minutes, then add the remaining ingredients, cover, reduce heat to low, and simmer for 20 minutes until slightly thickened.
4. **To make the Filling:** In a large nonstick skillet, warm the olive oil over medium heat, add the onions, garlic, and shrimp, and cook for 6 minutes or until the shrimp is pink and cooked through. Add the parsley and ricotta cheese and mix well. Salt to taste.
5. **To Assemble:** Place ½ tablespoon of filling on the overturned, flat dough sheet about ½-inch apart. Brush beaten egg around the mounds of filling. Place the other flat sheet of dough on top of the mounds, so that the stripes are facing up. Press a very small cup, bowl, or cookie cutter around each mound of dough and filling to create a cut-out ravioli. Use the extra dough to make more raviolis. Seal the dough edges with a fork. In a large stockpot of boiling salted water, drop 10 ravioli in at a time, and cook over medium heat, for 6 minutes, or until they are completely cooked and float up to the top. On each plate, combine 5 ravioli with ¼ cup of tomato sauce and serve.

Vermont

Backyard Garden Salsa Tortillas

Laura Printon, age 9 in 2012

Laura took a cooking class in the third grade, which inspired her desire to pick "salsa ingredients" from the garden, reports her mother, Catherine. Because Laura's brother likes soft tortillas, Laura incorporated chicken or tofu tortillas into the meal along with serving beans and fruit, like kiwi.

Makes 6 servings

INGREDIENTS

For the Salsa:

4 beefsteak tomatoes

2 Roma tomatoes

2 plum tomatoes

1 green bell pepper

1 yellow bell pepper

1 medium or large Spanish onion

1/2 cup chopped fresh cilantro

2 tablespoons lemon or lime juice

For the Tortillas:

6 whole-wheat flour tortillas

3 (4-ounce) skinless boneless cooked chicken breasts or tofu, cut into bite-size pieces

1 cup canned black beans, drained and rinsed

1 cup shredded mozzarella and Cheddar cheese

2 cups of shredded romaine lettuce

1 Granny Smith apple, diced

1 avocado, peeled, pitted, and sliced

PREPARATION

For the Salsa:

1. In a food processor or blender, combine all the tomatoes, bell peppers, onion, cilantro, and lemon or lime juice. Blend until the ingredients and blend until they are well combined but the salsa is still chunky.

For the Tortillas:

2. Preheat the oven to 350°F. Top each tortilla with equal amounts of the chicken, beans, and cheese, and bake until the cheese is melted and the chicken is warm, 10 to 12 minutes. Just before serving, add the lettuce, apple, and avocado, and serve with the salsa.

Champ's Maple BBQ Turkey Burgers

COLIN HURLIMAN, age 9 in 2013

"I chose this recipe because it uses ingredients that Vermont is known for. Some of my favorite Vermont products are apples, maple syrup, and cheese," says Colin. "Champ is the mascot of our local baseball team. He is active and fun and I bet he would love this burger! I bet he would also be happy that so many fruits and vegetables are hidden in the burger. I love to eat this with fresh apple slices or baked sweet potato French fries."

Makes 8 servings

INGREDIENTS

For the barbecue sauce:

Cooking spray

1/4 medium sweet onion, diced

1/2 cup chicken broth

3/4 cup ketchup

1/4 cup apple cider

2 tablespoons maple syrup

1 teaspoon apple cider vinegar (optional)

For the burgers:

Cooking spray

1 medium carrot, diced

1 medium stalk celery, diced

1/2 medium sweet onion, diced

1 pound lean ground turkey

1 apple, peeled and shredded

1 large egg, beaten

1/2 cup whole wheat bread crumbs

To serve:

8 whole-grain buns, cheddar cheese (1/2 ounce per burger), lettuce, and pickles

PREPARATION

Make the barbecue sauce:

1. Spray a sauté pan with cooking spray and place over moderate heat. Add the onion and sauté, stirring occasionally, until translucent, about 3 minutes. Add the chicken broth, ketchup, apple cider, maple syrup, and apple cider vinegar (if using) and continue to cook, stirring frequently, until thickened, about 20 minutes. Pour sauce through a sieve or strainer to remove any onion pieces and discard the onion.

Make the burgers:

1. Spray a medium nonstick sauté pan with cooking spray and place over moderate heat. Add the carrot, celery, and onion and sauté, stirring occasionally, until the vegetables start to soften, about 5 minutes. Remove the pan from the heat and let the vegetables cool.

2. Once the vegetables are cool, transfer to a large bowl. Add the ground turkey, apple, egg, and bread crumbs and stir until well combined. Divide the mixture into 8 equal parts and form each one into a ball. Using the palm of your hand, gently flatten each ball into a patty.

3. Heat a grill or sauté pan and cook the burgers, flipping once, until cooked through, about 5 minutes per side. During the last 2 minutes of cooking time, top each burger with cheddar cheese and let the cheese melt.

4. To serve, spread 2 tablespoons of barbecue sauce on each bun. Add the burger, top with lettuce and pickles, and serve with sliced apples. Enjoy!

384 calories; 28g protein; 39g carbohydrates; 14g fat (7g saturated fat); 786mg sodium

CHINESE VEGETABLE STIR-FRY

INGREDIENTS

♥ For the Sauce:

¼ cup scallions chopped fine
2 tablespoons low-sodium soy sauce
2 minced garlic cloves
1 teaspoon peeled grated ginger
1 tablespoon sesame oil
½ teaspoon honey
Juice of ½ an orange

♥ For the Stir-Fry:

2 tablespoons vegetable oil
2 cups sliced broccoli
1 block of firm tofu, drained and chopped
2 cups chopped watercress
2 cups sliced baby bok choy
Garnish: Brown rice, sliced orange

PREPARATION

Make the Sauce: In a medium bowl, combine all the ingredients and mix well.

Make the Stir-Fry: In a large sauté pan or wok over moderately high heat, warm the oil. Add broccoli and cook for 2 minutes, then add the tofu, watercress, and bok choy and cook for 2 minutes more. Add the sauce and cook down until sauce is reduced by half, about 2 minutes more. Serve with brown rice and orange slices.

Iris Hsiang, age 10 in 2014

"I have made this because I am half Chinese, so I wanted to make a stir-fry," says Iris. "We have a family garden, so I appreciate fresh vegetables. My recipe is lactose-free because I am lactose-free. This is one of my favorite dishes!"

Makes 4 servings • 254 calories • 18g fat • 13g carbohydrates • 16g protein

CHEF IRIS

Maya's Delicious Vegetarian Little Lasagnas

Makes 6 to 8 Servings • 337 calories • 7g fat • 43g carbohydrates • 24g protein

---

INGREDIENTS

½ pound lasagna noodles
1 tablespoon olive oil
2 cups chopped vegetables, such as onions, zucchini, carrots, and peas
½ cup grated Parmesan cheese
2 cups low-fat cottage cheese
1 large egg, whisked well
1 teaspoon pepper
3 cups tomato sauce
1 cup shredded low-fat mozzarella cheese

PREPARATION

1. **Preheat the oven to 350°F.** Fill a large pasta pot with water and bring to a boil over medium-high heat. Add the noodles and cook about 8 minutes, or until al dente. Drain the noodles and let cool.
2. **Meanwhile, in a large sauté pan,** heat the olive oil over medium heat. Add the vegetables and sauté for about 6 minutes, or until soft and lightly golden.
3. **In a large bowl,** combine ¼ cup of the Parmesan cheese with the cottage cheese, egg, and pepper.
4. **Cover the bottom of a muffin tin** or individual baking dishes with a small amount of tomato sauce. Cut the noodles to size and place 1 noodle in each cup/dish. Begin layering with vegetables, sauce, the cottage cheese mixture, and then another noodle, veggies, sauce, the cottage cheese mixture, any remaining Parmesan, and the mozzarella cheese. Bake for 30 minutes, or until the cheese is bubbling and brown. Remove from the oven and let sit for 10 minutes. Carefully loosen sides with a knife and remove gently. Serve with salad and fruit. Enjoy and stay healthy!

Chef Maya Elliott,

age 10 in 2015

"I first made this recipe yesterday," says Maya. "I was inspired by my family because we all love vegetables, but different vegetables. I decided to make little lasagnas so we could all choose our own vegetables to put in it. I put fruit and salad on the side because of ChooseMyPlate.gov!"

Go Local Lunch!

Makes 8 servings • 361 calories • 13g fat • 41g carbohydrates • 21g protein

INGREDIENTS

For Maple Veggies:

1 tablespoon olive oil
¼ teaspoon salt
3 cups carrots, peeled and chopped
4 cups cubed butternut squash
1 tablespoon butter
2 tablespoons maple syrup

For Chicken Salad:

1 tablespoon olive oil
1 pound skinless, boneless chicken breast
3 celery stalks, finely chopped
3 green onions, peeled and finely chopped
1 Fuji apple, peeled, cored, and cut into thin strips
⅓ cup raisins
½ cup nonfat plain Greek yogurt
¼ cup mayonnaise
¼ cup unfiltered apple cider vinegar
1 teaspoon curry powder
Pinch of salt

For Wraps:

8 whole-wheat tortillas
2 cups fresh spinach
½ cup low-fat sharp cheddar cheese, shredded

PREPARATION

1. **To make Maple Veggies:** Preheat the oven to 375°F. Spread all ingredients on large silicone baking mats or a large nonstick baking pan greased with nonstick cooking spray or oil and bake for 30 minutes, stirring occasionally, or until soft.
2. **To make the Chicken Salad:** In a large nonstick skillet, warm the olive oil over moderate heat and add the chicken. Cook for 6 minutes, turn, and cook for additional 7 minutes or until golden brown. Let cool for 5 minutes, then shred. In a large mixing bowl, combine celery, onions, apple, and raisins. In a small bowl, whisk together remaining ingredients. Add ¾ of dressing to chicken salad, saving the rest for people to add to wraps as desired. Top each wrap with spinach, chicken, and cheese, and fold. Serve Maple Veggies as a yummy side dish!

CHEF

Miranda Gallagher

age 8 in 2016

"Miranda works hard helping in our garden and raising our chickens," says Miranda's mom, Genevieve. "Last summer we would make entire meals using only foods that we grew or raised ourselves. She came up with this recipe because it includes some of her very favorite foods—our own chicken, apples, maple syrup, and veggies that we can usually find in our own garden or the farmer's market. She's been making wraps for a while now and cooks often with both me and her grandmother. She even has her own cookbook with all of the recipes she's learned to make by herself."

Virginia

Fish Chowder

Madeleine Steppel, age 9 in 2012

"Senator Mark Warner's recipe for 'creamless' Asparagus Soup, which I found in the Celebrate Virginia Cookbook, inspired me to create a chowder recipe," says Madeleine, who used milk in this recipe because it is the State Beverage of Virginia. She would serve this with a fruity salad of spring greens, cherry tomatoes, strawberries, dried cranberries, and a citrus vinaigrette, with whole-grain bread.

Makes 4 to 6 servings

INGREDIENTS

3 white potatoes (about 12 ounces total), peeled and cut into ½-inch cubes

1 pound bag frozen peas and carrots, thawed

3 tablespoons unsalted butter

1 small onion, finely chopped

1 garlic clove, minced

1/4 cup all-purpose flour

4 cups low-fat milk

1½ to 2 pounds skinless white fish fillet, such as bass, tilapia, or flounder, cut into 2-inch pieces

Salt and white pepper

PREPARATION

1. Place potatoes in a large glass microwave-safe bowl. Add enough cool water to just cover the potatoes, and microwave on high for 4 minutes. Add the peas and carrots, and microwave on high until the vegetables are tender, about 3 minutes. Drain the vegetables and set aside. (Or, boil the vegetables until soft, about 8 minutes.)

2. In a large saucepan over moderate heat, melt the butter. Add the onion and garlic, and sauté, stirring occasionally, until golden, 4 to 5 minutes. Lower the heat to moderately low, add the flour, and whisk for 2 minutes to make a roux. Gradually whisk in 1 cup of milk and stir until hot and creamy, making sure to whisk out any lumps. Gradually whisk in the remaining 3 cups milk and cook, whisking, until steaming hot, about 5 minutes.

3. Add the fish and the cooked vegetables, and cook over moderate heat, stirring often, until the fish is cooked through and flaky. Season to taste with salt and white pepper.

Orange Chicken Lettuce Wraps

CAMPBELL KIELB, age 8 in 2013

"Campbell has autism, and the changes we have made in our family's diet—eliminating processed foods and replacing with fresh fruits, veggies, and meat—have had the most effective impact on his behavior along with ABA therapy," says his mom, Erin. "He has embraced this new lifestyle and loves to help me cook. So when we read about this challenge, he wanted to create something new. These lettuce wraps are wonderful served warm or cold. And they have to be served with a side of blueberries and cantaloupe, which we call Campbelloupe because he eats so much of it."

Makes 8 to 10 servings

INGREDIENTS

4 cloves garlic, minced

3 medium boneless, skinless chicken breasts

2 oranges

1 (8-ounce) can water chestnuts, chopped

1/3 cup rice vinegar

1/3 cup honey

2 tablespoons Liquid Coconut Aminos (or regular soy sauce if no one is gluten- or soy-sensitive)

1 tablespoon grated fresh ginger

1 1/2 teaspoons crushed red pepper

8 scallions, chopped, white and green slices separated

3 yellow bell peppers, seeded and diced

3 red bell peppers, seeded and diced

3 orange bell peppers, seeded and diced

3 cups warm cooked brown jasmine rice

Romaine lettuce hearts, separated into large leaves

PREPARATION

1. Bring a large pot of water to a boil. Add the garlic and chicken and cook until the chicken is cooked through, about 10 minutes. Let cool, then transfer the chicken and garlic to a bowl and use a fork to shred the chicken into bite-size pieces.

2. Zest 1 orange then squeeze the juice from both oranges—you should have about 1 cup of juice total. Transfer both the zest and juice to a medium saucepan and add the water chestnuts, vinegar, honey, Liquid Aminos, ginger, crushed red pepper, and the white scallion slices. Place the saucepan over moderate heat and cook until the mixture comes to a boil, about 3 minutes. Add the shredded chicken and return the mixture to a boil, stirring to make sure the chicken is coated in the sauce. Reduce the heat and simmer for 5 minutes. Add the bell peppers and the greens from the scallions and cook until the peppers are tender, about 5 minutes. To serve, spoon the rice, chicken, and sauce into the romaine leaves.

219 calories; 8g protein; 46g carbohydrates; 1.3g fat (0g saturated fat); 295mg sodium

CHIA CHICKEN PITAS

INGREDIENTS

1 cup bulgur
Pinch of salt
2 boneless skinless chicken breast,
cooked and diced
1 cup fresh or frozen corn
1 cup fresh or frozen cooked peas
1 cup carrots, peeled and chopped
1 teaspoon olive oil
2 teaspoons lemon juice
Fresh pepper
1 tablespoon chia seeds
½ cup cilantro, chopped
1 cup cucumbers, peeled
and chopped
½ cup feta cheese
4 whole-wheat pitas

PREPARATION

In a large microwavable bowl, combine 1 cup water, bulgur, and salt. Cover with plastic wrap and put a fork through the wrap to vent the steam. Microwave for 3 minutes on high power, then remove from the microwave.

Add the chicken, corn, peas, and carrots, cover back up, and let sit for 10 minutes. Add olive oil, lemon juice, pepper, chia seeds, cilantro, cucumbers, and cheese. Slice pitas in half. Stuff pita shell with mixture until full.

Sophie Haga, age 12 in 2014

"I wanted a food that would last from lunchtime until after a gymnastics practice or a swim team practice," says Sophie. "I like to experiment with my mom in the kitchen, so I started experimenting with ingredients to come up with something I could eat for lunch to keep me energized all afternoon. I added chia seeds because my mom likes to sprinkle them on our meals. She says they add some protein. I like to have a fruit salad on the side. I think they're yummy!"

Makes 4 servings • 428 calories • 10g fat • 43g carbohydrates •t 29g protein

Chef Simone Spalding,

age 8 in 2015

"I love to eat colorful, flavorful food! That's why I created Rainbow Chili," says Simone. "It's an easy way for kids to eat a whole lot of vegetables—one from almost every color of the rainbow. I've been helping in the kitchen since I was 3. I like to cook because you get to put all sorts of different foods together and taste it before anyone else. I think we make better food at home than even fancy restaurants. And I think that kids will eat more vegetables if they look beautiful and taste delicious."

Rainbow Chili

Makes 6 to 8 Servings • 562 calories • 18g fat • 57g carbohydrates • 47g protein

---

INGREDIENTS

1 tablespoon olive oil
1 onion, peeled and diced
4 celery stalks, thinly sliced
2 tablespoons peeled and minced garlic
1 pound lean ground turkey
2 tablespoons chili powder
1 tablespoon ground cumin
2 teaspoons salt
2 (14-ounce) cans fire-roasted diced tomatoes
2 large sweet potatoes, peeled and diced
1 (16-ounce) bag frozen corn
1 bell pepper, seeded and diced
2 (15-ounce) cans black beans, drained and rinsed
1 bunch of fresh cilantro, finely chopped

PREPARATION

1. **In a large stockpot,** heat olive oil over medium-high heat. Add the onions, celery, garlic, turkey, chili powder, cumin, and salt and cook, breaking the meat up with a wooden spoon, for about 10 minutes, or until the turkey is cooked through.

2. **Add the tomatoes,** reduce the heat to medium-low, and simmer a few minutes before adding all the other ingredients, except the cilantro. Add 8 cups of water, bring to a boil, then reduce the heat to medium-low and simmer for approximately 45 minutes. Add the cilantro right before serving. Enjoy!

CHEF

Kathryn Duvall

age 10 in 2016

"We are a military family who have lived in many states and countries," says Kathryn's dad, Elven. "We have a tradition of trying local foods, then making our own versions and giving them memorable names to remind us of our time living there. While stationed at Langley Air Force Base, in Virginia, we visited the Yorktown Battlefield. That hot summer night we were in the mood for something light; this dish was originally made from local ingredients. The best part was brainstorming name ideas and laughing about all the ideas not chosen because they were too silly. Victory at Yorktown came up. Even though it doesn't really describe the wrap, it does remind of us of the day." Kathryn serves it with a side of fruit salad.

Victory at Yorktown

Makes 1 serving • 378 calories • 12g fat • 47g carbohydrates • 22g protein

---

INGREDIENTS

For Wrap:
1 whole-wheat tortilla
2 tablespoons hummus
½ cooked chicken breast, thinly sliced
3 avocado slices
1 tablespoon finely sliced carrots
2 slices cucumber, diced
2 tablespoons diced tomatoes
Drizzle sweet chili sauce
5 cilantro leaves

For Fruit Salad *(not pictured)*:
2 sliced strawberries
5 raspberries
5 banana slices
2 tablespoons of vanilla low-fat yogurt

PREPARATION

1. **To make Wrap:** On tortilla, spread hummus, then layer on strips of chicken breast and avocado. In a small bowl, combine carrots, cucumbers, and tomatoes, and arrange on top of the avocado. Drizzle with chili sauce just before serving and top with cilantro.
2. **To make Fruit Salad:** In a bowl, combine all ingredients and stir to combine.

Washington

Salad Noodle Wraps

Arla Sutton, age 9 in 2012

Arla reports that her recipe won a school student chef competition, part of the Farm-to-Cafeteria (F2C) program. "I love F2C because we get to go outside in our school garden and also cook and try yummy recipes like kale chips, nettle tea, and apple muffins," says Arla, who likes to serve this with an apple and milk.

Makes 6 servings (12 wraps)

INGREDIENTS

For the peanut dipping sauce:

1 (3-inch) piece fresh ginger, peeled and minced (about 2 tablespoons)

1/2 cup creamy peanut butter

4 tablespoons rice vinegar

2 tablespoons low-sodium soy sauce

2 tablespoons white miso paste

1/4 teaspoon dried red pepper

For the salad noodle wraps:

4 ounces rice noodles

12 rice paper rounds

2 carrots, peeled and cut into matchsticks

½ cucumber, peeled, seeded, and cut into matchsticks

1 cup snap peas, trimmed and cut into matchsticks

1 cup cooked shredded chicken

1/2 head green leaf lettuce, cut into strips

1/2 cup fresh cilantro, coarsely chopped

1/2 cup fresh mint, coarsely chopped

Optional:

Avocado, bell peppers, zucchini, and sprouts

PREPARATION

Make the peanut dipping sauce:

1. In a small bowl, combine the ginger, peanut butter, rice vinegar, soy sauce, miso paste, red pepper, and ¼ cup hot water. Whisk until smooth. The sauce can be made several hours in advance and kept, covered, in the refrigerator.

Make the salad noodle wraps:

2. In a pot of boiling salted water, cook the rice noodles until al dente, 3 to 4 minutes. Drain, rinse in cold water, and drain again.

3. Fill a shallow baking pan with warm water. Soak 1 rice paper round in water until soft, 30 seconds to 1 minute.

   Transfer the rice paper round to a work surface, and in the lower third of the round, pile a small amount of the rice noodles, carrot, cucumber, snap peas, chicken, lettuce, cilantro, and mint. Roll the bottom of the rice paper round gently and tightly around the filling, then fold each side toward the center. Continue rolling the bottom toward the top, as gently and tightly as possible, until completely rolled. Place the wrap, seam-side-down, on a plate. Repeat with the remaining rice paper rounds and fillings.

Cook's Note: The wraps can be made several hours in advance and kept, covered in a damp paper towel and plastic wrap, in the refrigerator.

Nummy No-Noodle Lasagna

AMBER KELLEY, age 10 in 2013

"Lasagna is delicious, but the noodles do nothing for you, and it can be super greasy. So we created this easy-and-fun-to-make, gluten-free, healthy lasagna packed with flavor," says Amber. "It uses zucchini as the noodles, and trust me, it tastes so good, we eat the whole pan every time! We serve it with a big green salad, and sometimes a piece of gluten-free toast on the side. Yum!" Adds mom Yohko: "The kids love to assemble the lasagna, and I welcome the quality family time!"

Makes 8 servings

INGREDIENTS

3 to 4 small zucchinis

2 tablespoons olive oil

1 medium onion, chopped

2 cloves garlic, minced

1 1/2 pounds sweet Italian turkey sausage, casings removed

1 (28-ounce) can crushed tomatoes in tomato purée

1 (6-ounce) can tomato paste

1 tablespoon dried basil

Freshly ground black pepper

2 ounces (or less) freshly grated Parmesan

8 ounces (or less) shredded mozzarella cheese

PREPARATION

1. Preheat the oven to 400°F.

2. Use a mandoline or knife to cut the zucchini into paper-thin slices. Place the zucchini slices on paper towels and let them dry out at room temperature while you make the sauce.

3. In a large sauté pan over moderate heat, warm the oil. Add the onion and sauté, stirring occasionally, until soft, about 5 minutes. Add the garlic and sauté, stirring occasionally, 1 minute. Add the sausage and cook, stirring to break up the meat, until cooked through, 8 to 10 minutes. Add the crushed tomatoes, tomato paste, basil, and pepper and simmer, uncovered, until thickened, about 20 minutes.

4. To assemble, spread about 3/4 cup of the sauce into the bottom of a 9- by 13-inch baking dish. Layer zucchini on the sauce, overlapping it slightly, then sprinkle with some of the Parmesan and mozzarella. Continue to layer the lasagna with the remaining sauce, zucchini, and both cheeses, finishing with sauce and a sprinkle of Parmesan. Bake the lasagna until the sauce is bubbling, about 30 minutes. Broil the lasagna until a crust develops, 1 to 2 minutes. Let cool slightly before serving.

422 calories; 13g protein; 17g carbohydrates; 28g fat (11g saturated fat); 922mg sodium

Maliha Amarsi, age 9 in 2014

"I enjoy salmon and I love maple syrup, so I mixed them together," says Maliha. "And hot soup on a cold day makes me warm and happy inside." Maliha serves this with a Caesar salad and adds, "Crunchy salad is fun to eat."

Makes 4 servings • 479 calories • 13g fat • 48g carbohydrates • 32g protein

THIS FISH HAS GONE NUTS!

INGREDIENTS

♥ For the Salmon:
2 6-ounce salmon fillets, halved
¼ cup maple syrup
¼ cup chopped walnuts
Fresh lemon juice
♥ For the Lentil Soup:
1 cup red lentils
1 red onion, peeled and chopped
1 medium potato, peeled
and chopped
2 carrots, peeled and chopped
Salt and pepper to taste
2 tablespoons dried mint

PREPARATION

Preheat the oven to 375°F. Place the salmon on baking sheets, and drizzle 1 tablespoon of maple syrup on top of each and top with a few walnuts. Bake for 20 minutes or until the fish is firm and lightly golden.

In a large pot, combine all ingredients and 2 cups of water and cook over moderately low heat for 45 minutes, or until the lentils and vegetables are soft. Let soup cool then blend with a handheld blender. Add a dash of lemon to taste. Serve with the fish.

Teriyaki Chicken with Cabbage Salad

Makes 4 Servings • 211 calories • 11g fat • 16g carbohydrates • 16g protein

INGREDIENTS

For the Teriyaki Chicken:

¼ cup low-sodium soy sauce
1 garlic clove, peeled and minced
2 tablespoons brown sugar
1 teaspoon honey
½ teaspoon ground ginger
2 skinless, boneless chicken breasts, thinly sliced
1 tablespoon olive oil

For the Cabbage Salad:

½ head green cabbage, shredded
1 peeled and shredded carrot
3 celery stalks, chopped
4 green onions (scallions), chopped
2 tablespoons low-sodium soy sauce
2 tablespoons rice vinegar
1 tablespoon sesame oil
2 tablespoons sesame seeds

PREPARATION

1. **To make the Teriyaki Chicken:** In a large bowl, mix together the soy sauce, garlic, brown sugar, honey, ginger, and 1 cup cold water. Place the chicken slices into a large plastic bag with a seal, add the marinade, and seal the bag. Set in the refrigerator and marinate for at least 1 hour.
2. **To make the Cabbage Slaw:** In a large bowl, thoroughly combine the cabbage, carrots, celery, and green onions. In a small bowl, whisk together the soy sauce, rice vinegar, and sesame oil. Drizzle over the slaw and toss thoroughly.
3. **In a large sauté pan,** heat the olive oil over medium-high heat. Add the chicken and sauté for about 8 minutes, or until cooked through. Serve with the slaw and sprinkle sesame seeds on top.

Chef Simone Harvey,

age 10 in 2015

"I first made this recipe when I was very little," says Simone. "My mom and I would always make this dish together, but because my mom is a vegetarian we would make teriyaki tofu instead of teriyaki chicken. A favorite story about this dish is my mom helping me learn the dish at a young age, and saying it was ok if I made mistakes—just try again."

Salish Sea Kedgeree

Makes 4 servings • 551 calories • 11g fat • 89g carbohydrates • 24g protein

INGREDIENTS

For the Kedgeree:

6 cups water
2 cups basmati rice
2 eggs
2 teaspoons butter
½ yellow onion, peeled and diced
3 garlic cloves, peeled and minced
1 teaspoon cumin
½ teaspoon cinnamon
¼ teaspoon cardamom
¼ teaspoon freshly ground black pepper, plus additional
¼ teaspoon clove
¼ teaspoon nutmeg
Salt
2 teaspoons mustard seeds
2 teaspoons curry powder
1 bunch asparagus, tough ends removed, cut into bite-sized pieces
6 ounces crimini mushrooms, quartered
1 bunch kale, stems removed, roughly chopped
Juice of 1 fresh lemon
1 tablespoon olive oil
6 ounces smoked wild salmon

Garnish:

Green onions, chopped (optional)

PREPARATION

1. **In a large saucepan,** bring salted water to a boil over medium-high heat. Add rice, cover, reduce heat to low, and simmer for 30 minutes. Meantime, in a medium saucepan, cover the eggs with cold water and bring to a boil. Cook over medium-high heat for 12 minutes, or until cooked through and hard boiled. When cooled, peel eggs and quarter.

2. **In a nonstick skillet,** melt butter on medium-high heat. Add the onion, cook for 2 minutes, then add garlic. Cook 1 minute more, then add all of the spices. Stir and cook for another 2 minutes. Add the asparagus, mushrooms, and kale. Season with the lemon juice, and cook about 5 minutes more, or until asparagus and kale are tender. Transfer to bowl.

3. **In the same pan,** warm the olive oil over medium heat and add the salmon. Cook until cooked through, about 3 minutes per side (if there is skin, remove and discard). Flake the salmon into bite-sized pieces, or keep whole. Add the cooked rice and the vegetables, and mix well. Divide into 4 bowls and top each bowl with 2 egg quarters. Garnish with scallions, if desired. Enjoy!

CHEF
Lukas Anderson
age 10 in 2016

"I first tasted Kedgeree, a classic British dish with Indian roots, at a friend's house," says Lukas. "We couldn't find smoked haddock. My mom thought our local smoked salmon might work. I love kale, which grows like crazy in Washington, so we added it. Washington is also the perfect climate for mushrooms. We added crimini for their woodsy, creamy taste. Instead of the traditional English peas, we used asparagus. I think wonderful and tasty things can happen when cultures mix together. This Northwest take on a British-Indian dish was a hit with my picky 7-year-old sister. My mom was happy to get my little sister to eat more veggies and said the garlic and spices might strengthen our immune systems. I plan to serve this dish with wild blackberries when they are ready to be picked."

West Virginia

Golden Moroccan Butternut Stew

Alexis Nelson, age 10 in 2012

"One of my favorite vegetables is butternut squash. My mom uses Moroccan spices to add flavor to our meals, and this inspired me to make this stew," says Alexis. "This butternut stew has all my favorite vegetables and spices; this stew is pretty much me in a pot." Alexis serves this on top of couscous and likes to have low-fat Key lime pie yogurt for dessert.

Makes 4 to 6 servings

INGREDIENTS

3 tablespoons extra-virgin olive oil

1 cup finely chopped shallots

4 garlic cloves, minced

1 (14-ounce) can crushed plum tomatoes

1 whole cinnamon stick

1/4 teaspoon ground ginger

1/4 teaspoon ground cumin

1/2 teaspoon ground coriander

1 teaspoon garam masala

1/4 teaspoon crushed red pepper

1 medium butternut squash, peeled, seeded, and cut into 1-inch pieces

1 (16-ounce) can chickpeas, drained and rinsed

3 1/2 cups low-sodium vegetable broth

1/2 cup golden raisins

3 cups chopped fresh baby spinach

2 cups cooked couscous

Juice of 1/2 lime

1 tablespoon golden honey

Salt and pepper

For garnish:

Fresh cilantro

slivered almonds

PREPARATION

1. In a large saucepan over moderate heat, warm the olive oil. Add the shallots and sauté, stirring occasionally, until soft, about 6 minutes. Add the garlic, tomatoes, cinnamon, ginger, cumin, coriander, garam masala, and crushed red pepper. Cook until the cinnamon stick unfurls and the tomatoes are cooked down, about 4 minutes. Add the butternut squash, chickpeas, vegetable broth, and raisins, and bring to a simmer. Cook, partially covered, until the butternut squash is tender, about 20 minutes. Add the spinach and cook until wilted, about 2 minutes.

2. While the stew is simmering, warm the couscous in the microwave.

3. Add the lime juice and honey to the stew, and season to taste with salt and pepper. Divide the hot couscous among four bowls, top with the stew, garnish with cilantro and toasted almonds, and serve.

Spicy Tofu Lettuce Cups

JESSICA WOLFE, age 9 in 2013

"I was born in China and adopted as a baby. Even though I haven't lived in China for a long time, I still love Chinese flavors," says Jessica. "This is a traditional Chinese dish called ma-po tofu that my mom and I added a lot of vegetables to, so it's healthier and easier to eat at lunch. The lettuce helps you to add a lot of veggies because you can wrap up whatever you want to include, then crunch them up together like you were using a tortilla."

Makes 10 to 12 servings

INGREDIENTS

For the sauce:

1 cup chicken broth

6 tablespoons reduced-sodium soy sauce

2 tablespoons sugar

2 tablespoons chili-garlic sauce

2 tablespoons sesame oil

For the tofu:

1 tablespoon vegetable oil

2 tablespoons minced garlic

2 tablespoons peeled and minced fresh ginger

1 pound ground chicken breast

1 (14-ounce) package firm tofu, drained of liquid (press between paper towels) and cut into cubes

2 tablespoons cornstarch

1 to 2 tablespoons water

1 head iceberg lettuce, leaves separated

1 red bell pepper, seeded and thinly sliced

1 medium cucumber, peeled and thinly sliced

1 medium carrot, thinly sliced

PREPARATION

Make the sauce:

1. In a small bowl, whisk together the chicken broth, soy sauce, sugar, chili-garlic sauce, and sesame oil. Set aside, stirring occasionally to ensure the sugar is dissolved.

Make the tofu:

1. In a large sauté pan over moderate heat, warm the vegetable oil. Add the garlic and ginger and sauté for 1 minute. Add the ground chicken and cook, stirring to break up the meat, until the chicken is cooked through and there are no pink spots, about 6 minutes. Add the tofu and the reserved sauce and simmer, covered, until the tofu is warmed through, about 5 minutes.

2. In a small bowl, whisk together the cornstarch and water. Add this to the pan and continue to simmer, stirring, until the mixture is hot, about 2 minutes.

3. Serve by taking one lettuce leaf, adding a few strips of red bell pepper, cucumber, and carrot then spooning some of the tofu mixture on top. Roll and eat.

154 calories; 11g protein; 8g carbohydrates; 9g fat (2g saturated fat); 386mg sodium

Adrianna Nelson, age 9 in 2014

"I love to create healthy recipes because I feel great when I eat healthy. Couscous is my favorite side, and it's very tasty," says Adrianna. "I decided to use couscous in my yummy stuffed peppers that are filled with my favorite veggies. I would serve fresh fruit salad as dessert!"

Makes 4 servings • 476 calories • 17g fat • 42g carbohydrates • 35g protein

CHEF ADRIANNA

MAGNIFICENT MEDITERRANEAN SPOTLIGHT PEPPERS

INGREDIENTS

4 assorted colors of bell peppers—red, green, yellow, and orange, halved and seeds removed
1 tablespoon extra-virgin olive oil
1 cup chopped shallots
1 tablespoon minced garlic
1 pound ground turkey
¼ cup fresh lemon juice
1 teaspoon Mediterranean herb seasoning
¼ teaspoon crushed rosemary
¼ teaspoon Mediterranean oregano leaves
1¾ cups vegetable broth
1⅓ cups couscous
⅔ cup fresh Roma tomatoes, diced
½ cup roasted red peppers, drained and chopped
¾ cup fresh parsley, chopped
½ teaspoon coarse sea salt
¼ teaspoon fresh ground black pepper
½ cup low-fat shredded mozzarella cheese

PREPARATION

Preheat oven to 450°F. On a large baking pan, place pepper halves, cut side down, and cook in oven for 15 minutes or until peppers are tender when pierced.

Meanwhile, in a large skillet over moderate heat, warm the oil. Add the shallots and garlic, and cook for 3 minutes. Add the ground turkey and cook for 7 minutes. Add 2 tablespoons of lemon juice, herb seasoning, rosemary, and oregano and cook for 3 minutes. Add vegetable broth, couscous, and remaining 2 tablespoons lemon juice and bring to a boil, cover, and remove from heat. Let stand until couscous is tender, about 8 minutes. Add tomatoes, roasted red peppers, and parsley. Season with salt and black pepper.

Turn the pepper halves over and fill each with turkey mixture. Top with shredded cheese and bake until cheese is melted, about 5 minutes. Transfer peppers to serving platter.

Chef Reagan Blasher,

age 10 in 2015

"I'm involved with my local Dairy Council through a nutrition program at my school," says Reagan. "I knew I had to incorporate dairy to make them proud, so I made a list of all of my favorite foods to see what kind of recipe I could come up with. I talked with a local chef at the university in my town and he explained what the new "super foods" were and how important they are to our health. I then created a recipe that I thought would be great. I worked through trial and error until I finalized my recipe that is now delicious and includes my favorite and super foods."

Honey Baked Salmon with Spinach Quinoa, Pineapple Salsa, and Cucumber-Dill Dipping Sauce

Makes 4 Servings • 394 calories • 12g fat • 48g carbohydrates • 27g protein

INGREDIENTS

For the Salmon:

4 (10-inch-square) pieces parchment paper
3 tablespoons honey
1 tablespoon coconut oil
1 garlic clove, peeled and minced
1 teaspoon dried thyme
4 (2-ounce) skinless salmon fillets
Pinch of sea salt and pepper

For the Pineapple Salsa:

½ cup fresh pineapple, diced
¼ cup corn kernels
¼ cup cucumber, peeled and diced
¼ cup red onion, peeled and diced
½ tablespoon fresh cilantro, chopped
½ tablespoon flax seed
½ teaspoon lime zest
1 tablespoon lime juice
1 teaspoon honey
Pinch of sea salt

For the Spinach Quinoa:

1 tablespoon coconut oil
¼ cup onion, peeled and diced
1 garlic clove, peeled and minced
¾ cup quinoa, rinsed
Sea salt to taste
3 cups baby spinach
1 tablespoon lemon zest

For the Sauce:

1 cup Greek yogurt
½ cucumber, diced
2 teaspoons fresh dill
1 teaspoon lemon zest
Pinch of ground cumin
Pinch of sea salt

PREPARATION

1. **To make the Salmon:** Preheat the oven to 375°F and line a large baking sheet with 4 pieces of parchment paper. In a small bowl, whisk together the honey, coconut oil, garlic, and thyme. Place 1 salmon fillet on each piece of parchment paper. Season with salt and pepper. Drizzle the honey mixture over the salmon. Roll the parchment paper into pouches around each piece of salmon and pinch the sides closed, making sure they are sealed well. Bake for 15 to 20 minutes, or until the fish flakes when touched by a fork.
2. **To make the Salsa:** In a medium bowl, combine all of the ingredients and toss to combine.
3. **To make the Quinoa:** In a large saucepan, heat the coconut oil over medium heat. Add the onion and sauté for 4 minutes, or until soft. Add the garlic and quinoa and cook 1 minute. Add 1 ½ cups water and salt and bring to a boil. Reduce the heat, cover, and simmer for 15 to 20 minutes, or until the water is absorbed. Add the spinach, lemon zest, and salt to taste.
4. **To make the Sauce:** In a medium bowl, combine the yogurt, cucumber, dill, lemon zest, cumin, and salt and mix together well.
5. **To plate:** Spoon the quinoa onto plates, place the salmon on top, and spoon the salsa onto the salmon. Serve the sauce in a small dish on the side.

CHEF

Grace Landini

age 12 in 2016

"Through our cooking camps and Kids in the Kitchen class, I was inspired to eat well and make healthy food for my own family," says Grace. "We joined Grow Ohio Valley, a group that turns vacant city lots into gardens. Each week my mom and I would pick out our vegetables. It was great to know we were eating really fresh vegetables and helping our community. As a child I always liked when my mom made couscous and this past summer I found out how easy it was to prepare. Now I have a meal that even my picky 7-year-old sister will eat. The dish can be made in less than 20 minutes and is great packed up for lunch the next day."

Grace's Supermeal: Cool Couscous and Berry Healthy Dessert

Makes 6 servings • 596 calories • 20g fat • 79g carbohydrates • 31g protein

INGREDIENTS

For the Cool Couscous:

2 cups low-sodium chicken broth (or water)
1 10-ounce box whole-wheat couscous
1 tablespoon olive oil
1 yellow onion, peeled and diced
1 bunch asparagus, white parts removed, chopped into bite-size pieces
1 cup shelled edamame
½ bunch kale or spinach, stemmed and chopped
1 cup peas
1 cup green beans, stemmed and halved
1 pint grape or cherry tomatoes, halved
⅓ cup nonfat plain Greek yogurt
1 store-bought medium rotisserie chicken or two cooked chicken breasts, shredded
Salt and freshly ground black pepper

For the Berry Healthy Dessert ***(not pictured)*****:**

3 tablespoons butter, room temperature
2 ripe bananas, peeled and sliced
1 cup blueberries
1 cup oats
½ cup walnuts, finely chopped (optional)
1 ½ teaspoons cinnamon
1 teaspoon sugar

PREPARATION

1. **To make the Cool Couscous:** In a medium saucepan, bring the broth to a boil over medium-high heat. Stir in the couscous, cover, remove from heat and let stand 5 minutes. In a nonstick skillet, warm the oil over medium heat, and add the onions, asparagus, edamame, kale, peas, and green beans and cook about 6 minutes or until vegetables are tender and golden brown. Add tomatoes and stir to combine. Stir Greek yogurt into couscous, add vegetables, and season to taste with salt and pepper. Add cooked chicken and stir to combine. Serve.
2. **To make Berry Healthy Dessert:** Preheat oven to 375°F. Grease an oven-safe ceramic or glass baking dish with 1 tablespoon butter. Layer banana slices on bottom and then a layer of blueberries. In a small bowl, combine oats, walnuts, cinnamon and remaining 2 tablespoons butter, and using your fingers, crumble the butter into the mix thoroughly. Sprinkle on top of the blueberries, add a few additional berries, sprinkle sugar over the top and cook for 30 minutes, or until topping is golden.

Wisconsin

Barbecue Cheddar Chickpea Burgers

Finwe Wiedenhoeft, age 9 in 2012

Finwe's mom, Kristina, says, "When my oldest son left for the U.S. Navy in September 2011, we showed solidarity by going on a strict vegan diet for the duration of boot camp, and stuck to it faithfully until we saw him at boot camp graduation. We ate (and loved) a lot of beans! I wanted to make a well-rounded recipe using readily available, affordable ingredients like broccoli and cauliflower stems, which might not otherwise be used." Finwe likes to have this on a whole-grain bun with lettuce, and fresh fruit on the side.

Makes 6 servings

INGREDIENTS

1 (15-ounce) can chickpeas, rinsed and drained

1/2 cup minced broccoli stems

1/2 cup minced cauliflower stems

3 tablespoons whole-wheat flour

3 tablespoons cornstarch

1/2 cup finely shredded Cheddar cheese

1/2 cup small-curd cottage cheese

1/2 cup barbecue sauce

1 large egg

1 teaspoon salt

1/2 teaspoon ground black pepper

2 tablespoons vegetable oil

For serving: Whole-wheat buns, toasted

PREPARATION

1. In a food processor or blender, blend the chickpeas so they are crumbled but not yet a paste, or mash with a potato masher. Transfer the chickpeas to a large bowl and add the broccoli and cauliflower stems, flour, cornstarch, Cheddar cheese, cottage cheese, barbecue sauce, egg, salt, and pepper. Stir to thoroughly combine.

2. In a large skillet over moderate heat, warm 1 tablespoon oil. Scoop three slightly heaping 1/2 cup portions of the chickpea burger mixture and drop them into the skillet. Using a spatula, shape and flatten the burgers so they will fit on the buns. Cook for 10 minutes, then flip, flattening the burgers slightly, and continue cooking until golden brown and cooked through, about 10 more minutes. Repeat with the remaining oil and burgers. Serve on hot toasted buns.

Wisconsin Solar Oven-Simmered Chili

LIAM KIVIRIST, age 11 in 2013

We love cooking with garden vegetables,
Which on our Wisconsin farm we grow.
We raise veggies with compost, mulch and love.
Organic agriculture is what we know.
But our favorite chili recipe comes with two twists:
First, pumpkin adds a dash of sweet.
Garden tomatoes, onions, garlic, and peppers,
Give it fresh, delicious flavor that can't be beat.
The second twist is how we cook on the farm,
We harness the heat of the sun during the day,
We put the chili pot in a solar oven and simmer,
It's super kind to the earth to cook this way.
Invite your neighbors as this makes a big pot,
Serve with fruit kabobs for a healthy meal sure to please,
Top with Greek yogurt and don't forget,
To sprinkle on some fabulous Wisconsin cheese!
--Lisa Cindy Kivirist

Makes 8 servings

INGREDIENTS

1/2 pound lean ground turkey

1 medium onion, diced

3 cloves garlic, minced

1 red bell pepper, seeded and diced

1 green bell pepper, seeded and diced

1 cup tomato sauce

2 medium tomatoes, diced

1 (15-ounce) can black beans, rinsed and drained

1 (15-ounce) can kidney beans, rinsed and drained

1 (15-ounce) can pumpkin purée

1 cup low-sodium chicken broth

2 teaspoons chili powder

2 teaspoons ground cumin

1 teaspoon paprika

1 teaspoon ground cinnamon

1 teaspoon sea salt

1/2 cup cooked quinoa

Optional toppings: Plain Greek-style yogurt, shredded cheddar cheese

PREPARATION

1. In a nonstick skillet over moderate heat, cook the ground turkey, stirring to break up the meat, until browned, about 5 minutes. Add the onion, garlic, and bell peppers and sauté, stirring occasionally, until tender, about 5 minutes.

2. In a medium-size slow cooker, combine the tomato sauce, tomatoes, black and kidney beans, pumpkin purée, chicken broth, chili powder, cumin, paprika, cinnamon, and salt. Add the turkey mixture and stir to combine. Cook on low for 6 hours or on high for 3 hours. (You can also simmer this in a large pot on the stove for about 3 hours or bake it in an ovenproof dish in a 300°F solar oven for about 3 hours.) Add the cooked quinoa and stir to incorporate. Serve with your favorite healthy chili toppings such as plain Greek-style yogurt or shredded cheddar cheese.

208 calories; 21g protein; 28g carbohydrates; 2g fat (.25g saturated fat); 917mg sodium

AMAZING AFRICAN SWEET POTATO STEW

INGREDIENTS

1 tablespoon olive oil
2 yellow onions, peeled and chopped
4 minced garlic cloves
2 red bell peppers, seeded and chopped
4 sweet potatoes, peeled, cut into ½-inch squares
2 (15-ounce) cans Great Northern beans, drained and rinsed
1 (15-ounce) can diced tomatoes
6 cups vegetable broth
1 tablespoon brown sugar
2 teaspoons fresh grated ginger
2 teaspoons ground cumin
½ teaspoon salt
¼ teaspoon black pepper
⅛ teaspoon allspice
1½ teaspoons ground cinnamon
¼ cup peanut butter
1 tablespoon cilantro, chopped, optional
Red pepper flakes, optional

PREPARATION

In a large sauté pan, warm the olive oil over moderate heat. Add the onions and sauté for 5 minutes. Add the garlic, bell peppers, sweet potatoes, beans, tomatoes, broth, brown sugar, fresh ginger, cumin, salt, pepper, allspice, cinnamon, and peanut butter, and bring to a boil.

Reduce heat to low and simmer until vegetables are soft, about 30 minutes. Serve with cilantro and red pepper flakes, if desired.

Sarah Ganser, age 12 in 2014

"My family loves warm, healthy soup on a cold Wisconsin day. The sweet potatoes, spices, and peanut flavors make this soup one of my all-time favorites," says Sarah. "The sweet potatoes, vegetables, and beans provide plenty of fiber and plant proteins to keep us going all day. The stew also helps lower our cholesterol and helps prevent cancer, which my family cares a lot about. We serve this amazing soup with warm whole-grain bread and a side of strawberries and grapes."

Makes 8 servings • 468 calories • 10g fat • 39g carbohydrates • 31g protein

Mediterranean Rockin' Roasted Vegetables in Cool Cucumber Boats

Makes 8 Servings • 294 calories • 8g fat • 44g carbohydrates • 14g protein

---

INGREDIENTS

½ pound fresh asparagus, cut into 1-inch pieces
1 cup red bell pepper, cut into ½-inch pieces
1 cup yellow bell pepper, cut into ½-inch pieces
1 small red onion, peeled and diced
¼ cup olive oil
8 ounces whole-wheat orzo
½ cup grape tomatoes, quartered
¼ cup Kalamata olives, pitted and quartered
1 (15-ounce) can great northern beans, drained and rinsed
1 cup cooked, shelled edamame
3 canned artichoke hearts, diced
¼ cup fresh lemon juice
¼ cup fresh key lime juice or regular lime juice
2 teaspoons Dijon mustard
1 teaspoon fresh rosemary, chopped
1 garlic clove, peeled and minced
½ teaspoon salt, plus more to taste
½ teaspoon pepper, plus more to taste
4 cucumbers, halved lengthwise and seeded
½ cup crumbled garlic and herb feta cheese

PREPARATION

1. **Preheat the oven to 425° F.** On a large baking sheet, combine the asparagus, red and yellow bell peppers, and red onion and toss with 2 tablespoons olive oil to coat. Spread the vegetables in a single layer. Sprinkle lightly with salt and pepper to taste. Roast for 20 minutes, or until softened. Let the vegetables cool for 15 minutes.
2. **Meanwhile, in a medium stockpot,** cook the orzo in boiling water for 7 minutes, or until tender. Drain and transfer to a large bowl.
3. **Add the roasted vegetables to the orzo.** Add the grape tomatoes, Kalamata olives, great northern beans, edamame, and artichoke hearts.
4. **In small bowl,** whisk together the remaining 2 tablespoons olive oil, the lemon juice, lime juice, Dijon mustard, rosemary, garlic, ½ teaspoon salt, and ½ teaspoon pepper. Drizzle over the roasted vegetable-orzo mixture. Spoon into the seeded cucumbers and sprinkle with feta cheese. Serve with homemade whole-wheat garlic pita chips. Enjoy!

Chef Anna Canser,

age 10 in 2015

"I love to go sailing with my grandpa in Sturgeon Bay, WI, and thought of him with this recipe," says Anna. "I am using the cucumber as an edible boat filled with flavorful ingredients, such as roasted vegetables, beans, herbs, and spices. My family also cares a lot about eating healthy to prevent heart disease and cancer. This Mediterranean-inspired recipe does just that. We serve my recipe with healthy homemade whole-grain pita chips and a side of berries. Yummy!"

Wisconsin Cranberry Chickpea Salad

Makes 4 servings • 312 calories • 12g fat • 38g carbohydrates • 15g protein

---

INGREDIENTS

2 15-ounce cans of chickpeas, rinsed and drained
1 bunch of parsley, finely chopped
Juice of 1 fresh lemon
¼ teaspoon salt
1 tablespoon olive oil
1 red bell pepper, seeded and thinly sliced
1 yellow bell pepper, seeded and thinly sliced
3 ounces feta, cubed
2 tablespoons dried cranberries

PREPARATION

1. **In a large mixing bowl,** combine the chickpeas and parsley. Add the lemon juice, salt and olive oil and stir thoroughly to combine.
2. **On a large serving platter,** arrange the chickpea salad, and add the red and yellow bell pepper slices around it. Sprinkle the feta and cranberries on top and enjoy with family or friends!!!

CHEF

Raya El-Hajjar

age 8 in 2016

"In my family we eat a lot of hummus, and lately I wanted to know where hummus comes from," says Raya. "I read an article that said that the main ingredient in hummus is chickpeas. I discovered that chickpeas are really a super food and they are so tasty, too! In the summer, my brother and sister and I love to pick fresh vegetables from our backyard and we make different kinds of salads with them. So, for this salad we used our parsley and red and yellow peppers. Wisconsin is famous for cheese and cranberries. This is an easy, delicious salad that has all the nutrients you need!"

Wyoming

Macaroni Casserole

Grace Ratchford, age 12 in 2012

"I love pasta, and I wanted to come up with something filling and healthy at the same time. Adding protein and a vegetable to one of my favorite dishes made it creative, healthy, and delicious," says Grace. She likes to serve this with a side of fruit, such as grapes or watermelon.

Makes 4 to 6 servings

INGREDIENTS

8 ounces whole-wheat elbow macaroni

2 tablespoons unsalted butter

2 tablespoons all-purpose flour

1 cup 1-percent milk

2 1/2 cups shredded sharp Cheddar cheese

1/2 teaspoon kosher salt

1/4 teaspoon freshly ground black pepper

3 organic turkey hot dogs, boiled and cut into bite-size pieces

1 small bunch broccoli, steamed and cut into bite-size pieces

1/2 cup crushed cornflakes

1 to 2 tablespoons chopped fresh flat-leaf parsley

PREPARATION

1. Preheat the oven to 350°F and grease a 9- by 13-inch baking pan.

2. In a large saucepan of boiling salted water, cook the macaroni according to the package directions. Drain in a colander and rinse with cold water until cool.

3. In the same saucepan over moderate heat, melt the butter. Add the flour and stir for 1 minute. Gradually add the milk and cook, whisking, until hot and thick. Add the Cheddar cheese, salt, and pepper and whisk to combine. Remove the sauce from the heat and add the noodles, stirring well to combine. Stir in the hot dogs and broccoli.

4. Transfer the noodle mixture to the greased pan and sprinkle with cornflakes and parsley. Bake until bubbly, about 20 minutes, and serve.

Scrumptious Chili with Zucchini Cornbread

BREEZE PETTY, age 11 in 2013

"I love warm comfort foods, and one of my favorites is chili and cornbread," says Breeze. "My favorite fruit and veggies are strawberries and zucchini, so if you add the zucchini to the cornbread and serve strawberries on the side, you have the perfect healthy meal."

Makes 12 servings

INGREDIENTS

For the scrumptious chili:

1 tablespoon oil

2 pounds ground lean turkey

1 medium onion, chopped

4 cloves garlic, minced

4 (15-ounce) cans chili beans in sauce

2 (15-ounce) cans petite diced tomatoes

2 (8-ounce) cans tomato sauce

3 teaspoons chili powder

For the cornbread:

1/2 cup unbleached all-purpose flour

1 1/2 cups cornmeal

1/4 cup sugar

1 teaspoon baking soda

1/2 teaspoon salt

1 cup plain nonfat yogurt

2 large eggs, beaten

1 cup shredded zucchini

PREPARATION

Make the scrumptious chili:

1. In a large sauté pan over moderate heat, warm the oil. Add the turkey and cook, stirring to break up the meat, until browned and cooked through, about 10 minutes. Add the onion and garlic and cook until translucent, about 5 minutes. Add the chili beans in sauce, tomatoes, tomato sauce, chili powder, and simmer, stirring occasionally, for 20 minutes.

Make the cornbread:

1. Preheat the oven to 400°F. Lightly grease an 8- by 8-inch baking pan or spray it with cooking spray.

2. In a large bowl, whisk together the flour, cornmeal, sugar, baking soda, and salt. Stir in the yogurt, eggs, and shredded zucchini. Be careful not to overmix—stir only until just blended. Pour the batter into the prepared pan and bake until the center springs back when gently pressed, 20 to 25 minutes.

364 calories; 30g protein; 56g carbohydrates; 3g fat (.5g saturated fat); 802mg sodium

STUFFED PUMPKIN

INGREDIENTS

4 small pumpkins
1 pound ground turkey
½ teaspoon garlic salt
½ teaspoon pepper
1 cup wheat crackers
½ cup diced onion
1 cup spinach

PREPARATION

Preheat the oven to 350°F. Cut the top off the pumpkins, remove seeds and pulp, and wipe clean.

In a large bowl, mix all other ingredients together and divide among the pumpkins. Bake for 1 hour, or until the turkey is cooked through. Serve in the pumpkins.

KyAnn James, age 11 in 2014

"Personally, I really love pumpkins, so one day I thought, Why not?" says KyAnn. "My mom is always making stuffed peppers, and really I don't like peppers, so I decided to try pumpkins. I would pair it with a side salad or some fresh strawberries from the garden."

Makes 4 servings • 463 calories • 17g fat • 39g carbohydrates • 31g protein

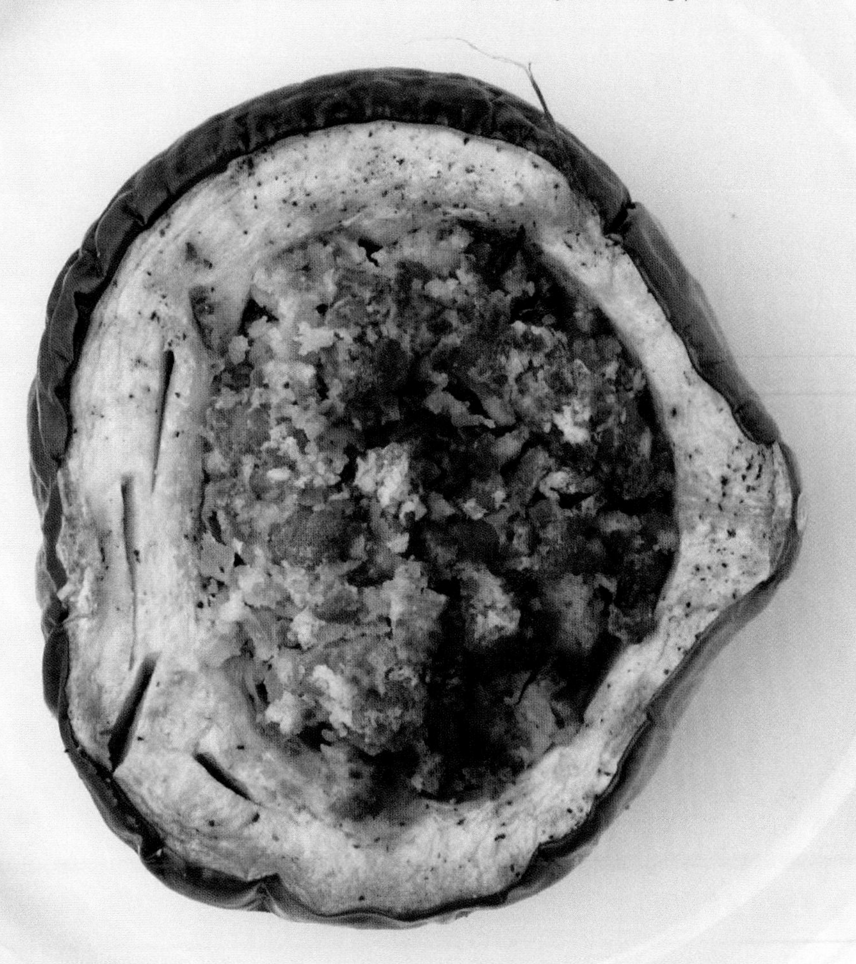

CHEF KYANN

Indian Tacos

Makes 6 Servings • 311 calories • 6g fat • 35g carbohydrates · 29g protein

---

INGREDIENTS

½ cup tikka masala simmer sauce
½ rotisserie chicken, shredded
½ can garbanzo beans, rinsed and drained
¼ cup fresh cilantro
¼ cup peeled and diced sweet onion
¼ cup diced bell pepper
½ cup diced tomatoes
½ lemon
Dash of salt
6 whole-wheat tortillas
¼ cup plain Greek yogurt

PREPARATION

1. **In a large sauté pan,** combine the tikka masala simmer sauce, shredded chicken, and garbanzo beans over medium heat and cook for about 5 minutes, or until warmed through.
2. **Meanwhile, in a large bowl,** combine the cilantro, onion, bell pepper, and tomatoes. Squeeze the lemon over the mixture and add a dash of salt. Gently mix the vegetables together.
3. **Top each tortilla with some chicken,** a generous helping of vegetables, and a tablespoon of yogurt. Roll up, serve, and enjoy!

Chef Dillon Andrews,

age 12 in 2015

"When I was little, I lived in San Francisco, and was exposed to all sorts of culture and food," says Dillon. "One of my favorites was Indian food, so I decided to make an Indian style dish. I would serve this dish with mango and chai."

Chicken and Veggie Salad

Makes 4 servings • 443 calories • 28g fat • 12g carbohydrates • 37g protein

INGREDIENTS

1 tablespoon olive oil
2 skinless boneless chicken breasts
1 head of romaine lettuce, chopped into bite-size pieces
1 red onion, peeled and thinly sliced
½ cup black olives, pitted and halved
2 tomatoes, seeded and chopped
⅓ cup sunflower oil
Dash of vinegar (optional)
1 teaspoon garlic salt
⅓ cup grated Parmesan cheese

PREPARATION

1. **In a large nonstick skillet,** warm the oil over moderate heat. Add the chicken and cook for 6 minutes per side, or until cooked through and golden brown. Remove from heat, let cool, then dice or shred the chicken.

2. **In a large salad bowl,** combine the lettuce, chicken, onion, olives, and tomatoes. Add the oil, vinegar if using, and toss. Add the garlic salt and Parmesan cheese, toss well, and serve.

CHEF

Hannah Andreen

age 11 in 2016

"The recipe I am making is very special to my family," says Hannah. "When we were kids we would always go to dinner with my Great Grandma and eat this chicken and veggie salad. She has since passed away, so we eat this in remembrance of her. We make this salad for dinner all the time. The reason that I like this salad is because it is a little bit tart. Also, this is healthy because it has sunflower oil and that is healthier than corn oil. It also has a ton of vegetables."

The table settings for the first Kids' "State Dinner" included copies of the winning recipes and Let's Move! bracelets for souvenirs.

Mr Hightower
Kids' State Dinner
Kale Chips
New York
Arizona
Kansas
North Carolina
WINNING
LUNCH
RECIPES

2013

In 2013, the colorful garden-themed table decorations included festive centerpieces made of fruits, vegetables, and flowers.

President and Mrs. Obama welcomed guests to the Kids' "State Dinner" from an East Room stage complete with a well-stocked "Farm Stand."

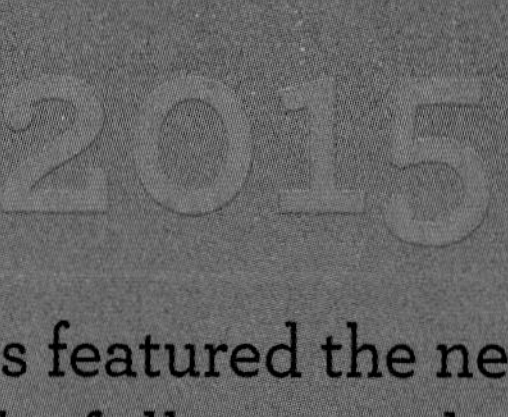

The 2015 place settings featured the new Obama State China and colorfully printed menus.

Kids' "State Dinner"

Mediterranean Rockin' Roasted Vegetables
in Cool Cucumber Boats
Wisconsin

Vegetable Confetti Spring Rolls
Washington, DC

California Rainbow Taco
Mic-Kale Obama Slaw
Barack-amole
California

Oodles of Zoodles
Avocado Pistachio Pesto
Arizona

Aloha Sorbet
Hawaii

Mary's Garden Smoothie
Iowa

Friday, July 10, 2015

2016

Decorative planters for the 2016 Kids' "State Dinner" flank doors to the Blue Room beneath the Great Seal in the White House Entrance Hall.

Kids'
State
Dinner

Marjoram
Rosemary
Sage
Chives

Acknowledgements

We would like to acknowledge the entities that were involved in and supported the Healthy Lunchtime Challenge and Kids' "State Dinner" over the course of the five years of the program.

FEDERAL GOVERNMENT

Office of First Lady Michelle Obama

U.S. Department of Agriculture

U.S. Department of Education

MEDIA PARTNERS

Epicurious

WGBH Boston

PROGRAM SUPPORT

Newman's Own

Newman's Own Foundation

Rachael Ray's Yum-o! Organization

TRAVEL AND LODGING SUPPORT

Delta Air Lines

The Westin Alexandria

The Westin Georgetown, Washington, D.C.

United Airlines

Oregano

Marjoram
Sage